THE DEVELOPMENT OF SHAKESPEARE
AS A DRAMATIST

LONDON IN 1610

(Drawn by Hondius. The circular theatre near the middle foreground is the first Globe.)

THE DEVELOPMENT

OF

SHAKESPEARE AS A DRAMATIST

BY

GEORGE PIERCE BAKER

PROFESSOR OF ENGLISH IN HARVARD UNIVERSITY

New York

THE MACMILLAN COMPANY

LONDON: MACMILLAN & CO., Ltd.

1920

Norwood Press
J. S. Cushing Co. — Berwick & Smith Co.
Norwood, Mass., U.S.A.

To

BARRETT WENDELL

IN GRATITUDE FOR MANY YEARS OF

STIMULATING COMPANIONSHIP AND UNREMITTING

ACTS OF FRIENDLINESS

CONTENTS

LIST OF ILLUSTRATIONS

THE DEVELOPMENT OF SHAKESPEARE
AS A DRAMATIST

DEVELOPMENT OF SHAKESPEARE AS A DRAMATIST

CHAPTER I

THE PUBLIC OF 1590 AND SHAKESPEARE'S INHERITANCE IN DRAMATIC TECHNIQUE

MUCH current appreciation of Shakespeare's plays treats them, both in bulk and in quality, as the only really significant part of the Elizabethan drama. By implication, at least, Shakespeare is held isolated by this relative insignificance of his contemporaries, the completeness of his original equipment, and the swiftness with which, in the years between 1590 and 1612, he took the foremost position as playwright. This is, of course, wholly uncritical, for it neglects a commonplace as true for the fine arts as for mechanics; namely, that almost never is the originator the perfecter. Any great work of art is neither accidental nor wholly individual. It is the product of the individual reacting on his inheritance of technique and his social environment. It marks the highest stage in some artistic evolution. In any genuinely critical study of Shakespeare's work these trite facts should never be forgotten.

In sharp contrast with this attitude which overlooks a commonplace of life is the position of a small group of would-be critics who maintain that Shakespeare, as dramatist merely, was little more than a man of respectable initial gifts and copious industry, who wrote always with his eye on the public and who had no idea of the meaning of that modern literary shibboleth, "Art for Art's sake." That is, this group, who may perhaps fairly be called hypercritical in distinction from the first, the uncritical, group, are busy commonizing even Shakespeare, just as we have already had the "real Lincoln" and the "real Washington."

Truth, as usual, lies between these two sharply contrasting views. On the one hand, any artist, no matter how great his genius, if he is ever to be more than an infant prodigy at first and later one of those pieces of human flotsam and jetsam, the quondam genius who has failed to arrive, must master the technique of his art. Shakespeare mellowed even in the powers with which he was originally endowed. He acquired powers he did not originally possess. He substituted better for poorer methods. On the other hand, Shakespeare knew better than any other dramatist of his day the real meaning of "Art for Art's sake," for time and again he moulded his material, not merely to accord with public taste of his time, or even, as was the case with Ben Jonson, so as to conform to standards drawn from the Classical drama, but so as to satisfy some inner standards drawn from his own increasing experience or from that constant beacon of the highest creative minds, the artistic conscience.

Before, however, I begin a detailed examination of the development of Shakespeare as a dramatist, there is another fallacy in current judgment of drama which I should like to dissipate from the mind of any reader. It is the idea that there are certain standards by which the plays of any period may be declared good or bad without regard for the time in which a play was written, the public for whom it was written, or the stage on which it was acted. Year by year intelligent people endeavor to criticise and appreciate Shakespeare, Racine, Congreve, Goldsmith, Henrik Ibsen, Mr. Pinero, Mr. Clyde Fitch, and Mr. George Ade by some common standards — with results that would be amusing if they were not sad. For is it not always sad to watch people enthusiastically doing what must end in futility because impossible? Mr. Pinero, in his illuminating address on *Robert Louis Stevenson, the Dramatist,* says: "The art of the drama is not stationary, but progressive. By this I do not mean that it is always improving; what I do mean is that its conditions are always changing, and that every dramatist whose ambition it is to produce live plays is absolutely bound to study carefully, and I may even add respectfully — at any rate not contemptuously — the conditions that hold good for his own age and generation. . . . One of the great rules — perhaps the only universal rule — of the drama is that 'you cannot pour new wine into old skins!'"

Think for a moment how little we care for the successes of the Restoration comedy, whether drastically Bowdlerized or not. Remember that of all the plays popularly approved by the eighteenth century in England only three — one of Goldsmith and two of Sheridan — hold the stage. And how outworn seem the ideals that dominate the Robertsonian comedy which was the rage of the day in the late sixties. Mr. Pinero's statement must be an axiom of any sane critical study of the drama.

Yet the feeling of the critically untrained public that there should be certain final and permanent standards by which values may be apportioned to plays of different sorts and different periods has an element of truth in it; namely, that throughout all periods plays show common properties which distinguish them as a species of composition from tales, essays, or poems, — the differentia which make them the species *play*, in the genus *fiction*. These common characteristics are, of course, the fundamental principles in dramatic composition, for without them the play could not be a play at all. For these the public has a right to look in any play, and when, as with some of our modern plays, for instance *Maternité* or *Les Avariés* of M. Eugène Brieux, audiences declare the performances not plays at all, but dramatic essays on social questions, they are, consciously or unconsciously, recognizing the absence of these fundamental differentiating characteristics. But these common characteristics are relatively

few as compared with the characteristics of the plays of
any epoch or of any writer which result from the public,
from the stage for which they are written, and lastly
from the individual genius of the workman. What
makes current judgment of plays the hodge-podge of
contradictions that it is; what makes even a self-respecting individual who recognizes this confusion fall
back, complacently or distractedly, according to his
temperament, upon the weakest standard of all, "I
like it because it pleases me," is that just this distinction between the permanent characteristics of the
form, drama, and the ephemeral differentia of plays
belonging to different periods or different nationalities,
has not been widely understood. Indeed, only thoughtful students of the drama, probably, could name
offhand these permanent characteristics common to
all plays as plays. In imitating the Shakespearian
drama, it is just because we have not kept this fundamental distinction in mind that we have too often
produced, as in the plays of Sheridan Knowles, mere
feeble reflections of Shakespeare's splendor foredoomed
to only a momentary success. The imitators forget
that no play can have lasting popularity which neglects
the prejudices, tastes, above all the ideals of its own
day. That we find delight in Shakespeare's plays
to-day does not alter the fact that had he written for
us he could not have written exactly as he did for the
Elizabethans. Therefore, to judge his plays technically
by other standards than those of the time for which

he wrote them is illogical, and likely, as in the case of the Restoration critics of Shakespeare or Mr. G. B. Shaw's strictures more recently, to throw more light on the critics than on their subject.

Why it is that the drama cannot at any time wholly break away from the prejudices, tastes, and ideals of the public for which it is written, M. Édelstand Du Méril has clearly stated:[1] "In the drama the personality of the author is effaced even more completely than in the epic or other forms of poetry. . . . It is no longer he who speaks. . . . All the figures return successively to life, a little more talkative than they were originally, and express in orderly sequence their feelings and their desires. . . . Each of the dramatis personæ acts for himself and speaks according to the ideas and sentiments that are peculiarly his own. You assist at a genuine representation of life, and follow step by step the consequences of acts; you see the characters developing by vivid and convincing action in which each will is expressed by its acts, each act is related to its causes, and is brought to completion in its first results. But the inspiration of the work hasn't at all that egotistical spirit, disdainful of the outside world, which characterizes the other forms of art; this is no longer a monologue of the poet singing to himself for his own pleasure; this author tries by what his drama represents to awake in others the poetical ideas which have

[1] Adapted from the *Introduction* to his *Histoire de la Comédie*, Vol. I.

inspired him and are for him real. . . . The serious end of the drama depends, then, upon the ideas of the poet in regard to nature and the destiny of man, and his ideas are intimately bound up with the religion and the philosophy of his time. . . . If in all the persons more or less imaginary that the drama summons from the past and revivifies for a moment in the life of the theatre the spectator does not always recognize himself even as he does in one of those mirrors which exaggerate objects without changing their nature, if through his own feelings he does not understand the passions which disturb them and the miseries that fall upon them, he will be an indifferent witness to griefs which to him will be strange enough. There is much more egotism in pity than is supposed — an extreme admiration most surely kindles sympathy. . . . If a dramatist doesn't wish to employ his gifts in an effort condemned to failure in advance, he must, — and this is one of the first duties of the artist, — he must consider his public, respect their sentiments, and skilfully conform himself to their ideas and customs." Nor, as the following chapters will show, is such desirable pliability at all synonymous with truckling to one's audience.

From what precedes it should be clear that rightly to estimate the accomplishment of Shakespeare as a dramatist, one must first understand the public for which he wrote, know what was his inheritance of dramatic technique, and be able to visualize his stage. Then one may with some accuracy distinguish his contribution to the development of the drama, and may even succeed in differentiating between his effect on the permanent characteristics of the drama, and any changes of his which were necessarily ephemeral because they resulted from the impact of his genius on such temporary conditions as his public and his stage. All this differentiating should, too, leave one clear what are the common, permanent properties of plays as plays.

Inasmuch, then, as the public plays so important a part in the development of the drama of any epoch, what was the public of 1590 like? I choose the date somewhat arbitrarily, for it is likely that Shakespeare was in London by 1586 and connected with the stage. However, we really know little or nothing of his London experiences before 1590; we surmise merely that he first belonged to the Earl of Leicester's players; that after Leicester's death in 1588 he became one of My Lord Strange's Men, and that he acted at the Theatre in Shoreditch. Moreover, the trend of later criticism is to place his earliest extant plays after 1590 rather than before that date. Finally, what follows would need little if any modifying for the earlier date.

The first point to remember in regard to the public of Shakespeare is that it was relatively very small. Within the walls, which ran from the Tower of London around the City till they met the Thames again near the site of the present Blackfriars Bridge, and in the regions just outside the walls into which the growing City had already pressed, there are said to have been, roughly speaking, a hundred thousand people. In the village of Westminster, centred about Whitehall and Westminster Abbey; in the villages on the higher land about the City; and in the Bankside, on the Southwark side of the Thames at the end of London Bridge, there may have been another hundred thousand persons. This second hundred thousand must, however, have fluctuated considerably, as the many inns on or near the High Street of Southwark were full or not. That is, the public for which Shakespeare wrote is not comparable to that of any of the leading American or English cities, but rather with those, by population, of the fourth class. He wrote for Birmingham rather than London or Liverpool, for Providence or Detroit rather than New York or Chicago. It is true that often when the plague raged in London, and during the summer season, the London companies made provincial trips; but there is no evidence that Elizabethan managers paid any more deference to the judgment of provincial towns than do our present-day managers. Though the regular theatres in 1590 were few,—only the Theatre and the Curtain, built near together in 1576–1577 in Shoreditch, — numerous inn-yards provided for the companies of men who could not act at the two theatres.[1] In order to limit undesirable competition, to improve the quality of playing, and to prevent some

[1] The question has been raised whether the Rose Theatre was not built in the decade before 1592, the date usually given. The slight and vague evidence at present available cannot settle the matter. See under Rose Theatre, in Chapter II.

unworthy occurrences of the past, Parliament had passed an act in 1571 requiring players to procure from a peer of the realm or "personage of higher degree" a license to pursue their calling; if they had not this permit, they were to be adjudged rogues and vagabonds.[1] Under these conditions there were in 1590 the companies of the Queen's Men, of My Lord Strange, the Lord Admiral, the Earl of Sussex, the Earl of Pembroke, and the boy actors of the choir of St. Paul's Cathedral. The last acted somewhere about the Cathedral precincts, probably, as will appear in the next chapter, in the yard of the Convocation House. That is, theatrical life in 1590, unlike that of the next decade, in which it was transferred to the Bankside region, centred either about the inns or in homes of its own just outside the Liberties.[2] It was organized, concentred, and subject to the wishes of a small and definite public.

Between this public of Shakespeare and our own there is one fundamental difference of large significance: his audiences came to the theatre, even if primarily for amusement and sensation, yet somewhat also for information. Indeed, only in the theatre could they gain much of the information without which to-day we seem to find it impossible to exist. Though the printing press was already beginning to pour out cheap books, the public had by no means acquired the reading habit

[1] *Life of Shakespeare*, p. 34. Sidney Lee.
[2] Any region outside the London wall over which the City fathers had jurisdiction.

as it is understood to-day. This was chiefly for the very good reason that popular education had only just begun to spread. Consequently, as has often been pointed out, the theatre filled not only the place it occupies now, but the place of the magazine, illustrated histories, biographies, and books of travel and even of the yellow journal. This is proved by the innumerable plays from such sources as Painter and Bandello, by the chronicle histories, by *Sir Thomas Wyatt, Sir Thomas Gresham, or the Building of the Great Exchange, The Adventures of Three English Brothers, Two Murders in One,* and *Arden of Feversham.* Nor was this combined desire for amusement and information anything new, for till well down to the middle of the century the attitude of the English public toward the drama had combined that of the person seeking amusement and the person seeking instruction. For generation after generation the forefathers of the men of 1590 had learned, while they enjoyed, from the miracle plays and the moralities; and the forebears of these Elizabethans, in the days of Henry VIII, had been trained in politics as well as in education by moralities of the type of *Albion's Knight* and the *Marriage of Wit and Science.*

This receptivity of mind in Shakespeare's auditors was also an alert receptivity, for they came to the theatre not at the end of an arduous and deadening day of business or after an elaborate dinner ending only just before the performance, but in the clear light of the early afternoon at two or half-past two; and they sat in a building which, open as it was to the air, had great advantages of ventilation as compared with our own. But this alertness had less superficial causes; one must not forget the immensely stimulating effect upon the people at large of the various influences of the Reformation and of the Renaissance as they had been permeating England for nearly a century. Later, through the disappearance of the Armada and the ending of conspiracies in behalf of Mary Queen of Scots by her death, the growth of a national spirit stirred the English to new interest in their past and present. No less stimulating were the stories of adventure, discovery, and conquest told by the English voyagers who came sailing homeward from all the known and unknown seas.

Naturally this varied, eager interest overstimulated managers and authors. Their straining to provide constant novelty is responsible for the very large number of Elizabethan plays and for the crudity of many of them. A play was not given for a number of consecutive performances, but if it could be run once or twice a week throughout the season, and then kept in the repertoire for occasional revivals, was considered a great success. Many a play saw but a single season and only a half dozen performances in that. I have, however, called the dramatists of the early nineties overstimulated, because their audiences were by no means as exacting as ours in their use of the word "new." For them what was re-presented, if skilfully

done, was as good as new. To those audiences belonged permanently what is for us in our recent vogue
of plays made from novels — something wholly unpre-
sentable a dozen years ago — a mere passing mood.
So popular in Shakespeare's day were made-over plays,
and plays made from well-known pamphlets or tales,
that one wonders whether the audiences perhaps found
it a little hard to follow the extremely condensed exposition of a play unless they already knew something
of the story. Whatever the reason, they were not in
the least exacting where our audiences to-day are most
exacting, namely, in the matter of plot. To-day we
sneer unless a man gives us what we call a "new"
story, or so disguises an old story under new conditions
and environment that we do not recognize it — and
we make these demands in the face of the fact that
dramatists as famous as Gozzi and Schiller have been
able to find in all human life but combinations and
permutations of thirty-six dramatic situations. The
fact is, the mood of the Elizabethan theatre-goer was
delightfully childlike. He came, as a child comes,
saying practically, "Tell me a story," and he cared not
at all, provided the story was interestingly told, if he
had heard another tell it before. It is doubtful if,
even when trained by the best work of Shakespeare
himself, Elizabethan playgoers rose as a group to the
interest of our audiences in characterization. What
they demanded first of all in a play was story. This
fact must be kept steadily in mind in reading the plays

of Shakespeare and his contemporaries, for it explains the great emphasis in the Elizabethan drama on plot as contrasted with the emphasis on characterization in plays to-day, written as the latter are for an audience trained not so much in seeing plays as in reading novels. And here is an illustration of the effect of the public on the playwright.

The advantage for the dramatist of this predominating interest in plot and this broad interpretation of the word "new" must be self-evident. It permitted everybody, since there was no law of copyright, to plagiarize with impunity, and, if the results were really artistic, with acclaim. No period has ever more fully realized the condition phrased by J. R. Lowell: —

> "We call a thing his in the long run
> Who utters it clearest and best."

No dramatist need have any trouble in finding a plot, because if, as is the case with so many a modern, his imagination or experience would not provide it, he could revamp an old play or he could use any tale, pamphlet, or ballad, no matter how well known. This permitted the better order of dramatists to give more time to seeing their people in the situations already provided, or to finding new situations to fill gaps in the material, or for substitution for what they felt to be inadequate either dramatically or as characterizing material. It permitted the best men to do not only this, but — and this is most exacting of all in time — to plan their structure carefully. The Elizabethan as good as appreciated a truth definitively phrased by Professor Royce: "As a fact, originality and imitation are not in the least opposed, but are in healthy cases absolutely correlative and inseparable processes, so that you cannot be truly original in any direction unless you imitate, and cannot imitate effectively, worthily, admirably, unless you imitate in original fashions. The greatest thinker, artist, or prophet is merely a man who imitates inimitably something in the highest degree worthy of imitation."

Nor was playwriting a wholly haphazard matter. Apparently few of the Elizabethans at first wrote independently. They worked in collaboration with more experienced men or with men who could supply the proposed play with some quality which they themselves lacked. That is, Shakespeare, in the first and second parts of *Henry VI*, probably made over, with Christopher Marlowe, work in the first instance by Marlowe, Greene, and Peele. One even finds three or four novices working together, apparently sometimes collaborating act by act, sometimes taking each man an act to himself. The value of all this is evident when one remembers that some of the foremost dramatists have declared collaboration to be the best possible training a young playwright can have. Moreover, as has already been implied, much of the time of a young dramatist in Shakespeare's day went to making over plays once popular, but out of date. It is as if our public to-day would allow the young men who are in vain trying to have their crude productions represented to make over in accordance with the taste of the moment *Uncle Tom's Cabin, East Lynne,* and *Meg Merrilies.* The chance which such work offers to see what in once popular plays has permanent interest for an audience, and what changes will make the ephemeral permanent, must have been invaluable in giving a young playwright an intelligent understanding of dramatic manipulation of his material for his particular audience. When he once understood that, he had acquired the chief means, as the words of M. Du Méril show, to make his dramatic ability widely recognized. Here, then, are two conditions at the outset of an Elizabethan dramatist's career — collaboration and adaptation of old plays to new social and intellectual conditions — very favorable to swift and large development of a man with inborn dramatic instinct. Nor must a third be forgotten. These dramatists of the great Elizabethan period, that is, for our purposes, 1585 to 1603, really lived in the theatres. Though it is true that the best of the dramatists were by no means equally famous actors, many of them did act; and therefore they could visualize their material not merely as dramatists but also as actors. The immense importance of that double power we shall realize as we watch the development of Shakespeare, himself an actor. Even those dramatists who did not themselves act made part of the group which, whether it centred in Shoreditch or on the Bankside, one can see from the diary of Philip Henslowe and the letters of Edward Alleyn was much like a large family or, perhaps better, a club of Bohemians. From year's end to year's end they wrote, talked, and lived drama.

Indeed, the Elizabethan dramatists, with the exception of Ben Jonson, wrote with an eye single to the stage. When they sold their plays they seem to have disposed of all rights in them. In the absence of any copyright law, and in the presence of intense competition among the companies, every reason urged a company to keep a successful play as long as possible from publication. Most plays, therefore, came into print because the company owning them went to pieces, because the plays were no longer great successes on the stage, or because they were published surreptitiously. The whole case of the self-respecting Elizabethan playwright is stated, even as late as 1633, by Thomas Heywood in his address *To the Reader* before his play, *The English Traveller*: —

"If, Reader, thou hast of this play been an auditor, there is less apology to be used in entreating thy patience. This tragi-comedy (being one preserved among two hundred and twenty in which I had either an entire hand, or at least a main finger) coming accidentally to the press, and I having intelligence thereof, thought it not fit that it should pass as *filius populi*, a bastard without a father to acknowledge it. True it is, that my plays are not exposed to the world in

c [17]

volumes, to bear the title of works (as others); one reason is, that many of them by shifting and change of
companies have been negligently lost; others of them
are still retained in the hands of some actors, who
think it against their peculiar profit to have them come
in print; and a third, that it never was any great
ambition in me, to be in this kind voluminously read.
All that I have further to say at this time is only this:
censure I entreat as favourably as it is exposed to thy
view freely. Ever

"Studious of thy pleasure and profit,
"Thomas Heywood."

It is doubtful whether the widespread idea that each
dramatist confined his labors entirely, or almost entirely, to some one company is true except when the
author was also a shareholder or an actor. On the
other hand, a company would naturally make association with them as attractive and binding as possible
for any man who could provide them with successful
plays, and doubtless many who had been free lances
settled down early to working, at least for long periods,
for some one company. Think of what this meant for
these playwrights in concentrated work visualized to
the utmost for stage purposes. They knew every
peculiarity and device of the stage on which their play
would be presented; they did not write, as do playwrights to-day, for countless stages of innumerable
differences in England, America, and Australia. They

did not write for many companies, some of which the dramatist of to-day never sees in his plays, but for a company so well known to them that even as they wrote they could hear the very voices of the men and lads who would play their heroes and their heroines. They did not write for a hydra-headed, sated composite, which we call the public, but for a group of people almost as definitely known to them from repeated watching as are regular customers to the tradesman of to-day. What wonder that these Elizabethan plays, with all their faults from the point of dramatic technique as it is understood to-day, show when revived an acting quality that surprises! This very acting quality means merely that they were so skilfully fitted to one public as to acquire certain permanent qualities of dramatic appeal.

The chief fault of our theatrical public is that it rests its critical judgments on a confusion of misunderstood criteria. Sometimes people hesitate to judge statuary, paintings, even music, because they feel their lack of standards, but who hesitates to criticise a play? Shakespeare's task was simplified because for the greater part of his audience there was only the one standard, "Does it interest me?" Plays were given at Court, and there were courtiers in the public audience, even sitting upon the stage; but the strength of the Elizabethan drama as contrasted with that of the time of James, or, more accurately, the drama of 1608–1642, is that it reflects the interests and ideals of the great body of the people rather than of the Court or any literary coterie. Only a few in Shakespeare's audience were so travelled that they could compare his plays with those of other countries. Very few, comparatively, knew the Classical drama well enough to be able to hold him to its methods. The great majority, comparing his work only with that of his predecessors and contemporaries, were satisfied if their attention, stimulated quickly at the opening of the play, was held unswervingly to the end. The fact is, the English drama was so much in the making that the audience had no standards to apply, and even among the dramatists themselves everything was still formative and experimental. Till 1580–1585 it may be said, speaking roughly, that there was no such thing as technique of the drama. The plays immediately preceding that date can be divided into two groups, — interludes influenced by the Classical drama and those uninfluenced. The aim of the interlude was, in whatever time was allowed the dramatist, to amuse and interest or to interest and move. It told its tale, when uninfluenced by the Classical drama, in whatever way its author willed, or perhaps more strictly in whatever way his somewhat limited dramatic endowment permitted. If it was influenced by the Classical drama, as in *Ralph Roister Doister* or *Gorboduc*, it borrowed certain types and showed a division into five acts, but the real significance of the five-act division was not grasped till long after. Whatever technique existed is to be found in the work of John Lyly, Thomas Kyd, George Peele, Robert Greene, and Christopher Marlowe. Indeed, it must chiefly be looked for in the work of Greene and Marlowe. That it must be sought in these two men is true mainly because if one is to understand the technique of any dramatist, one must know the sources of his play and must study them in connection with the play evolved from them. His shifts in order, the differences in emphasis, the material developed or supplied — all these matters will throw light upon the technique of the dramatist himself. We lack this source-material for Lyly and Kyd; and Peele shows but little technique. It is just because such comparative study of the sources and the completed work has been neglected that people have been so ready to assume that Shakespeare is really the creator of the Elizabethan drama — even if that term is confined to the technical side of the drama.

However, examination of the sources of *Friar Bacon and Friar Bungay* and *James IV* by Greene and of *Edward II* and the first part of *Tamburlaine* by Marlowe show that these two dramatists understood the fundamental characteristics of successful story-telling on the stage. Mr. Pinero has said that there are two parts of technique, — "strategy and tactics." "Strategy is the general laying out of a play; tactics, the art of getting characters on and off the stage, of conveying information to the audience." [1]

[1] *Robert Louis Stevenson, the Dramatist,* p. 13. A. W. Pinero.

The fundamental need in strategy, that is, in laying out the play, selective compression of life so that it may be represented within the limits of five acts at most without falsification of its real values, even though historical sequence suffer, both Greene and Marlowe understood. Perhaps one instance will suffice. Marlowe wished to tell the story of Edward II and his favorites. He knew perfectly well that Spenser, the second favorite of Edward II, rose into power only some time after Gaveston, the first favorite, was killed; but he knew also that to follow the custom of the earlier playwrights and put in a scene to kill time would drop the interest of his audience, besides splitting his play into two parts, the first dealing with Gaveston and the second with Spenser. What did he do? Disregarding history, he brought the Spensers in early as followers and friends of Gaveston, — they were nothing of the sort, — and had Gaveston introduce them to the notice of the king. Even by the time of Gaveston's death the position of the young Spenser is so well assured that it seems quite natural the king in his grief for Gaveston should turn his affection toward Gaveston's follower, young Spenser. Note that though history is tampered with, the human problem which interested Marlowe, namely, the way in which the unbridled affection of the king threw his kingdom into confusion and brought him to an ignominious death, is not disturbed at all. Here, too, is an illustration of the imperative necessity that a critic should first find out what a dramatist means to do, and then, and then only, berate him for turning history from its natural course.

Such selective compression as I have just been noting makes, of course, for unity in the telling of the story, and if the first step in dramatic composition be so to select your incidents that you can illustrate within five acts the idea or the character which obsesses your mind for the time being, the second essential is that you shall not scatter the interest of your audience, but shall so order your details that at the end your purpose, if any, is clear, or that your story, at least, develops clearly and interestingly from start to finish. Marlowe understood this perfectly. He found in his sources for *Tamburlaine* merely the statement that the great conqueror had one wife of several whom he loved devotedly. In Perondinus, from whom Marlowe took Zenocrate, she is unnamed and without even a nationality. With Marlowe she is the daughter of the Soldan. Made prisoner by Tamburlaine, she becomes his devoted and admiring wife. Her chief desire is to reconcile her father and her husband, for her father has taken up arms to revenge her capture. Why all this elaboration? That the desire of Zenocrate, who is captured in Act I, may connect that act and every other place where it is mentioned with Act IV, in which the Soldan, her father, first appears. Above all, this elaboration takes place in order that what has been a slight element of suspense in the body of the play, interest to learn whether her desire is accomplished and how, may give a climatic effect to the fifth act. There, amidst the waving of banners, the blowing of trumpets, and the marching and countermarching of the two little stage armies, Zenocrate reconciles her husband to her father.

What I have just been citing from *Tamburlaine* shows also that Marlowe understood motivation, that is, making the action of his characters result from causes in accord with human experience. Even in small things Robert Greene provides for this in a play not usually ranked high technically, namely, *Friar Bacon and Friar Bungay*. In the *History*, the source of the play, the story of the quarrel of the two fathers who have been lifelong friends, has no other connection with the rest of the material used by Greene than that their sons, also devoted friends, see the quarrel through a magical glass, the property of Bacon, the necromancer. Greene makes the fathers suitors for the hand of Margaret of Fressingfield, and in their jealousy provides the cause of their quarrel. Moreover, as the sons watch this quarrel through the magic glass, they hear their fathers, as they wrangle, mention the loyalty to them of their sons. This sufficiently motivates the hot words between the sons and the fatal fight which ensues.

Two other causes of success in playwriting are proper suspense and climax. Indeed, it may be said that the business of the dramatist is the creation of suspense and the sustaining of it when created. Robert Greene, in the first act of *Friar Bacon and Friar Bungay*, creates sus-

pense in four scenes in the following clever fashion:
The first arouses interest in the love story and intro-
duces the two plots — that of the love of Prince Edward for Margaret and that of Bacon's necromancy;
the second increases the interest in Bacon's necromancy
and promises marvels ahead; the third scene complicates the love plot, but offers no hint of the solution;
the fourth, bringing in nearly all the remaining characters, leads the play, as did the first act, toward Oxford, threatens by bringing the King and the Prince
together to complicate the love plot, increases the desire
to see what Bacon can do in conjuring, and arouses
national pride by suggesting a contest in necromancy
between Bacon, of England, and Vandermast, repre-
sentative of the German Emperor. Surely, with all
those reasons for wishing to see Act II, suspense has
been intentionally created.

Too often, in judging the Elizabethan dramatists,
we blame them for a lack of climax at the end of acts
or in the closing scene because in modern practice till
very recently we find at these points a moment of intense emotional expression. We forget, in the first
place, that the modern curtain and the long waits
between the acts are largely responsible for this heavy
stressing of the final moments of scenes and acts; an
effect strong enough to hold over is required. For
the Elizabethan, as the next chapter will show, scene
melted swiftly into scene. Moreover, as he was primarily interested, not in character but in story, he

was content if the act closed at an interesting point in the plot and left him eager for more. The silent climax so popular in recent years, depending as it does on complete understanding by the audience of the train of thought of the hero or the heroine, can never be as widely popular as the climax emphasized by speech or unmistakable action. For the bulk of the great theatrical public to-day the leap of the heroine of melodrama from the window of the burning building is more moving than the sobbing departure of Iris from the rooms of Maldonado. That is, except for the critically trained, action produces larger emotional returns than does speech, and speech is more effective than merely connotative action. That both Greene and Marlowe understood climax well, so far as pomp and spectacle in themselves or by symbolizing the mental triumph of those upon the stage produce it, the ends of *James IV* and *Tamburlaine,* Pt. I, show. Indeed, the last act of the second part of *Tamburlaine,* showing the slow yielding of the great unconquered of mortal forces to the steady, insidious attacks of death, would in action work up to a superb climax in that last shuddering, sobbing line —

"For Tamburlaine, the Scourge of God, must die."

In brief, the absence of persistent climax in the modern sense among these early Elizabethans is due, not to ineptitude, but to their conception of the nature of dramatic narrative for the stage.

If, then, the pre-Shakespearian dramatists were

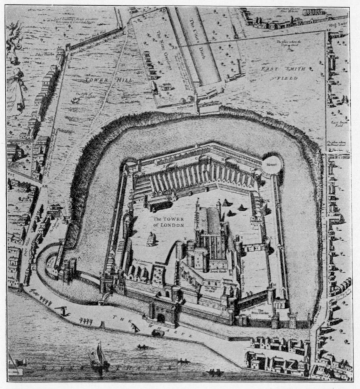

THE TOWER IN 1597

A. The Middle Tower.   *T.* The Bloody Tower.
D. Beauchamp Tower.   *V.* St. Thomas's Tower.
                W. Cæsar's or White Tower.

primarily story-tellers, certainly they had discovered ways of making their story arouse and maintain interest which, compared with the novel of their own day, are succinct. But, in another essential of the strategy of playwriting, they were very uneven, namely, characterization. Too often their figures said what was necessary for a clear development of the story rather than what made them, I will not say individuals, but even types. Incident these men understood; the related incident which is plot they had begun to understand, and they were steadily making essays at characterization; but far too often it was colorless as in John Lyly, conventional as is usually the case with Thomas Kyd, or only fitfully true to life, as in George Peele. Yet at times their sympathetic imagination kindled their vocabulary to accurate responsiveness, and they struck out perfect speeches, scenes, and even rarely, as in *Tamburlaine*, consistently conceived and strongly phrased central figures. It must be noted, too, that they often felt the situation entering into it emotionally, but were unable to phrase it with simplicity and truth. This is particularly true of Marlowe's *Tamburlaine*, and of all the known work of Kyd. But both of these men, and Greene as well, have moments in which they defy criticism. Take, for instance, the passionate cry with which Margaret, the heroine of *Friar Bacon and Friar Bungay*, yields to the pleadings of her lover Lacy that she put off the nun's garments just assumed for the wedding robes he has prepared: —

> "The flesh is frail; my lord doth know it well,
> That when he comes with his enchanting face,
> Whate'er betide, I cannot say him nay,
> Off goes the habit of a maiden heart,
> And, seeing fortune will, fair Framlingham
> And all the show of holy nuns, farewell!
> Lacy for me, if he will be my lord.
> *Lacy.* Peggy, thy lord, thy love, thy husband."

Nor can any student of the Elizabethan drama forget Greene's Dorothea, the first real woman of any complexity in that drama — tender, pure, wise, and loyal to the last. When her friends advise her to arouse her father against her husband James IV, who has wronged her greatly, this is her answer: —

> "As if they killed not me, who with him fight!
> As if his breast be touched, I am not wounded!
> As if he wailed, my joys were not confounded!
> We are one heart, though rent by hate in twain;
> One soul, one essence, doth our weal contain:
> What, then, can conquer him, that kills not me?"

Even amidst the conventional phrase of Thomas Kyd in the *Spanish Tragedy*, which is so pervasive as to make the characterization almost completely inadequate for a modern reader, there are purple patches. Take, for instance, the first two lines of Hieronimo's last speech in the scene in which the King and the Viceroy, whose nephew and son respectively he has killed in revenge, keep the old man from suicide: —

> "*King.* Hold Hieronimo, —
> Brother, my nephew and my son are slain.
> *Viceroy.* We are betrayed, my Balthazar is slain:
> Break ope the doors; run, save Hieronimo.
> *[They run in and hold Hieronimo.*

<blockquote>

	Hieronimo, do but inform the king of these events,
	Upon mine honour, thou shalt have no harm.
Hieronimo.	Viceroy, I will not trust thee with my life,
	Which I this day have offer'd to my son, —
	Accursed wretch, why stay'st thou him that was resolved
	to die?
King.	Speak, traitor! damnèd bloody murderer, speak!
	For now I have thee, I will make thee speak:
	Why hast thou done this undeserving deed?
Viceroy.	Why hast thou murdered my Balthazar?
Castile.	Why hast thou butchered both my children thus?
Hieronimo.	O, good words: as dear to me was my Horatio,
	As yours, or yours, or yours, my lord, to you,
	My guiltless son was by Lorenzo slain,
	And by Lorenzo and that Balthazar
	Am I at last revengèd thoroughly;
	Upon whose souls may heav'ns be yet avenged
	With greater far than these afflictions."

</blockquote>

What could be more final in phrase than that agonized cry of the opening two lines of the last speech? Moreover, to point out that these men just preceding Shakespeare were uneven in characterization, even faulty, is to judge them in the light of modern drama or at least of the Shakespearian work of 1595 to 1610, something wholly unfair, for their own audiences, comparing the plays with the wooden figures and the frigid dialogue of the novels of the day, probably waxed enthusiastic over the very great advance in characterization. At least, then, these men were grasping the fundamentals of playwriting, — selective compression, the unification of material which makes plot, characterization including motivation, and dramatic dialogue. They were acquiring the knowledge which any man must have if he is to write acting plays at all, and consequently were as yet stronger in the laying out of their plays, strategy, than in tactics, — the methods of conveying information to an audience, of getting characters on and off the stage, and of creating atmosphere. By the latter I mean witching an audience into believing itself in any land, real or unreal, which the dramatist may desire to represent. These early Elizabethan dramatists are for modern readers wearisomely fond of monologues and of self-exposition, nor do they scruple to use prologues and chorus as means of simplifying their problems of exposition. The idea of making entrances and exits count in characterizing, or dramatic in themselves, seems hardly to have occurred to them. Atmosphere they tried for but rarely, and even then only in single speeches. Yet the way in which these men piece out their chief source in order that the play may teem with interest or add a subplot for the same purpose, and their use of humor, show that they were keenly sensitive to the moods and interests of their coarse-minded, story-loving audiences. Consequently it is probable that the defects just pointed out are more faults from the modern than the Elizabethan standpoint. Their audiences allowed them the faulty exposition, for they themselves knew no better till these very men or their successors taught this public higher standards. Such details as characterizing entrances and exits would and could come only as the art of playwriting refined. The same is true of atmosphere.

Yet the *Arraignment of Paris*, by George Peele, has touches of it. The following curious mixture of pseudo-classicism and genuine observation of nature somehow does transport one to a slow-slipping brook in some flower-bespangled English valley: —

> " Not Iris, in her pride and bravery,
>   Adorns her arch with such variety;
>   Nor doth the milk-white way, in frosty night,
>   Appear so fair and beautiful in sight,
>   As done these fields, and groves, and sweetest bowers,
>   Bestrew'd and deck'd with parti-colour'd flowers,
>   Along the bubbling brooks and silver glide,
>   That at the bottom do in silence slide;
>   The water flowers and lilies on the banks,
>   Like blazing comets, burgen all in ranks;
>   Under the hawthorn and the poplar trees
>   Where sacred Phœbe might delight to be,
>   The primrose and the purple hyacinth,
>   The dainty violet, and the wholesome minth,
>   The double daisy, and the cowslip, queen
>   Of summer flowers, do overpeer the green;
>   And round about the valley as ye pass,
>   Ye may ne see for peeping flowers the grass."

That is, these men were learning the tactics of play-writing by experience, and, as they learned, provided their audiences with higher standards of judgment. Nor were these men without some feeling for literary expression. Blank verse had been gaining in popularity through increasingly frequent experimentation since *Gorboduc* in 1562. So popular was it by 1591 that Robert Wilmot, one of the authors of *Tancred and Gismunda*, first acted in 1568, when he printed his play, polished the rhymed quatrains, "according to the decorum of these days," into blank verse. It was by 1590 as definitely established as the medium for serious dramatic expression as was prose for farce and low comedy. These men were not without, too, what they and their public regarded as excellencies of style meant to give additional charm to the inherent interest of their story and the worth of their plays as drama purely. Undoubtedly much which is to our ears fustian, or mannered to excess, gave their audiences something of the delight which we have been gaining from Walter Pater and George Meredith. Perhaps a century hence our descendants may think our taste as queer as we find the delight of an Elizabethan audience in a passage like the following from Kyd's *Spanish Tragedy :* —

> "O eyes ! no eyes, but fountains fraught with tears:
> O life ! no life, but lively form of death:
> O world ! no world, but mass of public wrongs,
> Confus'd and fill'd with murder and misdeeds:
> O sacred heav'ns ! if this unhallow'd deed,
> If this inhuman, and barbarous attempt;
> If this incomparable murder thus,
> Of mine, but now no more my son,
> Shall unreveal'd and unrevenged pass,
> How should we term your dealings to be just,
> If you unjustly deal with those that in your justice trust?"

Read that passage without entering into it emotion- ally, and it is almost fantastic in its mannerisms. On the other hand, turn the imagination loose upon it sympathetically, assuming that an audience that had gone wild with enthusiasm over Lyly's intricate, cumbrous, and intensely artificial prose style is listening, and you will find it carries surprisingly. Just here is an admirable illustration of the way in which any play derives a large part of its immediate value from the closeness of its relation to the audience it addresses. Here, too, is illustration of another point far too little understood by the general public, but entirely clear even to these early Elizabethan dramatists, that in any phrase it is not, on the stage, so much the thought as the emotion called out by the words which tells with an audience. Did even the remotest spectator in the old Elizabethan theatre, in order to understand that here was an aged father agonized at the death of his son, need more than to see the poses, facial expression, and gestures of the actor, and to hear the tones of his voice? What do the words matter? Enter sympathetically into the feeling of the lines, disregarding the separate words, and then let the voice color the lines. In spite of the highly mannered phrase, the speech will carry its emotional appeal direct to an audience to-day.

In 1590, therefore, beginnings were on every hand: beginnings of an understanding and a competent use of the essentials of the drama and of special methods which would be effective for the epoch or half century, but not thereafter; beginnings, as the interest in phrase shows particularly, of a complete union between the drama and literature. These beginnings were not, however, persistently maintained by individuals, even

D [33]

the best of them. Even when Marlowe understands and feels, he often falls short in phrase of recreating in us instantaneously his thought and his emotion. A man was needed to bring the somewhat ragged experimentation to an orderly science. In one respect, also, this drama just before Shakespeare was almost inchoate: it did not differentiate clearly, indeed, hardly at all, between what we know as different dramatic forms. These pre-Shakespearian dramatists leave us uncertain whether they are writing chronicle history, melodrama, or tragedy, not distinguishing the last from the two preceding allied forms; nor had they at all discerned the boundaries of farce, extravaganza, low comedy, and high comedy. The drama, too, except in Marlowe, was mere story-telling. It had not gone deep into characterization. Moreover, except in the best men, it was an everyday affair, with no beauty of content. Even in Marlowe there was not the pervasive beauty that raises a piece of dramatic composition to the level of dramatic art. Some one was needed to chart, to develop, and to beautify this dramatic wilderness.

In 1590, then, when Shakespeare emerges as an experimenter in playwriting, the drama had two equipped homes, the Theatre and the Curtain, and was run on an orderly business basis; the companies had been reorganized under self-respecting conditions; and playwriting meant, not mere haphazard experimentation, but a period of apprenticeship under desirable conditions, and writing with the idea, above all, that "the play is the thing." A public, eager for information as well as amusement, unprovided with information by many of the purveyors of news of the present time, came to the theatre day after day asking little more, if anything more, than to hear a story, new or renewed, interestingly told. Already a group of plays existed in which any constant attendant at the theatres who aimed to be a playwright might distinguish certain principles, permanent and ephemeral, — though he probably would not distinguish between them, — which could steady him as he moved to an accomplishment more significant than any which had preceded him on the stage for which he was writing. What that stage was the next chapter attempts to show.

CHAPTER II

THE STAGE OF SHAKESPEARE

IN order to understand with any completeness the theatrical conditions under which Shakespeare worked, one must first recreate the London of 1590–1600. It was not only a small place, but, strange as it seems to-day, airy and clean. To any one who knows the region of London Tower now the description of it in 1597 by Haughton the dramatist may be surprising: —

> "I promise you this walk o'er Tower-hill
> Of all the places London can afford,
> Hath sweetest air."[1]

One reason for this great change is that, though Shakespeare speaks cosily of "the latter end of a sea coal fire," the authorities still regarded coal so dubiously that at one time in the reign of Elizabeth burning it during the session of Parliament was forbidden, lest the health of country members (accustomed only to wood fires) be injured.

The great highway was the Thames, not because it gave access to the sea, but because, as William Smith's map of 1588 shows (p. 18), it ran between the City and the many inns on the opposite bank, in the High

[1] *A Woman will have her Will*, Act I, Sc. 2.

[36]

Street, Southwark, and because narrow and ill-paved streets which wound tortuously from point to point made travel difficult and sometimes dangerous. It was much quicker to go to some one of the numerous "stairs" which lined the river bank on both sides, and to summon one of the many hundred boatmen who flitted hither and thither across the Thames. Taking the order, the man would swing off into the stream, crying to approaching boatmen, "Eastward Ho," "Westward Ho," " Northward Ho," as he chanced to be going in any one of these directions. When he landed his passenger, he charged a penny or two for a short distance with the tide, but could exact sixpence for the same distance against it. Only one bridge spanned the river, a forerunner of the present London Bridge.

Ryther's map of London in 1604 shows clearly the wall surrounding the City proper, and also the outlying territory. The wall ran in a rough semicircle from the Thames by the Tower to the Thames just below the Fleet Ditch and Bridewell Palace. It was punctured by seven gates: Aldsgate, Bishopsgate, Moorgate, Cripplegate, Aldersgate, Newgate, and Ludgate. Three of these are specially memorable for students of the Elizabethan drama: Bishopsgate, because just outside it, in Shoreditch, to the right of the Moorfields region, the Theatre and the Curtain were built in 1576-1577; Cripplegate, because in Golden Lane, straight out beyond it, the Lord Admiral's Men opened the Fortune Theatre in July, 1601; and Ludgate, because between that gate and the river, in Play House Yard where the *Times* building now stands, the Blackfriars Theatre was built in 1596. Within the walls and the Liberties, that is on all land controlled by the City Fathers, a public theatre was never permitted in either Elizabeth's or James's reign. All public dramatic performances allowed by the City authorities must be given in inn-yards. Nor were even the two private theatres, the Blackfriars and that of the Children of Paul's, exceptions, for the Liberties of the Blackfriars were exempt from the jurisdiction of the Common Council,[1] and the Dean of St. Paul's controlled the Cathedral precincts. This opposition of the City authorities, though grounded in Puritanism, was undoubtedly strengthened by jealous conserving of the rights of the City government independent of the Crown. Outside the Liberties the Crown was supreme, but royalty could not formally enter the City without permission of these City Fathers. The actors holding patents from the highest of the nobility and even from royalty itself, pressed just as near the City walls as they could. The resulting conflict in theatrical authority caused constant irritation.

In order better to understand where these Elizabethan theatres stood, let us traverse rapidly this London of 1590. Imagine that we have taken boat at Tower Stairs — the Tower was then much as it is now except for the disappearance in Cromwell's troublous

[1] *Works of John Lyly*, R. W. Bond, Vol. I, p. 24, note 6.

times of the Private Apartments of the Queen.[1] As
the tide is with us, we can make our way swiftly to
London Bridge.[2] Like some of the great Continental
bridges to-day, it was really a great street of dwellings,
with shops facing upon the street. With its fortress-
like towers, provided with portcullises, it could easily
be transformed into a stronghold. At both ends there
were water mills for grinding grain. All day long traffic
and pleasure surged and jostled across its narrow length,
while high above all the heads of traitors to the realm
bleached in the sunlight. It must have been a place
most familiar to Shakespeare, where he met day after
day figures he has made live again in his comedies.
We find on passing under the arches — at certain conditions of tide this would be impossible so swiftly does
the Thames run at this point — the river bank from
just above us to Westminster wholly different from
what it is to-day. The Victoria Embankment has
changed the Thames frontage as completely as developing parkway systems are now metamorphosing the water
front of many American cities. If to-day, in London, one
goes down Essex Street from the Strand, one will find
just at its end a curious old arched gateway with steps
leading to a lower level, now a greensward that stretches
many hundred feet away to the Thames. In 1590–1600
the Thames at this spot lapped the garden wall of
York House. The completion of the Victoria Embank-

---

[1] Just within the right-hand corner of the Tower walls as shown in
the print on p. 26. [2] See Frontispiece.

ment in 1870 finished the work of destruction and transformation which had been going on for centuries, and there is little along the water front now to set the imagination working in any attempt to reproduce the old conditions.

In Shakespeare's day building after building intimately associated with the reigns of the kings who figure in the Chronicle Plays stimulated curiosity in the passer-by as to their lives and deaths. That fact must not be overlooked when one seeks to account for the swift development of this so-called form of the Elizabethan drama between 1585 and 1600. To-day we satisfy the same curiosity which the Elizabethan felt by visiting historic spots in huge motor cars and listening to the hoarse voice of a guide as he shouts through a megaphone. Our forebears learned most of their history from dramatic and sometimes poetic presentation of it in their theatres. Is it clear that we have really advanced?

The palaces which lined the river bank were of two sorts,—single buildings looking much like fortresses and dating from an early period, or congeries of buildings constructed from decade to decade, often of conflicting styles of architecture. The first type was built because in the factious days before the realm became as settled as it was during the rule of Elizabeth and James, he who lived outside the walls needed a dwelling which he might easily defend. Indeed, these palaces outside the City were originally almost exclusively the property

BAYNARD'S CASTLE

ARUNDEL HOUSE

(This is but one-half of the square made by the buildings.)

of men whose position to a large extent protected them, namely, the bishops of the Church. From their sees the buildings took their names; on the City side of the Thames were Worcester, Durham, and York houses, and on the Southwark side were Winchester House and Lambeth Palace, the home of the Bishop of London. By 1590–1600 most of these places had passed into possession of the Crown or the nobility. They took the names of their successive owners. A good type of fortress palace was Baynard's or Barnard's Castle (p. 40), in the time of Shakespeare the property of the Pembroke family. In the inner court, Scene 7 of Act III of *Richard III* took place: Richard, at the urgency of the people, who have been egged on by his tool Buckingham, with pretended reluctance accepts the crown for which he has been scheming. Passing rapidly by Bridewell Palace and the Temple Gardens, with the notorious Whitefriars region lying in between, we come upon a good specimen of the other form of palace, Essex House. It was here that Robert Devereux, so long a favorite of the Queen, dwelt, and in it had lived another favorite of hers, Robert, Earl of Leicester.

Just beyond it, by Arundel House, the river curved, giving a view (see p. 46) of Durham and Worcester houses, the Savoy, once the home of John of Gaunt, and, in the distance, Whitehall and Westminster. Diagonally across the river from Whitehall stood Lambeth Palace (p. 50), the limit to the southwest of the inhabited region on the Bankside. As Smith's map shows, little but open fields lay between it and the theatrical centre on the Bankside. Striking almost straight across the river from Lambeth Palace, we face interesting buildings at Westminster (see p. 46), the Abbey, St. Stephen's, — now built into the vestibule of the modern enormous Houses of Parliament, — and Westminster Hall, where the courts of justice were held for centuries, till the New Law Courts were built in 1874–1880 opposite the gate of the Temple. That famous speech of the Duke of Buckingham, on his way to death in the Tower, beginning: —

> " All good people,
> You that thus far have come to pity me,
> Hear what I say and then go home and lose me."
> —*Henry VIII*, Act II, Sc. 1.

was given as he walked from this hall to the landing stage where we leave our boat. Just outside the gate, at the opposite end of the yard, stood the two garrulous gentlemen in *Henry VIII* who gossip so helpfully [1] for the auditor as they wait for Anne Boleyn to return up King Street — now wiped away — from her coronation at Westminster. Going up that street ourselves, we should come out, under a beautiful archway by Holbein, in front of the banquet house and Whitehall Palace. In the former many Elizabethan plays and many masks, notably Jonson's, were given. From this point we can easily make our way to Charing Cross, — one of eleven crosses placed by Edward I wherever the

[1] Act IV, Sc. 1.

body of his queen, Eleanor, rested in its long journey from Lincoln to London. Standing at this spot, we shall get something the view up the Strand toward Ludgate, which the print on p. 60 shows. Though the picture is only a modern attempt to reproduce the old conditions, it is approximately right. The space between the Strand and the river, where were the gardens of the palaces, should be much wider, but the view does show the row of palaces which lined the bank, the unevenness and ill-paved condition of the streets, the open fields to the left, and the curious way in which buildings were placed even in the middle of the street, notably the still existing churches, St. Mary's in the Strand and St. Clement Danes. At best this Strand, in 1590–1600, was little better than an ill-kept country lane. Making our way rapidly up the Strand by the fronts of Somerset and Arundel houses on the right, and the home of Lord Burleigh on the left, and passing by the two churches already mentioned, we reach, just by the entrance to the Temple, Temple Bar.[1] Originally there was here only just what the name implies,—a bar which was at times placed between two stone posts in order to mark off the territory governed by the City from the royal village of Westminster. When Queen Elizabeth went to St. Paul's to give thanks

[1] Some construction stood here much before 1590, for Stow, (*Annales*) under May 31, 1533, writes of Queen Anne Boleyn: " Shee with all her Companie, & the Maior rode forth to Temple bar, which was newly paynted and repaired," etc. — *Old Time Aldwych, Kingsway and Neighbourhood*, p. 62, C. Gordon. See also map, p. 36.

for the defeat of the Armada, she paused here till the waiting City Fathers had given formal permission to enter their jealously guarded territory.

If we pass inside the walls by Ludgate (p. 68), and bear a little to the right, we shall see a particularly ugly building, the Blackfriars Theatre.[1] Built in 1596–1597 by the Burbadges, it was occupied from its completion till 1608 for the public performances of the Children of the Chapel Royal. Blackfriars was made over from a house which had originally been one of the priory buildings of the monastery of Blackfriars,[2] and was always what was known as a private theatre — that is, it was roofed in, had locks on the box or "room" doors, gave its performances by candlelight, and charged higher prices. Such theatres grew from private and court performances even as the public theatre developed from performances in inn-yards. Here, between 1608 and 1625, were given many famous plays, notably Webster's *Duchess of Malfy*, "presented privately at the Blackfriars and publicly at the Globe by His Majesty's Servants," and Beaumont and Fletcher's *Philaster*.

Going up the rise of land to the northeast of this theatre, we shall come in sight of St. Paul's Cathedral. It was burned in the great fire of 1666. In the

---

[1] I found the original of this print in London in the great private collection of views kept together and developed by Henry Gardiner, Esq., as a memorial to his father, who began it. The print seems to have been lost sight of, but Mr. Gardiner and antiquarians to whom I have submitted it believe it genuine. See p. 78.

[2] See article by Charles William Wallace, *London Times*, Sept. 12, 1906.

houses which surrounded it (see p. 85) — in monastic days they had belonged to the petty canons — were the bookshops of Shakespeare's day. If you wish to buy a copy of *Midsummer Night's Dream*, you can find it at the shop of James Roberts in this yard. It is said that he had for many years the right to print such programmes as were used in the Elizabethan theatres,[1] but no specimen survives. The place was noisy enough, for there were not only the customers whom the shops attracted, but as the Yard was the connecting link between the City proper and the Strand, a human flood flowed through it all day long. In the crypt of the Cathedral, once the church of St. Faith's, it is reported, too, that coopers loudly plied their trade; and up and down the nave of the great cathedral a parti-colored, noisy crowd promenaded or jostled, for the nave was one of the great rendezvous of the day. Before we go into that nave notice the little church of St. Gregory's,[2] snuggling close by one corner of the great cathedral front, for in it was the music room of the choir boys of St. Paul's. That room, report says, was the theatre in which from long before 1579, when we first hear of the boys as actors of John Lyly's plays, till about 1608, they acted to the great delight of Elizabethan audiences. Another report,[3] however, says that they acted somewhere about

[1] *Annals of Dramatic Poetry*, Vol. III, p. 186.

[2] It disappeared, of course, in the fire of 1666. See p. 95.

[3] Malone's *Shakespeare*, Prolegomena, III, p. 46, notes 8 and 9. *History of Stage*, p. 56, Fleay.

the Convocation House, and I believe that their theatre was the yard enclosed by the high wall seen in the print on p. 95. If we make our way by the eastern transept and aisle to this yard, we shall find ourselves in the enclosure illustrated on p. 115. Is it not strange that students of our stage have not before seen the fitness of the place for the theatrical needs of the St. Paul's Boys? A platform easy to remove could have been built out from the door below the Convocation House. The yard itself formed the pit. The ambulatory provided spaces for the boxes or "rooms" preferred by those able to pay higher prices. The audience could enter at either side under the Convocation House, or perhaps by doors leading directly from the aisle of the Cathedral into the ambulatory. Necessary properties could be kept in the Convocation House, where the boys could dress, and any needed instrumental music could be placed. The high wall at the end of the enclosure in large part shut off the noise of the Cathedral Yard. So easily could this nook be adapted to the needs of the boy actors that I have little doubt it was their theatre in good weather, even if in bad they had to use their music room.

If now we leave the Cathedral Yard by its northeast corner and go down Cheapside to the third street on our left, we can pass quickly by Great and Little Wood streets, to Cripplegate.[1] Thence Red Cross Street takes us speedily into Golden Lane, midway on the left of

[1] See Ryther's map, p. 36.

[46]

1. Palace of Westminster.	9. The King's Stairs.
2. St. Stephen's Chapel.	11. Lambeth Palace.
3. Westminster Hall.	15. Whitehall.
5. Old Palace Yard.	21. St. Mary's Hospital.

THE

(From V

which stood the Fortune Theatre, opened in July, 1601. It belonged to the Lord Admiral's Company, of which Edward Alleyn was the leading actor, and Philip Henslowe, his father-in-law, was manager. From 1594 this company had acted at the Rose, on the Bankside, with decided success. The money made there led to this new venture. The original theatre (see the print on p. 125) was built as nearly as possible like the Globe,[1] its rival on the Bankside, except that it was not circular but square inside. This building burnt in 1621, and was replaced by the structure well known from the very common print of it (see p. 125). This later theatre, as the print well shows, was not circular or even hexagonal without, as were the other theatres. Even inside it was not circular, but square like the original structure.

To the left of Golden Lane and farther from the Cathedral stood St. John's Gate (p. 135), the office of the Master of the Revels, without whose consent no play could be given. In his hands, too, were all performances at Court. At his office were kept the costumes and properties used for masks and plays at Greenwich, Whitehall, Hampton Court, or any of the royal residences. Near by, in St. John's Street, stood after 1608 the Red Bull Theatre. This was patronized by the unfashionable, and from contemporary reference and the print we have of its interior[2] was evidently less

---

[1] See the contract for the Fortune, in the *Appendix*.
[2] See p. 230.

fully equipped than its competitors. No print of its exterior exists.

If, instead of going westward to St. John's Gate, we had returned up Golden Lane, we could have walked rapidly by Beech Lane and Chiswell Street to Moorfields and thence to Bedlam. Just to the left as we enter the Bedlam region stood the Theatre, the first of the buildings specially devoted to plays (see p. 135). Just beyond it the Curtain[1] was built the next year, in 1577.

Both the earlier Fortune and the Theatre have been rescued from oblivion by applying a magnifying glass to the map of Ryther, on which they appear as little more than specks. They must be taken as only approximations to their originals, for any one who has studied the details of the old maps of London knows that to their makers it was the total effect which was the desideratum and that the theatres naturally meant no more to them than do our gasometers to typographers to-day. Consequently they drew them in with little or no care for accuracy, often, I suspect, conventionalizing them to a type form, and never suspecting that centuries later we should try to make these maps authoritative as to the exact form and position of each of these Elizabethan theatres.

If now we go directly across the City by Bishopsgate, Gracechurch Street, and New Fish Street, we shall be at the entrance to London Bridge.[2] As we cross that we

[1] See *Shakespeare Society's Papers*, Vol. I, p. 29.
[2] See Ryther's map, p. 36.

may meet a band of players with banners and trumpets who are announcing a performance of one of Shakespeare's plays at the Globe at two o'clock.

Once across the Bridge, let us stop some distance up the High Street to look back. We shall see that the Duke of Suffolk's Palace on the left has given place to tenements, and that both sides of the street are lined with inns. The Bear was in Bear Alley, the Green Dragon in Foul Lane. The Bull, with the pillory in front of it, stood about where the print from Wyngrerde's map on p. 46 ends; the Boar's Head, the property of the real Sir John Fastolfe, was nearly opposite. On the right were the White Hart, the George, and the Chaucerian Tabard. The Queen's Head was near the Bridge on the right. We are now in a region which for generations has been a centre of entertainment, for at one time a bull ring had stood at the fork in the streets seen in this view, and long before any theatre was built on this side of the river there had been a place for bull baiting and another for bear baiting, where the Globe and the Hope theatres will stand. By 1600 the theatres in this region looked much as they do in the view from the Visscher map (p. 155). By 1584 the property where the Rose Theatre stood later had been leased [1] by Philip Henslowe, although the theatre was probably not constructed until 1592.[2] The Rose

---

[1] *Memoirs of Edward Alleyn (Old Shaks. So.)*, p. 189, J. P. Collier.
[2] *Henslowe's Diary*, ed. Greg, pp. 7–10; but see, for question of a theatre in 1587, *Catalogue of Dulwich Mss.*, p. 233, G. F. Warner.

(p. 165) seems by 1603 to have been given up as a theatre, but it was still used for prize fighting. In 1594 Francis Langley had built the Swan Theatre (p. 165), considerably beyond the others, in the precinct of Paris Garden.[1] It was meant for bull and bear baiting as well as for plays, and its stage could, therefore, be removed. By 1632 it had fallen into decay.[2]

In December, 1598, Richard Burbadge became involved with Giles Allen in a dispute over a new lease of the Theatre, originally erected for his father, James Burbadge. Consequently, early in 1599, he connived with his brother Cuthbert in carrying the wood of the Theatre to the Bankside and there erecting a new play-

---

[1] The Lord Mayor, writing to the Lord High Treasurer in 1594, said: "Francis Langley, one of the Alnagers, for sealing cloths, intends to erect a new stage, or theatre, on the Bankside." (*City Remembrancia*, p. 354: 1579–1664.) In 1598 it was "ordered by the Vestry that Mr. Langley's new buildings shall be viewed, and that he and others shall be moved for money for the poor in regard to the playhouses and for tithes." (*Minutes St. Saviour's Vestry*.) In 1600 Peter Bromville was recommended from the Court to the Justices of Surrey as one known to the French king for his skill in feats of activities. Wishing to appear in some public place, he "has chosen the Swann, in Old Paris Garden, being the house of Francis Langley." (Quoted by William Rendle from a note lent him by Halliwell-Phillips.) For later particulars as to this theatre, see William Rendle's *The Playhouses at Bankside in the Time of Shakespeare*, originally printed in Walford's *Antiquarian*, but separately reprinted.

[2] In 1632, in the play *Holland's Leaguer*, the lady of the leaguer, speaking of three famous amphitheatres which can be seen from its turret, mentions "one other that the lady of the leaguer, or fortress, could almost shake hands with, now fallen to decay, and, like a dying swanne, hangs her head and sings her own dirge."

THE PALACE OF WHITEHALL

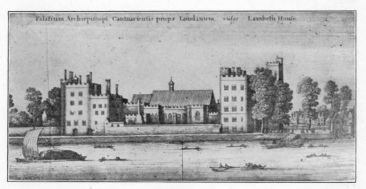

Palatium Archiepiscopi Cantuariensis propè Londinum. vulgò Lambeth House.

LAMBETH PALACE

house,[1] the Globe, on or near the site of the old bull-
baiting ring. The only authentic view we have of this
first Globe Theatre is from a map of London in 1610
by Hondius. (See Frontispiece).

Notice that the building, in distinction from the
structures shown in the group of theatres, is circular
rather than hexagonal or octagonal, for the circular
was the earlier form. It is thatched, too, not tiled
as were the later buildings, when the companies had
learned to their sorrow the inflammability of thatch.
The flagpole rises from the centre of the enclosure
rather than, as in the later theatres, from a turret
jutting inward from the tiled roof. These characteristics should be noted, for they help to identify some
views which have been misnamed. On June 29, 1613,
the first Globe was destroyed, for some lighted paper
from a piece of ordnance fired in a performance set fire
to the thatch and within an hour burned the house to
the ground. It was rebuilt (p. 175) as speedily as possible, and stood until 1644, when it was pulled down.[2]

The Hope Theatre, built "neare or uppon"[3] the site of
the old bear-baiting ring, was put up rapidly in 1613 (see
p. 165), to catch the custom temporarily lost to the
Globe by its fire. It was successful at first, but as the

[1] *Early London Theatres*, T. F. Ordish, pp. 75–76.
[2] It was "pulled doune to the ground by Sir Matthew Brand (owner
of the land), on Monday, April 15, 1644, to make tenements in the
room of it." Collier's *Life of Shakespeare*, p. ccxlii.
[3] See the contract in Malone's *Shakespeare*, Vol. III, Prolegomena,
p. 144.

theatrical centre, in the years after 1620, shifted to the region between Ludgate and Drury Lane, it fell into disuse as a theatre, though prize fights and bull baitings continued there till as late as 1682.[1]

For a long time it was thought that no view of the Rose Theatre existed, but a building on Hollar's map of London in 1647 usually identified as the first Globe Theatre is now believed by some to be the Rose.[2] The building is evidently an old theatre, for it is thatched, circular, and shows a flagpole rising from the pit. Moreover, it is too near the river for the Globe and does not agree with the view of that building by Hondius. Yet Hondius made his drawing when the Globe was in the full swing of its popularity and the original building still stood, but Hollar drew it when the old Globe had for over thirty years been replaced by a building of different construction, and when all the theatres had been disused and neglected for five years. The view cannot be the old Globe; it may reproduce roughly the Rose; possibly it is merely a conventionalized theatre.

There was also some building at Newington Butts which could be used as a theatre. Mr. Fleay shows that on account of the prevalence of the plague in June, 1592, My Lord Strange's Men were ordered by the Privy Council to play at Newington Butts instead of at the Rose Theatre. The restraint was not re-

[1] See Rendle, *The Playhouses at Bankside in the Time of Shakespeare*, p. 17.
[2] See p. 165.

moved till December of the same year.[1] In June, 1594, we find in *Henslowe's Diary*, " In the name of God Amen begininge at newington my Lord Admeralle men & my Lorde chamberlen men As ffolowethe 1594." [2] Again the plague and the Privy Council were responsible for this shift of about a mile into the fields. After ten days the company returned to the Rose.[3] Probably the structure used was an amphitheatre for sports, such as bull baiting, rather than a regularly equipped theatre. Stow speaks of it, in 1598, as built " in former times." [4]

There were in any of the large companies three groups of actors: the sharers, men who had acquired sufficient reputation to be allotted shares in order to bind them to the company; the actors employed at regular salaries, apparently in most cases actors of secondary rank or the younger men who had not yet won their spurs; and the boys. The last, dramatic apprentices, appear to have belonged to individual actors who were paid for their services, and sometimes they seem to have been sold by one actor to another.[5] That the means by which these boys were obtained were sometimes more

[1] *A Chronicle History of the London Stage*, p. 86.

[2] *Henslowe's Diary*, Greg, p. 17. For reference to plays " about Newington," in 1586, see *Old London Theatres*, T. F. Ordish, p. 147.

[3] *A Chronicle History of the London Stage*, p. 140.

[4] Rendle, *The Playhouses at Bankside in the Time of Shakespeare*, p. 18, says that the Newington Butts Theatre stood about where the Metropolitan Tabernacle, famous in the ministry of Mr. Spurgeon, now is.

[5] " bowght my boye, Jeames brystow, of william augusten, player, the 18 desembr 1597 for viij li ." *Henslowe's Diary*, Greg, p. 203.

than doubtful is shown by some old documents discovered a few years ago, in which a father has invoked the aid of the law to restore to him a son who had, according to the parent's story, been kidnapped on his way to school by the men at the head of the Children of Her Majesty's Revels.[1] Probably, however, such instances were rare, for there must have been many parents glad to apprentice their children to an art so full of glamour and so well rewarded.

Doubtless many men drifted into connection with the theatre, at least as far as managers and sharers are concerned. Until the theatres were built in London, and, indeed, to how late a date we do not know, the actors gave their performances in inn-yards. It is not difficult to see the advantage of such performances to innkeepers, nor is it difficult to imagine that sometimes the players left an inn decidedly in debt for lodging and food. What more natural than that some of these innkeepers should have become, willingly or unwillingly, financially interested in some one of the companies, or that younger members of their families should have gone upon the stage? We know, for instance, that the father of the great Edward Alleyn was an innholder in Bishopsgate, and that his brother John, after some experience as an actor, succeeded his father as innholder.[2] As for the famous Philip Henslowe, he was

[1] *History of the Stage*, F. G. Fleay, pp. 127–132.

[2] *Memoirs of Edward Alleyn*, J. P. Collier (*Old Shaks. So. Pubs.*), pp 3–4; *Catalogue of Mss. and Monuments of Dulwich College*, G. T. Warner, pp. xvi–xvii.

originally a dyer, and whether he went into theatrical management purely as a speculation or was drawn in because of money advanced by him to actors, — later in life he certainly seems to have been a money lender, — or whether at first he meant to do no more than to let his building, the Rose, to whatever company cared to use it, are unsettled questions. In any case, sources from which these dramatic companies could at need get fairly large sums of money are sufficiently evident.

As one turns the pages of such a book as Mr. Fleay's *A Chronicle History of the London Stage*, one is fairly bewildered by the number of companies and the different titles, but closer examination shows that the changes are often merely in name. If a new company was formed, it must get the right from some one of the nobility to bear his title. Originally, undoubtedly, and perhaps till the theatres were built in London, a company had some close relation to the man whose title it bore; for instance, the members may have been required to act in his presence when he wished; but certainly by 1590 the relation seems to have been largely a nominal one — except when the company wished favors from City or provincial authorities or got into trouble. In such cases the interest of the patron was invoked.[1] Of course, when the patron

---

[1] See Lord Hunsdon's letter to the Lord Mayor in October, 1594, asking permission for his men to play at the Cross Keys Inn, *Illustrations of Shakespeare*, Halliwell, p. 31. For letters of the Earl of Nottingham in behalf of his players, see *Memoirs of Edward Alleyn*, J. P. Collier (*Old Shaks. So.*), pp. 55–57.

gained a new title or died, the name of the company must be changed, so that the company of Shakespeare was in succession My Lord Strange's Men, My Lord Derby's Men, and the Lord Chamberlain's Men. After the succession of King James, the company became the King's Men. Meantime, of course, the company underwent, also, the changes that death, necessary retirement from the stage, and the addition of needed young players must mean. Now and then, as in a time of prolonged plague, — for the Privy Council closed the theatres whenever they thought danger of infection too great,[1] — some of the companies, especially the smaller ones, could not, as the phrase went "save their charges" and so went to pieces. At such a time their wardrobes, and their plays in part, passed to other companies. Other plays went to the publishers and were printed for the first time. The actors themselves scattered among the other companies or formed some group to perform English plays in Germany, Holland, or Denmark, where the English players were very popular between 1585 and 1600, and where their plays strongly affected the German and Dutch drama. The only other resource in hard times was to take to the country, but it is not likely that when the plague raged in London the actors would have been very welcome anywhere.

Much of the current wonder that Shakespeare's heroines could have been adequately represented by boys and youths vanishes if one knows the contem-

[1] *History of Stage*, F. G. Fleay, p. 162.

porary evidence as to their exceeding skill and realizes
how long, thorough, and varied the training of an
Elizabethan actor could be. As I have already said,
the men's companies were made up of the sharers, the
actors on regular salaries, and the boys; but acting
was by no means confined to these companies. In the
first place, with the revival of learning and the spread of
general education in England, the custom of presenting
Latin plays in the great schools such as Westminster
and the Merchant Taylors' School became widespread.
Here was an impulse to send some youths upon the
stage and by no means wholly unequipped, but it was
undoubtedly slight as compared with the effect on
acting of the companies of choir boys, such as, in
particular, those of the Chapel Royal and St. Paul's
Cathedral. Words of Shakespeare in the first quarto
Hamlet [1] as to the wandering players show that at the
opening of the seventeenth century the performances
of these choir boys roused jealousy among the men's
companies. Nor was this popularity probably wholly
a mere fad of the moment. For generations the selection of these boys for their abilities as singers and,
prospectively, as actors, had been carefully organized

[1] *Hamlet.*   How comes it that they travell? Do they grow
                 restie?
Gildenstern.   No, my Lord, their reputation holds as it was wont.
Hamlet.   How then?
Gildenstern.   Yfaith my Lord, noveltie carries it away,
                 For the principall publike audience that
                 Came to them, are turned to private playes,
                 And to the humour of children.

[57]

under the favor of royalty itself. So, too, had their training. For instance, the following writ of the days of Richard III is merely the earliest of a long list of similar documents reaching down to the second decade of the seventeenth century:—

"Ric., etc. To all and every our subjects, as well spiritual as temporal, these letters hering or seeing, greeting. We let you wite, that for the confidence and trust we have in our trusty, wel-beloved servaunt John Melyonek, and of the gentilmen of our Chapel, and kenning also his expert habilitie and connying in the science of music, have licensed him, and by these presents licence and give him auctoritie, that within all places in this our realme, as well Cathedral-churches, colleges, chapels, houses of religion, and all other franchised and exempt places, as elliswhere, our College Roil, at Wyndesor reserved and except, to take and sease for us and in our name all such singing men and children, being expart in the said science of musique, as he can find and think sufficient, and able to do us service. Wherefore, etc. (1484–1485)." [1]

The early age at which these boys were taken up and the severity of their training are shown by some autobiographic lines of the poet, Thomas Tusser. They

[1] *Cheque Book of the Chapel Royal*, pp. vii-viii. Rimbault. Camden Society Publications. A rare series of privately printed pamphlets, compiled by Miss Maria Hackett, in 1812–1814, in her effort to recover for the St. Paul's Boys some of their ancient privileges and rights, show how carefully the education and care of the boys had been provided for up till the end of the eighteenth century.

trace, too, his progress from a provincial choir to St.
Paul's Cathedral and even Eton: —

"I yet but yong, no speech of tongue,
    Nor tears withall, that often fall
    From mother's eyes when child outcries,
        To part her fro,

"Could pity make good father take,
    But out I must to song be thrust,
    Say what I would, do what I could,
        His mind was so.

"O painful time, for every crime!
    What touzed ears, like baited bears!
    What bobbed lips, what jerks, what nips!
        What hellish toys!

"What robes how bare, what college fare!
    What bread how stale, what penny ale!
    Then Wallingford, how wast thou abhorr'd,
        Of seely boys!

"Then for my voice, I must (no choice)
    Away of force, like posting horse,
    For sundry men had placards then,
        Such child to take:

"The better breast, the lesser rest,
    To serve the choir, now there, now here;
    For time so spent, I may repent,
        And sorrow make.

"But mark the chance, myself to 'vance
    By friendship's lot to Paul's I got;
    So found I grace, a certain space
        Still to remain

"With Redford[1] there, the like nowhere,
    For cunning such and virtue much,

[1] Master of St. Paul's choir, *fl.* 15–.   Author of the morality, *Wyt and Science.*

[59]

> By whom some part of musick art,
>   So did I gain.

> "From Paul's I went, to Eton sent,
>   To learn straightways the Latin phrase,
>   Where fifty-three stripes given to me
>   At once I had.

> "For fault but small or none at all,
>   It came to pass thus beat I was:
>   See Udall,[1] see the mercy of thee,
>   To me, poor lad."

Acting occasionally at Court and daily before the public was, at least from 1580 to 1608, as important a part of the duties of these boys as their work as choristers. Trained at first chiefly to act what was graceful, what called out all their skill in singing the many songs scattered through the plays, or what depended chiefly upon its story for effect, they passed to creation of exceedingly difficult rôles in the work of Thomas Middleton, Ben Jonson, George Chapman, John Marston, and Beaumont and Fletcher. So wonderfully did these little fellows act that a critic as severe as old Ben Jonson paid the highest possible praise to one of the Children of the Chapel Royal, little Salathiel Pavy, in, if it can be believed, the parts of old men.

> "Weep with me all you that read this little story;
>   And know for whom a tear you shed,
>   Death's self is sorry.
>   'Twas a child that so did thrive
>   In grace and feature,
>   As heaven and nature seemed to strive
>   Which owned the creature.

[1] Master of Eton School, 1534–1541. Author of *Ralph Roister Doister*.

THE STRAND

(Looking from Charing Cross toward Ludgate and St. Paul's Cathedral)

Years he numbered scarce thirteen,
When fates turned cruel;
Yet three filled zodiacs had he been
The stage's jewel.

"And did act,
What now we moan
Old men so duly,
As, sooth, the Parcæ thought him one
He played so truly.
So, by error, to his fate
They all consented;
But viewing him since (Alas, too late!)
They have repented;
And have sought, to give new birth,
In baths to steep him;
But being so much too good for earth,
Heaven vows to keep him."

Think what these companies of boys must have meant to acting as an art! Of course not all the boys, when their voices broke, took advantage of the provisions existing to send them to the higher schools or universities, but some must have gone into the men's companies; and it is by no means unlikely that even some of those who went to the schools, and even perhaps to the universities, turned to acting or to dramatic writing later. Certainly the career of Nathaniel Field illustrates the development of a member of the St. Paul's company into a player, with men's companies, of women's as well as men's rôles and into a playwright. How much all this training at the most pliable period must have expedited development into mature actors or playwrights! When one recalls this training and remembers that in all the companies there were, also,

[61]

"players' boys" who were learning the art of acting, one sees that by the age of twenty a youth might have had twelve years of steady practice in a great round of male and female parts under instruction from the best actors, musicians, and dancing masters of the time. Does it still seem strange that Shakespeare, with such schools of acting existing, consented to intrust his heroines to these beardless youths? To-day we constantly intrust our modern stage heroines, much subtler than most of the Elizabethan drama, to graduates of grammar schools or of society who have had but a year or two of experience upon the stage and have never learned the rudiments of the art they pretend to exemplify. So clearly did Charles II see the value of these children's companies to acting as an art that he endeavored, though in vain, to establish such a company in 1660.[1]

The danger for dramatist and manager of free competition among the companies for the services of any specially gifted actor was provided for by making the leading men sharers in the company and by binding the men on salary as follows: —

"Mandom that the 6 of aguste 1597 J bownd Richard Jones by & a sumsett of ijd to contenew & playe wth the companye of my lord admeralles players frome mi[x] helmase next after the daye a bowe w^{r}itten vntell the eand & tearme of iij yeares emediatly folowinge & to playe in my howsse only known by the name

[1] *Shakespeare Society's Papers*, Vol. III, pp. 80–81.

of the Rosse & in no other howsse a bowt london pub-
licke & yf Restraynte be granted then to go for the tyme
into the contrey & after to retorne agayne to london
yf he breacke this a sumsett then to forfett vnto me
for the same a hundreth markes of lafull money of
Ingland wittnes to this E Alleyn & John midleton." [1]

The supply of plays was large because production of
them was rapid. On this point there has been far too
much readiness among students of our older stage to
argue from present to past conditions, and to insist that
this or that play could not have been written at a given
date because it would have come but a few weeks after
another play by the author which is clearly dated.
But this from *Henslowe's Diary* shows that a man later
proud of the slowness and care of his dramatic composition had at first to write at top speed : —

"lent vnto Bengemen Johnson the 3 of desemb₃
1597 vpon a boocke wch he showed the plotte vnto the
company wch he promysed to dd vnto the company
at cryssmas next the some of xx s." [2]

In the prologue to *Volpone* Jonson speaks of five
weeks as the time usually spent in composing a play.
We find, too, a dramatist of considerable repute in his
own time, Daborne, agreeing to write a play between
the twenty-fourth of December and the tenth of the
following February.[3] Nor can one explain this ra-

[1] *Henslowe's Diary*, W. W. Greg, Pt. I, p. 202. For similar agreements, see *idem*, pp. 201, 203–204.

[2] *Idem*, p. 82.

[3] *The Alleyn Papers*, J. P. Collier (*Old Shaks. So.*), p. 73.

pidity of composition by saying that these dramatists doubtless mulled over their material a long time before submitting their plots, for their receipts were not sufficient to allow them to produce a few plays per year. Between 1590 and 1600 the price for a play seems to have been between £6 and £8.[1] Allow that money had then eight times its present purchasing value, and also that, as D'Avenant alleges,[2] it was the Elizabethan custom to give an author the proceeds of the second day, yet an income sufficient for a year is hardly evident. Unless a dramatist had, like Jonson, some patron to aid him, or had other wares to sell, he must keep on pouring out plays as rapidly as possible. Just here the readiness of the Elizabethan public, already explained, to hear a good story retold, must have been of great aid.

Nor were plays lightly selected. Henslowe, when deciding to advance earnest money to some playwright for a proposed play, seems to have depended largely on recommendations from some member of his company of the "booke" containing the plot.[3] Always, too, he had at hand the trained judgment of his son-in-law

[1] *Henslowe s Diary*, Greg, p. 85 *et seq.*

[2] "There is an old tradition
That in the times of mighty *Tamberlaine,*
Of conjuring *Faustus,* and the *Beauchamps* bold,
You poets us'd to have the second day."

— *Play-House to be Let.*

[3] "Lent vnto Thomas Dowton the 10 of febreary 1598 to bye a boocke of m^r hewode called Jonne as good as my ladey the some iijli." *Henslowe's Diary*, Greg, p. 102 *et seq.*

and theatrical partner, the great actor Edward Alleyn, and there is evidence that he used it.[1] Undoubtedly, the chief criterion was, "Is the story likely to act well?"

These glimpses into the life of the Shakespearian actors must show that they were financially well backed, had protectors of high rank, were well organized as a body, and even managed the selection of their plays in businesslike fashion. In brief, the profession of the actor was well established in the decade of 1590–1600.

Performances at the theatres began at two or at three o'clock, except at St. Paul's, where the choir boys were not allowed to act till after prayers, that is, at four o'clock, and must finish by six, when the gates of the Cathedral were closed. Performances lasted from two hours to two hours and a half. All that can be said with safety as to prices at the theatres is that they were not the same at all theatres, were raised for first nights, and tended upward. Admission to the pit, at various places and times between 1600 and 1640, ran from a penny to sixpence. The contract for building the Fortune calls for "gentlemens roomes" and "twoo-pennie-roomes."[2] This suggests that the two-penny

[1] Daborne writing to Henslowe in regard to one of his plays, said, "If y{u} please to appoynt any hower to read to Mr Allin, I will not fayle." _The Alleyn Papers_, J. P. Collier, p. 60.

[2] This passage in the contract is ambiguous and is not so easily disposed of as students have thought. It reads, "All which stories shall containe twelve foot and a half of lawful assize in breadth through-oute, besides a juttey forwards in eyther of the saide two upper stories of ten ynches of lawful assize; with fower convenient divisions

F   [65]

rooms were in the top gallery, for the price is commonly named for seats there. According to the date and the theatre, prices for places in the lower rooms or boxes ranged from sixpence to half a crown, the highest charge probably being for such seats as those in the "gentlemens roomes" named in the Fortune contract. If one hired a stool for use on the stage, — for gallants were allowed to sit on the stage during the performance, — one paid from sixpence to a shilling. It is not clear whether in the public theatre stools could be hired for use in the pit, but this was the custom in such private theatres as the Blackfriars. I suspect that at least occasionally it was possible even in the public theatres. The range of prices in October, 1614, on a first night in a not fashionable theatre, the Hope, is seen from the Induction to Ben Jonson's *Bartholomew Fair*. "It is further agreed that every person here have his or their free will of censure, to like or dislike at their own charge, the author having now departed with his right; it shall be lawful for any man to judge his six pen'worth, his twelve pen'worth, so to his eighteen pence, two

for gentlemens roomes, and other sufficient and convenient divisions for twoo-pennie roomes; with necessarie seates to be placed and sett as well in these roomes as throughoute all the rest of the galleries of the said house." (See *Appendix*.) This shows that each "room" contained several places, and does it not raise the question whether there were not "four gentlemen's rooms" and some "two-penny rooms" in each story? That is, perhaps, the Jacobean managers were wise enough to grade prices according to the desirability of the seat either in point of seeing or being seen. If so, our present-day method of treating the Elizabethan galleries *en bloc* as to prices is amusingly wrong.

shillings, half a crown, to the value of this place; provided always his place get not above his wit."[1] Certain passages in the *Papers* of Edward Alleyn[2] suggest that at least at the Fortune a theatre-goer paid for admission at the door, and then when he had picked his place by observation of the house paid a "gatherer" or "box-holder" for the particular seat chosen. Certainly there were "gatherers" at each door. Gallants taking seats on the stage probably entered through the tiring house.

Now that we have seen the exterior of the theatres and the formation of the companies, let us look at the stage itself. No place is more tenacious of old customs than is the theatre, and actors in their art are conservatives. The very evolution of the English stage proves this true. When playing passed from the monks to the guilds, the performances were given on pageant wagons much like the floats at our modern carnivals, but by the time of the Moralities, in the fifteenth and sixteenth centuries, performances outdoors were often on scaffolds such as that shown on p. 190. A curtain could be stretched at the back of the platform so as to give a middle and two side entrances. The musicians played at the back of the stage. The per-

---

[1] For the evidence as to prices, see especially *English Dramatic Poetry and Annals of the Stage,* ed. 1879, J. P. Collier, Vol. III, pp. 146–157.

[2] In the articles of Dawes, a player, "suche moneyes as shal be receaved at the Galleres and tyring howse" are mentioned. *The Alleyn Papers,* J. P. Collier, p. 76.

formance took place in front of them without scenery of any kind, without any protection from the weather, and with no possibility of any dividing up of the stage unless some space was left behind the curtain where tableaux effects could be disclosed. So crowded, at best, must have been this space, however, that free use of such an arrangement does not seem likely. Of course such a platform in the middle of a city or town square must have been much disturbed by noises round about, and the actors must have found it difficult to collect money from the attending crowd, for it could easily melt away just as the collection began. We do not know when it first occurred to actors to use inn-yards, but those of the olden time (see p. 200), with their two or three galleries running all round a courtyard, were well fitted for the actors' purposes. They could easily control the exits and entrances of the audience, and could treat the spaces in the galleries which adjoined the rooms of the inn as the equivalent of our modern boxes. Indeed, the Elizabethan word "room" for a theatre box held a memory of these spaces next the rooms of the old inns. The courtyard was the pit, where the audience stood or sat on stools hired for the purpose. The actor hung his curtain at the back of an improvised platform and just at the edge of the gallery. He used a room or rooms across the passage behind the curtain for a dressing or "tiring" room. Now, however, he had gained a second stage, namely, the space in the first balcony just above his curtain, for

of

ON

Nego layne

Spitle

Artillerie lane

Artillerie garden

Spittle feildes

on wall

Howndes Ditch

Bishopsgate

Streete

Aldgate

white Chapell

Leade n hall Streete

Carne s hill

Fanchurchs Streete

Harstrete

Rosmary la:

Tow er hill

East smithfeild

Towre Streete

The Tower

ames Streete

Tower wharfe

THAMES

St Toolies Streete

604

(Ryther)

LUDGATE

there people supposed to be on a balcony, looking out of a window, or on the walls of a town, might appear.

When the actors could plan for a home of their own, in 1576, they deftly combined the facilities offered by certain existing buildings, namely, the bull-baiting and bear-baiting rings, with conditions to which they had become accustomed in the inn-yards, and also provided for some needs hitherto unsatisfied. The rings, like the inn-yards, provided a pit, surrounding galleries, the upper stage in the first gallery, and space for a tiring house behind the curtain of the stage. But the circular shape of the ring brought all of an audience nearer than some were under the conditions of the quadrangular inn-yards, — a decided improvement. There was added by the actors a long-felt want, a sort of hood projecting from the wall in front of the tiring house over some third or half of the depth of the stage. The space within the hood permitted machinery by which gods and goddesses in their chariots or cars could be lowered among the mortals. Technically known as the "Heavens," this hood was supported by pillars at its front, or, as in the case of the Hope Theatre in 1613, rested on beams projecting from the rear wall.[1]

On certain characteristics of the Elizabethan theatre there is agreement; namely, that the flying of a flag above the "Heavens" gave notice of a performance; that the stage was strewn with rushes; that the trumpet

[1] See *Appendix* for the building contract.

sounded thrice before the prologue came out to speak; that he appeared on a little balcony high up on the right side of the "Heavens"; that the music room was on one side of the stage or at times just behind it; that the tiring room was but a short distance behind the rear exits of the stage; that the earlier Globe at least, the Swan, the earlier Fortune, and the Hope had "Heavens"; that there were both an upper and a lower stage, as in the inn-yards; and that mechanism concealed somewhere, probably in the hut of the "Heavens," allowed heavy properties to be lowered upon the stage. Where dispute occurs or vagueness exists, is in regard to the seating capacity; spectators on the upper stage; signs for the name of the play and the placing of the scenes; the number of exits; the use of hangings or curtains on the stages, whether they be called "curtain," "curtains," or "arras"; the presence of scenery of any kind; and the exact purpose of the second hut, behind that over the "Heavens," seen in pictures of the second Globe Theatre (see p. 175).

Before I begin my discussion of these mooted questions, let me remind a reader that there was probably no one Elizabethan or Jacobean playhouse which was completely typical, but that they differed according to their age and the finances, as well as the ingenuity, of the companies. That there were elaborate properties and ingenious mechanical devices not merely at Court performances, the stage directions of many plays, notably Heywood's *Ages* and also Henslowe's inven-

tory of his properties, clearly prove. The audience
saw the great horse of Troy on the stage and watched
the Greeks steal out of it to surprise the city.[1] Of course,
some properties made heavy demands on the imagination of the audience, as Henslowe's "a robe for to goo
invisibell," but this was unusual. The stage was high
enough for music underneath and for Hamlet's father to
walk with such ease as was possible for so perturbed a
spirit. Other spirits descended from the "Heavens"
or ascended from the depths below. Transformations
of persons to trees and of trees to persons took place
before the eyes of the spectators. Heads rose from
practicable wells and answered questions. Remember,
too, it is quite conceivable that an age which could
produce some of our greatest imaginative writing may
have had craftsmen imaginative and skilled enough to
meet any difficulty met by the actors in mounting
their plays. At Court throughout this time there were
very elaborate performances with curtains and, apparently, perspective scenery.[2] The foremost architect
of the time, Inigo Jones, who was thoroughly informed
as to the conditions of the theatrical representations in
Italy, at the time the country most advanced in scenic
display and ingenuity, was concerned in the Court productions. He was, too, the friend of the dramatists.
In the light of all this is there not a strong probability

[1] *Henslowe's Diary*, ed. J. P. Collier, pp. 271–277 (*Old Shaks. So.*).
[2] See entries in *Accounts of the Revels at Court*, P. Cunningham
(*Old Shaks. So.*).

that we have underestimated the equipment of the best Elizabethan and Jacobean theatres? It must be remembered, too, that these older dramatists supervised, or at least attended, the rehearsals of their plays, and that it was not, therefore, necessary to give as minute directions for the staging of them as must the modern writer whose play may be produced in half a dozen places at the same time. The text, both when acted and when read, was the thing in those days; even for the reader the stage direction had not assumed at all its present importance. Consequently, Elizabethan stage directions make but a weak basis for argument. At best they are the hints of the writer to the experienced stage managers of the day, their shorthand correspondence, so to speak. To us, with our incomplete knowledge of the detailed conditions of the Elizabethan stage, they can convey but half truths. Summed up in a sentence, modern investigation of the presentation of Elizabethan plays amounts to this: we are gradually correcting much misapprehension and are just beginning to understand those conditions. There is, however, much that in the light of present evidence cannot be finally settled.

The seating capacity of an Elizabethan theatre has usually been estimated as somewhere between three hundred and twelve hundred. Recently Mr. John Corbin, in an acute and brilliant argument in behalf of the plasticity of the Shakespearian stage,[1] maintained

---

[1] *The Atlantic Monthly*, March, 1906, pp. 371–372.

in passing that the Fortune and probably other Elizabethan theatres held nearly three thousand people. He
rests on the testimony of Johannes de Witt accompany-
ing the famous sketch of the Swan Theatre.[1] In the
first place, Mr. Corbin's witness is very suspicious, for
if one asks a half dozen persons in any audience to guess
the seating capacity of the room, they will, unless some
of them know it already, give as many different esti-
mates. Nothing can be more untrustworthy than
approximate estimating of an audience, especially in
the retrospect. Moreover, this particular witness, De
Witt, commits himself to the statement that the Swan
was built of a peculiar kind of flint stones. Mr. Corbin
admits that this is a mistake. De Witt probably mis-
took a cross-timbered plaster construction for real
stone. Mr. W. W. Lawrence pointed out some time
ago [2] why Van Buchell's sketch of the Swan stage from
De Witt's description must at best be taken as only a
somewhat confused memory. In the first place, one
cannot deduce from the size of the Fortune that the
other theatres were equally large. It is clear from
the very wording of the contract for the Fortune that
that theatre was larger than the Globe, not only
because it was square inside instead of circular, but

[1] De Witt wrote, "The largest [theatre] . . . seats three thousand
persons, [and] is built of a concrete of flint stones which abound in
Great Britain." See print of interior, p. 210.
[2] *Englische Studien*, 1903, Vol. 32, *Some Characteristics of the Eliza-
bethan-Stuart Stage*, p. 44.

because built on a larger scale.[1] The price of the Hope shows that it must have been smaller than the Fortune, yet it was to be of "suche large compasse, forme, wideness, and height, as the plaie house called the Swan."[2] It is surprising, too, that if the audiences were as large as Mr. Corbin conceives, the return to Philip Henslowe as his share of a first night at the Rose was but between £3 and £4.[3] As he owned the theatre and was manager of the company most often playing at the Rose, is it likely at all that this amount represents his share in more than a total of £10 or £20? Moreover, we know that when the players acted at Court they were given £10 for an evening performance, for that allowed them to play also in their theatre in the afternoon, but that they exacted £20 when they lost their income of the afternoon by acting at Court.[4] Indeed, that looks as if £10 came nearer even than £20 to their profits from a single performance. Necessary expenses were, at the late date of 1628, when prices had risen, estimated at £2–5 a performance.[5] We know, too, that when Herbert, Master of the Revels, was, in 1628,

[1] Street the builder was to "make all the saide frame in every poynte for scantlings lardger and bigger in assize than the scantlings of the timber of the saide new-erected house called the Globe."

[2] The Fortune in 1599–1600 cost £440; the Hope in 1613 cost £360.

[3] *Henslowe's Diary*, W. W. Greg, p. 13 *et passim*. From a partnership agreement of Henslowe with John Cholmley, in 1587, we learn that the Rose property, on which at least one small building besides the theatre stood, was but 94 ft. square. *Memoirs of Edward Alleyn*, J. P. Collier (*Old Shaks. So.*), p. 189.

[4] Malone's *Shakespeare*, Vol. III, Prolegomena, pp. 167–68.

[5] *Idem*, p. 176.

given twice a year the second day of a revived play, his returns ran from £1–5 to £17–10.[1] As he was charged £2–5 for actual expenses, that made the largest return, even at this late date, but about £20. Moreover, when Taylor, the water poet, in 1613, writes complainingly of the loss of custom because the theatres, except the Globe, are now all on the Westminster side of the Thames and ferrying is no longer generally required by theatre-goers, he says that the theatres — at least two and possibly four — draw off from him some three or four thousand possible customers. Surely, as he is making the strongest case for himself that he can, he would have said, were Mr. Corbin's figures correct, that some nine or ten thousand were drawn off. What becomes, too, of the admitted intimate effects of the Elizabethan drama if the plays were given in theatres equalled in size only by the largest of the American theatres? Long since Americans realized that buildings so large seriously hamper the best dramatic work. Even longer England has recognized the fact. At most, then, the question of the seating capacity may be regarded as open; certainly not as settled.

The De Witt print is largely responsible for the persistence of the idea that seats in the upper stage were used and even coveted by the richer part of the audience. It is by no means clear that the persons seen in this gallery in the print are not actors in the play watch-

<hr />

[1] *Idem*, pp. 176–77.

ing the scene on the front stage, so that any argument from it starts from an exceedingly weak premise. Secondly, the great majority of the Elizabethan plays call for use of the upper stage. How convenient and how probable, to turn the occupiers of the upper stage seats out when the exigencies of the play demanded! Above all, why should rational theatre-goers wish to gaze on the backs of the actors and to sit in the one part of the house where hearing would be most difficult? Because we do not know exactly where the Lords' Rooms, the Gentleman's Rooms, were, does not prove that they were in the upper stage. Rather, Henslowe's contract for the Hope Theatre requires "two boxes in the lower most storie, fitt and decent for gentlemen to sitt in."

One of the deeply rooted ideas in regard to Shakespeare's stage is that the place of each scene was indicated by signboards conspicuously placed, and changed whenever necessary. Undeniably, signs were sometimes used. Doubtless, in more than one representation in the country, and even perhaps in theatres no better equipped than the Red Bull, there was real significance in such a direction as has come down to us with one old play of 1603, that if any of the properties "will not serve the term by reason of concourse of the people on the stage, then you may omit the said properties which be outward and supply their places with their nuncupations only in text letters."[1] We have, too,

[1] *Faery Pastoral*, 1603, St. Paul's Boys.

[76]

the following direction in a play written in 1601 and produced by the St. Paul's Boys: —

"Harwich. In middle of the Stage Colchester with Image of Tarlton, Signe and Ghirlond Under him also. The Raungers Lodge, Maldon, A Ladder of Roapes trussed up neare Harwich. Highest and aloft the Title. The Cuckqueanes and Cuckolds Errants. A Long Fourme." [1]

That is, there were three doors labelled respectively Harwich, Colchester, and Maldon, with necessary properties arranged near each. Again, in the *Famous Contention of the House of York and Lancaster*, one finds the following direction, "Alarmes to the battaile, and then enter the Duke of Somerset and Richard fighting, and Richard kills him under the sign of the castle in St. Albones." [2] Of course, too, every one remembers the lines in Sir Philip Sidney's *Defence of Poesy*, "What childe is there that comming to a Play and seeing *Thebes* written in great letters on an olde doore, doth beleeve that it is *Thebes?*" [3] Yet one must move with exceeding caution from these instances, or even from others which are sometimes cited, to the generalization that during the period from 1575 to 1620 it was the custom in public performances by professional actors to distinguish the scenes by signs. Very likely the title of the play was usually displayed "highest and aloft,"

[1] *Cuckqueens' and Cuckolds Errants*, 1601, acted by the St. Paul's Boys.

[2] *Shakespeare's Library*, W. C. Hazlitt, Pt. II, Vol. I, p. 516.

[3] *The Defence of Poesy*, ed. A. S. Cook, p. 36.

that is, on the front of the "Heavens," where that structure existed. Clearly, in some instances, the place of the play, and even the places, were shown by signs, but that these signs were shifted as often as the scene changed, that any indication of scene by signs was characteristic of the whole period, or was general in any division of that period, remain to be proved. In the first place, in the quotation just given from the *Defence of Poesy*, Sidney is not writing of the stage, but is illustrating his point that not even a child takes literally all that he is told. How do we know that he is thinking of public stage performances rather than of those which more appealed to him, the plays at Court modelled on the Classic drama and set in classical fashion? No one denies that at these Court performances there were signs. Even if he did have the public stage in mind, he was writing of the crude conditions before 1583. Even the *Famous Contention* provides a weak basis for deduction, for it belongs before 1590. Grant all that may be asked for both as evidence for their own time, and you merely have a custom which may have in the main disappeared by 1600. As for the play given by the St. Paul's Boys, it hardly seems fair to draw conclusions for the public theatres and the men's companies from the plays given by boys in private and special theatres. Finally, if the use of signs was general, why all the care of the dramatists between 1590 and 1642 to place their auditors exactly? Surely not from an irrepressible desire to run into poetic description.

THE BLACKFRIARS THEATRE

Nowadays one sometimes hears lines of Sidney's widely separated from those just quoted given with them as proof that the public stage of his day used signs widely, when really the second quotation clearly demonstrates that in many plays seen by him the audience had no means, till helped out by the poet, to tell where the scene was supposed to take place.

"You shall have Asia of the one side, and Afric of the other, and so many other under-kingdoms, that the player when he cometh in must ever begin with telling where he is, or else the tale will not be conceived. Now ye shall have three ladies walk to gather flowers, and then we must believe the stage to be a garden. By and by we hear news of a shipwreck in the same place, and then we are to blame if we accept it not for a rock. Upon the back of that comes out a hideous monster with fire and smoke, and then the miserable beholders are bound to take it for a cave. While in the meantime two armies fly in, represented with four swords and bucklers, and then what hard heart will not receive it for a pitched field?"[1]

Does that picture a stage with doors carefully marked to indicate the places in which the play takes place? Certainly not. Just the opposite, in fact. Nor should we in considering the probabilities in this matter forget that the use of elaborate and suggestive properties was steadily increasing after 1590. For myself, I believe that there never were signs saying merely,

[1] *The Defence of Poesy*, ed. A. S. Cook, p. 48.

"This is a street," "This is a house," etc., and that, though signs bearing the titles of the plays may well have been displayed, the use of signs to denote special places was old, decreasing, and by 1600 unusual.

Another subject of doubt which any careful consideration of the stage directions of the old quartos and folios will settle is as to the number of doors on the Shakespearian stage. But any such consideration must be of originals and not of reprints in which modern editors have self-satisfiedly interpreted or improved on the old directions. Of course, the theatres were not alike in this matter, but clearly they had whatever number of doors was necessary. For, so far as I have been able to ascertain, these Elizabethans were no less intelligent or ingenious than the managers and the actors of the present day. Evidently the space under the balcony at the back of the stage was sometimes hung with arras, which, parted in the middle, gave three approaches to the stage, or without this parting one at each end; or there were doors in the space as one sees them in the De Witt print; or, as there are directions which call for what seem to be practicable gates, both doors and arras seem to have been dispensed with and the gate built in for the performance. After all, why should there not have been great folding doors, with one or more smaller doors in each, which, when closed, would present the appearance of the De Witt print and which, when folded back against the side walls, would allow the arras to be hung, a practicable gate to be built in, or properties to be so placed that the recess represented a cave? Unless the space under the gallery could be widely opened, how could the entrances through the arras sometimes hung there be easily managed? How else, too, provide for bringing on the cumbersome properties often called for in Elizabethan plays; for instance, the frequently recurring dais? Is this plan for big folding doors too ingenious to have occurred to a man as shrewd as Philip Henslowe, as imaginative as Edward Alleyn, as skilled as Inigo Jones? All intelligence is not of the present, nor is it wholly the property of the stage antiquarians.

I believe, too, that not only were as many doors as might be needed provided for, but that they were placed wherever the action of the play demanded, not merely under the "Heavens" in the space just beneath the upper stage. First of all, we have many bits of evidence to show that three entrances were often used. Take, for instance, the opening stage direction of *Eastward Ho!*: "Enter Master Touchstone and Quicksilver at several doors. At the middle door, enter Golding discovering a goldsmith's shop and walking short turns before it." There are three entrances clearly enough. Moreover, two of the entrances must be beyond the space under the "Heavens," for that was too limited to allow a set shop to be discovered and give an entrance on each side of the shop. Evidently Touchstone and Quicksilver enter at left and at right of the space under the upper stage. In *Lucrece* (Act V,

G [81]

Sc. 3) we find this also, "Enter in severall places, Sextus and Valerius above." That is, there was an entrance at each end of the upper stage. The fact is, any close study of Elizabethan and Jacobean stage directions should convince the student that dramatists of those days never thought of their stage as rigid, but as supremely plastic, and calmly planned for whatever they desired, trusting to skilled carpenters and mother wit to create what they had planned. Perhaps the direction in Brome's *Covent Garden Weeded* that Dorcas, who has just appeared above "upon a bellconie," shall "run down the stairs" means only that she shall be heard running down them behind the scenes, but one is not so sure in *Two Murders in One*,[1] that some construction connecting the lower and the upper stage was not used. Merry, the murderous innkeeper, states his plan to lure his neighbor, Beech, to the garret and there kill him. He says: —

> "And therefore I will place the hammer here
> And take it as I follow Beech up staires,
> That suddenly, before he is aware,
> I may with blowes dash out his hatefull braines."

Later he bids Beech "Goe up these staires, your friends do stay above," picking up the concealed hammer as his victim precedes him. Later when Rachel, the sister, goes to see who is above, the direction is, not as elsewhere, *Exit*, but *Exit up*. Moreover, in this same play it looks as if the actors may have used one of the

[1] *A Collection of Old English Plays*, A. H. Bullen, Vol. IV, pp. 19–22.

nearest boxes as the home of Beech. After the villain has stated his murderous scheme, comes the direction, "Then Merry must passe to Beeches shoppe, who must set in his shop, and Winchester his boy stand by: Beech reading." If the shop were set under the upper stage, Merry must originally enter well at one side, as must Rachel and Williams when they enter because they have heard some one going upstairs. Yet as the speeches at all these entrances are important, and the "garret" is just above centre entrance, it would be much more natural and more effective to give the speeches at centre back. That, however, necessitates using one of the neighboring boxes as Beech's shop.

Nor can we forgot the tents set up in full sight of the audience in many of these plays. Sometimes, as in *Lucrece* (Act III, Sc. 3), a single tent was probably represented by curtains shutting in at least the front of the space under the "Heavens," but this is not the case with the following from *The Platt of the Secound Parte of the Seven Deadlie Sinns*, "A tent being plast on the stage for Henry the Sixt." [1]

Let us remember, too, as we try to enforce for the Shakespearian stage limiting conditions, that in the use of traps and mechanical devices it was both ingenious and prolific. Is it likely, then, that either dramatist or actor would have consented to the use of only three doors at most, and those always at the same spot?

Now to the extremely complicated question of cur-

[1] Malone's *Shakespeare*, Vol. III, Prolegomena, p. 348.

tains on the English stage between 1590 and 1642. Curtains, in our modern sense of hangings at the front of the stage which could be drawn together, were undoubtedly used in a large number of performances at Court,[1] and in some of these professional actors played. Every one grants that a hanging of some sort was often placed at the back of the public stage, falling from the lower edge of the upper stage. We know from a print of the Red Bull Theatre late in its history that the upper stage could be curtained off,[2] and in the *Thracian Wonder*, assigned to John Webster, we have the direction, "Pythia above behind the curtain." In *Henry VIII* (Act V, Sc. 2), after the direction, "Enter the King and Buts, at a window above," the King says: —

> "Let 'em alone, and draw the curtain close:
> We shall hear more anon."

In *Lady Alimony*, a play not printed till 1659, but written before 1642, we find the lines, "Be your stage curtains artificially drawn and so covertly shrouded, that the squint-eyed groundling may not peep in?" That implies curtains drawing together at the middle. Moreover, if it referred only to a curtain at the very back of the stage, would the groundlings be near enough to give point to the remark?

The epilogue to *Tancred and Gismunda* (1568) has this line, "Now draw the curtains, for the scene is

---

[1] *Accounts of Revels at Court*, Cunningham (*Old Shaks. So.*), pp. 85, 86, 90, for curtain-rings, wire, and curtains.

[2] See p. 230.

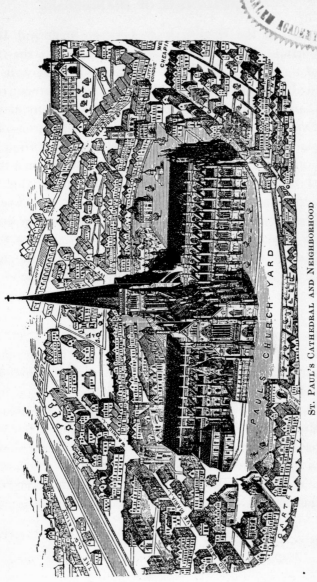

ST. PAUL'S CATHEDRAL AND NEIGHBORHOOD

(The upper spire, burned with the rest of the spire and roof in 1561, was never restored.)

done." Even if it be urged that *Tancred and Gismunda* was given by the gentlemen of the Temple in a hall and not a theatre, it shows what can be perfectly established for performances at Court, that front curtains were not unknown in dramatic performances of the time. The only question is, Were they used in public theatres?

Evidently any such curtains were impossible on a stage like that of the Red Bull. That is, the stage of the strictly public theatres forbade front curtains unless the theatre had "Heavens." It certainly is not clear that all of the theatres between 1590 and 1600 had this structure. Is it likely, however, that in those theatres where the "Heavens" made it easy to hang a curtain or curtains between the front pillars, no actor or manager would have seen the opportunity for shifting properties to better advantage and marking off scenes clearly? Even if they did not reach this subtle discovery for themselves, how could they fail, after taking part in Court performances in which curtains greatly simplified and improved the stage management, to reproduce the desirable conditions as closely as their stage permitted?

It would seem that the stage directions of the old plays ought to settle this question, but in the use of the word "arras," "curtain," and "curtains," on the lower stage, there is great confusion. Out of a hundred and thirty plays of the period examined, the word "curtain" appears twenty-two times apparently referring to the stage proper. Sometimes it appears as "a curtain," sometimes as "the curtain." In these plays the "traverse," curiously enough, is mentioned but three times.[1] From the various cases of the arras it is clear that it might be either a hanging at the back of the stage or some curtain farther out. For instance, we have in *The Merry Wives of Windsor* both "Falstaff stands behind the arras," and "He steps between the arras," which require nothing but the hanging at the back of the stage, and in *Tamburlaine*, Pt. II, "The arras is drawn, and Zenocrate is discovered lying in her bed of state; Tamburlaine sitting by her; three physicians about her bed tempering potions; her three sons and others." The last direction demands a large space, and, to be well seen, must have been given in the space under the "Heavens." That is, the stage directions of the plays provide no decisive proof on the question. I think, however, that no one who studies them carefully, especially if he has also an opportunity to stage a revival of one of the Elizabethan plays, can fail to feel that some of the theatres at certain times had a curtain or curtains somewhere on the front stage, probably between the pillars of the "Heavens." I say not only "some theatres," because not all had "Heavens," but also "at certain times," because it is likely that as the popularity of a theatre lapsed necessary repairs may not have included rebuilding the "Heavens." At least, we know that the Globe had this structure, and we see in the print of the second

[1] Twice in *Godly Queen Hester* and once in *The White Devil*.

Globe two huts projecting into the pit from the wall back of the stage just where the "Heavens" should be; yet in the *Lancashire Witches*, played at the Globe in 1634, we have the direction, "A bed thrust out, Mrs. Gener(ous) in't, Whetstone, Mall Spencer by her." [1] As, in the presence of such conflicting evidence, every piece of testimony is of possible value, it is worth noting that in the revivals under Mr. Poel by the Elizabethan Stage Society of London and in the revivals at Harvard University, two wholly independent experiments, a front curtain has been used.

Treating this question resolves itself into limiting it very narrowly and then reaching a conclusion phrased as a query. In the first place, caution is necessary. Tableaux effects meant to produce a result only as wholes could perfectly well be revealed by drawing the arras at the back and showing a group posed in the space underneath the upper stage. There, or in the upper stage itself, the procession of kings appearing to Richard III or to Macbeth could perfectly well be placed. But there are other scenes which because of the numbers in them, their complicated movements, and the necessity that they should be clearly seen and heard, must have taken place at least as far forward as the space underneath the canopy. For instance, it is not easy to believe that any dramatist as sensitive

---

[1] Possibly, as the play is held to be a reuniting of a Heywood play by Richard Brome, the stage direction belongs not to the Globe performance, but the earlier one.

to stage effects as Marlowe, or that any group of men as sensitive as are actors to making their effects reach their audience, would have united in playing one of the most lyrical and emotional scenes of *Tamburlaine* — that quoted in treating of the arras — so far back that it must have been out of sight for many of the audience, and inaudible to even more. It seems to me, too, that the repeated directions in the plays, such as, "She's drawn out upon a bed," "They bring him in in a chair," have no significance if the space under the balcony was a perfectly good place for other than tableaux effects. Why not simply draw the arras and discover her in bed or him in his chair? That they are brought down means two things: the space under the balcony was a bad place for important scenes, and in some of the theatres of Shakespeare's day there was no curtain on the main stage except that at the back. It is notable that these cruder arrangements are much more common before 1595 than after that date. Let us remember at the outset, too, that the proof in favor of a curtain or curtains between the pillars of the "Heavens" is not that certain scenes cannot be presented without them, but that the use of them makes possible a concealed placing of heavy properties, provides a larger stage for important dialogue, increases the movement of the play because one scene could be set while another was playing on the front stage, and was a very simple and obvious means to these important ends. In Scene 4, Act V, of Webster's *White Devil*, the stage directions run, "Enter Flam[ineo] and Gasp[aro] at one dore, another way, attended, Giovanni." These entrances are by the doors opening on the spaces to left and right outside the canopy or "Heavens." After the exit of Giovanni and the coming of a courtier with news that Flamineo is banished from the Duke's presence, Francisco enters overcome with the pity of Cornelia's mourning for her son Marcello. He reports that he has just left her winding, with other women, the dead lad's corpse. Flamineo cries: —

> "I will see them.
> They are behind the travers. Ile discover
> Their superstitious howling.

Cornelia, the Moore, and 3 other Ladies discovered, winding Marcello's coarse. A song."

Then follows a scene in which the grief-maddened mother prattles to the men like another Ophelia. Of course the scene could be given by treating the traverse as a curtain hanging at the back of the stage under the upper stage, but how cramped and ineffective the scene would be as contrasted with playing all the early part on the front stage, letting Francisco enter through curtains hung between the pillars, and having Flamineo draw these when he speaks of the traverse. A scene even more ineffective if played on the back stage under the balcony is the third in the fifth act of the same play. After Brachiano has been borne off very ill, Francisco and two others stand gossiping, when suddenly Francisco cries, "See, here he comes!" and the direction follows, "Enter Brachiano, presented in a bed; Vittoria and others." The death of Brachiano is preceded by very dramatic ravings which are to be given, as the old stage directions says, as "several kinds of distractions and in the action should appear." Does it seem likely that all this would take place at the back of the stage? Grant that a curtain is drawn between the pillars at the words, "See, here he comes!" and all is simple.

Note, too, how much a front curtain simplifies and improves the presentation of such a succession of stage directions as the following from *Henry VIII* (Act II, Sc. 2, of modern editions), "Enter Lord Chamberlain reading this letter." When the letter is read, "Enter to the Lord Chamberlain the Dukes of Norfolk and Suffolk." After the three have talked of Wolsey's unloved influence with the King, "Exit Lord Chamberlain, and the King draws the curtains and sits reading pensively." When Suffolk comments to Norfolk on the King's looks, Henry cries out angrily, as if interrupted in his meditations. Very shortly Wolsey and Campeius enter and an important scene for understanding the plot follows. Of course this scene could be played by using the whole stage for the Chamberlain, Norfolk, and Suffolk, letting the King draw back the curtain at the edge of the gallery stage; but in that case he could not sit long reading pensively, for what is said and done is so important that it must be played far enough forward to be seen and heard. Moreover, unless we admit the use of doors to left and right outside the "Heavens," Wolsey and Campeius enter through the place where the King is sitting or where his table or chair still stands. All this a front curtain simplifies and strengthens. The Chamberlain and the two Dukes would hold their converse on the front stage with the curtain of the inner stage drawn. When the first has gone out, the King would draw the curtain and be seen at his table, centre stage, in meditation. From that place he could for some time talk with the Dukes without rising. Wolsey and Campeius would enter either by the side doors or under the gallery. Is it not noteworthy, too, that the scene following this, that in which the Chamberlain brings to Anne Boleyn and her attendant news of her creation as Marchioness of Pembroke, could perfectly well be played on the front stage; but the next is the crowded scene of the trial with its elaborate entry and its large properties such as the chair of stage? Curtains drawn at the end of the scene with the King allowed, while the scene with Anne was playing, the placing of the properties essential for the final scene of the act. If it be maintained that the next act opens with what may have been a curtain scene, the answer is that the pause between the acts gave time, behind the drawn curtains, for any necessary change of properties. Indeed, it is difficult to understand how these long plays which, because of the exigencies of modern scenery, we must cut severely if they are to be given in two hours and a

half, were given in an afternoon unless time was econo-
mized by the placing of any elaborate properties during
the course of a preceding scene. In Scene 3 of Act I
in *Henry VIII* there is talk of a banquet at Cardinal
Wolsey's, to which Sir Henry Gilbert and the Lord
Chamberlain depart in the latter's barge. This scene
could perfectly well be played upon the front stage, and
then as soon as it was cleared the curtains of the inner
stage could be drawn and this setting revealed: "A
small table under a state for the Cardinal, a longer table
for the guests. Then enter Anne Boleyn and divers
other ladies and gentlemen as guests at one door;
at another door enter Sir Henry Guilford." Moreover,
any delay is at times fatal to the full dramatic effectiveness of the scene. For instance, the poignant irony
of Scene 2 of Act III in *Romeo and Juliet* can be felt
only if the audience turns instantly from watching the
banishment of Romeo to Juliet waiting for his coming
in a very ecstasy of unforeboding happiness. We lose
these effects to-day because of our cumbersome scenery.
So, too, did the Elizabethan dramatist in certain instances unless he could arrange his properties for one
scene while a preceding was acting.

Cymbeline, too (Act II, Scs. 1 and 2), argues for
this front curtain in its theatre. If we hold to only a
curtain at the back, then Scene 1, of Cloten and the
two lords, has taken place on the full stage, — a waste
of good room; Imogen in bed is either revealed under
the balcony or is thrust out from under it, and the trunk

containing Iachimo is brought on, not by his men, as in a preceding scene he said it would be, but by stage supers. At the end of the scene, when Iachimo has entered the trunk again, the bed is drawn out of sight or the rear curtain dropped, and the trunk removed. What a clumsy and ineffective presentation of the central scene in the play! With a front curtain all is simple. Cloten plays his scene on the front stage. The curtain shutting off the inner stage is drawn, revealing Imogen in bed, her candle on her table near at hand, her woman waiting, and the trunk well placed for the needs of the scene. At the end the curtain is drawn, and bed and trunk can be removed without any destroying of the illusion.

The *Sophonisba* [1] of John Marston shows in Act IV a set of directions hard to interpret without the front curtain. "Scena prima. Organs, viols and voices, play for this Act. Enter Sophonisba and Zanthia, as out of a caves mouth," presumably from some setting at the back of the stage under the balcony, but possibly from some set piece on the centre stage. The scene is the Forest of Belos (l. 4). Exit Zanthia in search of food. "Through the vautes mouth, in his night gowne, torch in his hand Syphax enters just behind Sophonisba." After the exit of Sophonisba, Syphax declares that he will fly to the "wonder-working spirits" for aid in winning her, and speaks of the scene as a desert. He summons Erictho, "Infernall musicke playes softly,

---

[1] *Works of John Marston*, J. O. Halliwell, Vol. I, pp. 191–199.

whilest Erictho enters, and, when she speakes, ceaseth."
After a long scene, she promises to aid him, and goes
to prepare her charm. Again there is "infernall
musicke softly" and a voice within cries, "Erictho."
"A treble viall, &c., a base lute, play softly within the
canopy." Then there is "a short song to soft musicke
above." The next direction is, "Enter Erictho in the
shape of Sophonisba, her face vailed, and hasteth in
the bed of Syphax." Now where is that bed, if the
cave's mouth occupies either centre stage or the space
under the gallery? Finally we have, "Syphax hast-
neth within the canopy, as to Sophonisba's bed."
What is this mysterious canopy? The next act opens
with the direction, "Syphax drawes the curtaines,
and discovers Erictho lying with him." Any setting
without a front curtain makes this difficult to handle
and leaves the "canopy" vague. With the front curtain, the directions mean this: Sophonisba and Zanthia
enter through the cave, either on centre stage, or, more
probably, under the gallery. Through this Syphax
also enters. After the exit of Sophonisba, Syphax,
with his words as to flying to the wonder-working spirits,
steps out to the front stage, and the front curtain is
closed. This allows the cave to be disposed of and the
bed to be put on. The music of the late part of the
scene, "within the canopy," comes from behind the
curtains, that is, within the "Heavens" space. Erictho
and Syphax both make exits into the "canopy," that
is, through the front curtain. At the opening of the

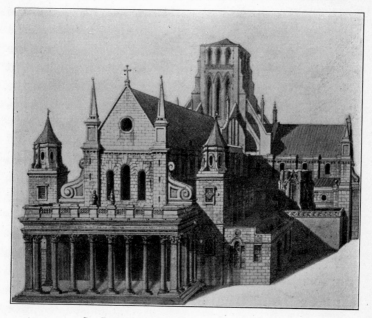

St. Paul's Cathedral and St. Gregory's

(The Music Room of the "Children of Powles" was in St. Gregory's.)

next act, Syphax draws this curtain, revealing Erictho lying by him.[1]

Two objections are especially raised against use of the front curtain: the first is, that for complete protection when properties were shifted there must be curtains between the pillars of the "Heavens" and the wall quite as much as in front. Is there any really strong protest even to-day when many of the side seats in our theatres get very disillusionizing glimpses of the wings, the shifters, and the prompter? Certainly, so far as mechanical difficulty was concerned, there could have been no trouble in drawing not only the front but two side curtains from behind the scenes.

The other objection is more serious. Plays exist in which the action is transferred from front stage to upper stage. If the front curtain were as high as in the reproductions by the London Elizabethan Society and the Department of English at Harvard University, such a change would be impossible. The prints on pp. 240 and 250 will make this clear. A lower curtain — just what a traverse is technically — running a little

---

[1] Were not *What you will* (1601) of Marston evidently acted in a private theatre, probably by the Chapel Children at Blackfriars, it would be strong testimony for curtains in the public theatres. "Induction: Before the musicke sounds for this Acte, enter Atticus, Doricus, and Phylomusus; they sit a good while on the Stage before the candles are lighted, talking together." Later Atticus cries: "Come, we straine the spectators patience in delaying expected delightes. Lets place ourselves within the curtaines, for good faith the stage is so very little, we shall wrong the generall eye els very much."

below the edge of the upper stage would meet this difficulty. But it is nearly useless to discuss, in the light of present evidence, any particular arrangement of the front curtain. On the other hand, from much study of the quartos and folios, and from repeated experience in reproducing Elizabethan plays, I have no doubt that Shakespeare during the greater part of his career as a dramatist could use practically four divisions on his stage: front, inner, back, and upper stage, with three curtains, one in the balcony, another under the balcony, and a third somewhere in front. I would not maintain, however, that this held good for all theatres, nor even for any one theatre throughout its whole history. These possibilities permitted any skilled dramatist an alternation of scenes when he desired, but did not exact it as some writers seem to think, and allowed him to run off his play rapidly, finishing it easily in two hours and a half.

Were the properties so often referred to, the occasional sign, and the poetical description, the only stimulations to the imagination of the Elizabethan and Jacobean audience? What backed the rear of the upper balcony? Of course it had some backing. Was it a mere dead wall? Henslowe, in an inventory of properties made on the 10th of March, 1598, mentions "The sittie of Rome." [1] That sounds like a cloth with a perspective on it of Rome. Henslowe names, too, a "cloth of the Sone and Mone." [1] Where did he hang

---

[1] *Henslowe's Diary,* J. P. Collier (*Old Shaks. So.*), p. 273.

that? Some years ago an architect who was reconstructing from the old contracts for the Fortune and the Hope an Elizabethan theatre suggested to the writer that the second of the huts seen in the print of the later Globe must at least in part have overhung the upper stage, and that consequently it would have been perfectly easy to lower from the hut any backing desired for that upper stage. In three performances at Harvard University a painted cloth has been dropped into this upper gallery. Of course this was done with full recognition of the fact that, though "painted cloths," "frames," and "citties" are common enough in the *Accounts of the Revels at Court*, the instances already cited are the only ones occurring in *Henslowe's Diary*, our only satisfactory record of the properties of an Elizabethan theatre. Yet the results in *Epicœne*, in *Hamlet*, and in *Ralegh in Guiana*, a play in imitation of the Elizabethan manner, were such as to leave any fair-minded observer more than ever doubtful whether the dramatist of Shakespeare's day could have missed the chance a painted cloth in the upper stage at times gave him. In *Ralegh* it was necessary to suggest to the audience a ship's cabin (p. 280). A companionway, with a rope railing, was built over one of the rear entrances. A painted cloth showing the rigging and the rail of a ship was dropped into the upper stage. A few sea chests were placed on the main stage. The suggestion of a ship and its cabin was complete. In face of the facts that Henslowe's inventory con-

H   [97]

tains the "cloth of the Sone and Mone," and also "3 payer of stayers for Fayeton," [1] can it be said that any real violence was done to Elizabethan staging? Of course this use of any painted cloths about the public stage is the most dubious of all the matters thus far considered, but against our lack of references to them may be offset the need of some backing for the upper stage, the frequency of their use at Court, the imitativeness of the actor, and the large result given by them.

All this examination of detail amounts to just this. Though the stage of Shakespeare was different from our own, and though in the opening chorus of *Henry V* he may have written somewhat mournfully of "this wooden O" when his company were acting at the old-fashioned Theatre, it was by no means ill equipped from 1598 when the Globe was built, and adequately responded to the developing needs of the drama. It did call for more imagination and sympathetic response from the audience than does our own; but the actors, thrust out into the midst of the audience as they were, could get a quicker response than can our own, who are always framed in like a picture. In a word, the conditions of the Shakespearian stage were intimate to an extent we scarcely realize and permitted a detail not always possible in our larger theatres. Above all, everything in the performance tended to make the play the thing : no lavish scenery drew off the attention, properties were usually employed only to the extent that

[1] *Henslowe's Diary*, J. P. Collier (*Old Shaks. So.*), p. 273.

the play demanded; there were no "stars," and both actor and hearer must give themselves up to the author, the one to interpret, the other to understand, if the play was to produce its full effect. Is it not evident that, for the dramatist, conditions were far better than to-day, indeed, well-nigh perfect?

NOTE. — The best of recent special studies of the Elizabethan stage are *Die Shakespeare-Bühne nach den alten Bühnenanweisungen*, Dr. Cecil Brodmeier, and *Some Principles of Elizabethan Staging*, Dr. G. F. Reynolds, first published in *Modern Philology*, April and June, 1905, but since republished in pamphlet form. This pamphlet of Dr. Reynolds' is noteworthy for its sanity and thoroughness. Malone's *Prolegomena* remains even yet the best collection of citations illustrating all the aspects of the Elizabethan theatre.

CHAPTER III

EARLY EXPERIMENTATION IN PLOTTING AND ADAPTATION

A T present our public is badly confused as to the right use of the word "dramatic." Starting with the undeniable assertion that the novels of our chief writers contain many a dramatic scene, the public reaches the wholly false conclusion that because of this dramatic feeling these same writers should be equally successful as dramatists. Mr. Pinero, in his lecture *Robert Louis Stevenson: The Dramatist*, makes a fundamental distinction in regard to the use of the word "dramatic" which I must ask the reader to bear constantly in mind throughout the rest of this book. He says: "What is dramatic talent? Is it not the power to project characters and to cause them to tell an interesting story through the medium of dialogue? This is *dramatic* talent; and dramatic talent, if I may so express it, is the raw material of *theatrical* talent. Dramatic, like poetic, talent is born, not made; if it is to achieve success on the stage, it must be developed into theatrical talent by hard study, and generally by long practice. For theatrical talent consists in the power of making your characters not only tell a story by means of dialogue, but tell it in such skilfully devised form and order as shall, within the limits of an ordinary theatrical representation, give rise to the greatest possible amount of that peculiar kind of emotional effect, the production of which is the one great function of the theatre." [1]

In this book we are to try to discern in Shakespeare's plays both such permanent principles and such ephemeral experimentation as lay behind the form and the order which gave rise to that intense emotional effect of which Shakespeare undoubtedly became a master. That is, in studying how, under the conditions of his stage, he accomplished his artistic purposes while so adapting his material as to gain from his particular audience the greatest possible amount of emotional response to his material, we shall try to arrive at his technique. "There are two parts of technique, — its strategy and its tactics." Strategy is the general laying-out of a play. Tactics is "the art of getting characters on and off the stage, of conveying information to the audience, etc." [2] These two essentials of technique we shall look for first in *Love's Labour's Lost, The Two Gentlemen of Verona, Titus Andronicus*, and *The Comedy of Errors*—all plays usually dated not later than 1594.

It is not necessary here to discuss mooted questions in regard to the exact date at which Shakespeare began to write for the stage or his earlier years in London.

---

[1] *Robert Louis Stevenson: The Dramatist*, pp. 6–7, A. W. Pinero, Chiswick Press, London, 1903.

[2] *Idem*, p. 13.

It is enough for us to be sure that by 1592 he had been declared excellent as an actor, and that by that year he had already begun as a dramatist.[1] It is certainly interesting as indirect evidence of contemporary opinion of his earliest efforts, order them as we may, that his first widespread popularity came to him through his *Venus and Adonis* (April, 1593) and his *Rape of Lucrece* (1594).   Their reception was enthusiastic and lasting.[2] In the dedication of *Venus and Adonis*, to the Earl of Southampton, Shakespeare calls the poem the "first heir of my invention," so that it may even have been written or planned before any of his dramatic work.   Viewed in one way the two poems are but two specially successful examples of a vogue for erotic verse which was marked in the decade of 1590–1600. Yet the willingness the young Shakespeare shows in both poems to try his hand on a subject and in a form particularly acceptable to the public at the moment, and his widely acclaimed success, prove that, at the outset of his career, he possessed some chief requisites of a successful playwright.   Here are readiness and ability to tell his audience something it wished to hear, in such a way as to gain a wide response and

---

[1] Chettle, in 1592, declared Shakespeare "exelent in the qualitie he professes." "Qualitie" was the Elizabethan word for the actor's profession. In *A Groats-worth of Wit bought with a Million of Repentance* (1592) Robert Greene, attacking him as "Shake-scene," is evidently jealous of his success as a playwright.

[2] For some proof of this see *Life of Shakespeare*, pp. 78–79, Sidney Lee.

yet keep his product on the high level of literary art. There can, too, be no question as to the dramatic power of these poems, for surely both "project characters and cause them to tell an interesting story through the medium of a dialogue." On the other hand, any thoughtful reading of *Venus and Adonis* and *The Rape of Lucrece* must demonstrate that a poet rather than a dramatist is at work. The very wealth of sensuous imagery accumbers the dramatic movement, particularly in the latter half of *Venus and Adonis*. Each poem shows Shakespeare doing what the poet may freely do, but the dramatist only very rarely: namely, lingering over his material by the ingenious or richly imaginative repetition of the same idea, situation, or conceit. In both these poems it is not primarily the situation, not primarily the characterization, but the opportunities the material offers for sensuous imagery and the display of conscious artistry in poetic narrative which attracted Shakespeare. Yet, undeniably, he could already by his imagination closely sympathize with some intense, human experience. Essentially untheatric, then, as the treatment is, one may yet discern in these two poems a promising endowment; poetic narrative is already Shakespeare's; sympathetic understanding of passionate experience and the power to phrase it, are his; and he has proved himself successful in so presenting material desired by his public as to give it wide and lasting success. But if this youth is to become a great dramatist, if he is not to remain a Thomas Dekker, whose rich early promise never ripened into a mastered art equal to all demands made upon it, that sympathetic understanding of human beings must be widened and deepened infinitely; that ability in poetic dramatic narrative must be metamorphosed into dramatic narrative for theatrical purposes by repeated, conscientious, self-criticising practice; and that readiness to serve the public must be checked and guided by a stern artistic conscience, if its own facility is not to land all the endeavor in accomplishment of great ephemeral success, but no permanent value.

Before we analyze Shakespeare's earliest dramatic work, just a word of warning as to a qualification with which any conclusions as to the plays of this first decade of Shakespeare's must be drawn: we do not know that we possess the whole body of Shakespeare's dramatic composition — original, collaborative, and, above all, adaptations of older materials. It certainly seems odd that in a period when plays were turned out very rapidly and at a time in Shakespeare's career when, for financial reasons, he would need to turn out plays as speedily as possible, he should have produced, so far as we know, between 1590 and 1594, only some eight or nine plays, fully half of those adaptations of dramatic material already existing. Moreover, that mysterious title given by Francis Meres in 1598 [1] for

[1] In his *Palladis Tamia*, where he gives a rough list of plays of Shakespeare whose titles he recalls at the moment.

NAVIS ECCLESIÆ CATHEDRALIS S. PAVLI
PROSPECTVS INTERIOR

THE NAVE

St. Paul's Cathedral

one of Shakespeare's plays, namely, *Love's Labour's Won,*
means either another name for a play now known to us
or a lost product of his pen. I mention this because it
must always be borne in mind, when one hears generalization in regard to the swiftness of Shakespeare's
development between 1590 and 1594, and particularly
as to the marked contrast between the plays written
before and after that date. The evidence for some
stages in his development may be wholly lost to us.

As I shall take up the three parts of *Henry VI* when
treating the Chronicle Plays in the next chapter, let us
now examine *Love's Labour's Lost.* We know that
it was first printed in 1598 in quarto, bearing on the
title-page the words, "as presented before her Highness
the last Xmas, newly corrected and augmented by W.
Shakespeare." As Mr. Sidney Lee has said: "There is
no external evidence to prove that any piece in which
Shakespeare had a hand was produced before the spring
of 1592. No play by him was published before 1597,
and none bore his name on the title-page until 1598.
But his first essay has been with confidence allotted to
1591. To *Love's Labour's Lost* may reasonably be
assigned priority in point of time of all Shakespeare's
dramatic productions. Internal evidence alone indi-
cates the date of composition, and proves that it was
an early effort." [1] What complicates generalizations in
regard to it is internal evidence that the statement of
the title-page, "newly corrected and augmented," is

[1] *Life of Shakespeare,* p. 50.

true. In the first place, the acts are singularly disproportionate in length. The first, fourth, and fifth, as printed in the Globe edition, run respectively 4, 6½, and 10 pages and the second and third 2½ and barely 2 pages. It is noteworthy that in the fourth and the fifth act there is evident addition,[1] and that the long acts

[1] In Act V, lines 827–832, when the Princess and her ladies are naming for their respective lovers the tests of devotion which they wish them to undergo, Biron, immediately after the King has heard his test from the Princess, speaks as follows: —

Biron. And what to me, my love? and what to me?
Rosaline. You must be purged, too, your sins are rank;
You are attaint with faults and perjury;
Therefore, if you my favor mean to get,
A twelvemonth shall you spend, and never rest,
But seek the weary beds of people sick.

Following this comes the similar dialogue between Dumain and Catharine of some dozen or more lines, after which Biron and Rosaline again speak as follows: —

Biron. Studies my lady? mistress, look on me.
Behold the window of my heart, mine eye,
What humble suit attends thy answer there;
Impose some service on me for thy love.
Rosaline. Oft have I heard of you, my lord **Biron**,
Before I saw you, and the world's large tongue
Proclaims you for a man replete with mocks;
Full of comparisons and wounding flouts,
Which you on all estates will execute,
That lie within the mercy of your wit:
To weed this wormwood from your fruitful **brain**,
And, therewithal, to win me, if you please,
Without the which I am not to be won,
You shall this twelvemonth term, from day to **day**,
Visit the speechless sick, and still converse
With groaning wretches; and your task shall **be**,
With all the fierce endeavor of your wit,
To enforce the pained impotent to smile.

contain all except one scene of purely comic material. It is usually conceded, too, that the large amount of rhyme in this play shows it was written early in Shakespeare's career, when blank verse and prose had not completely superseded the older forms of dramatic expression.

One must hesitate a little, also, in generalizing about *Love's Labour's Lost* because the play suggests more than once that it was written for some special occasion or audience. If this be true, the circumstances governing its writing may have led even the young Shakespeare to vary what was at the time his dramatic practice. For instance, no wholly satisfactory reason has been suggested for the curious ending, which defers the complete settlement of the love story for a year and deprives the audience of its time-honored satisfaction in seeing every Jack sure of his Jill. The general attitude of the play toward women, the sonneteering,

Clearly this is merely an amplification of the first quotation. Again there is repetition in the very long speech of Biron near the end of Scene 3, Act IV, lines 302–305 and 350–354. Biron says first: —

> "From women's eyes this doctrine I derive:
> They are the ground, the books, the Academes,
> From whence doth spring the true Promethean fire."

Some forty-five lines later in the same speech, he says: —

> "From women's eyes this doctrine I derive:
> They sparkle still the right Promethean fire;
> They are the books, the arts, the Academes,
> That show, contain, and nourish all the world,
> Else none at all in aught proves excellent."

Evidently the printer allowed both the original and the insert to slip into the quarto.

and, above all, the eulogy of woman which Biron utters near the end of Act IV, suggest strongly that originally, as well as in 1598, it may have been performed before the queen and her court, or that as first written it was given before an audience mainly composed of women. Throughout, the characters so much play with love rather than become its subjects that one wonders whether it was not composed as a whole with a definite view of pleasing the Virgin Queen, who was such an adept in coquetry and who was so fond of putting off her admirers just as they seemed nearest to the attainment of their wishes.

Whatever the conditions of the original production, however, it seems wholly unnecessary to search for the source from which this play was developed. Everybody admits the thinness of the story and the meagre dramatic incident. The fact is, *Love's Labour's Lost* is just the sort of play a young man of poetic and literary endowment — which we have seen Shakespeare had in *Venus and Adonis* and *The Rape of Lucrece* — would write, in 1590–1595, for some special audience in which the feminine element predominated. Such an audience would be best pleased if lightly entertained rather than called upon to appreciate either fine characterization or a skilful telling of a complicated story. By such an audience the play would be judged, not only as a play, but for its literary finish. It would delight in a love story which idealized woman and sang her praises. Moreover the story, as it stands, is made up of material already well tested by 1590. Shakespeare knew that audiences delighted in confusion brought about by the wrong delivery of love letters — here that of Biron to Rosaline and that of Don Armado to Jaquenetta; that they derived keen satisfaction also from confusion resulting when lovers, mistaking their mistresses, poured out their affections to the wrong persons; that they were amused by any contrasting of the loves of a noble and a comic figure, as in Biron and Don Armado; and that they were infinitely entertained by such burlesques as that of *The Nine Worthies*. Weave these strands together, even if loosely, and the result for an audience not critical in dramatic technique must be alluring. Recognizing that a particular audience finds a keen zest in listening to whatever is couched in an elaborate style popular at the moment, to whatever exhibits rich and various imagery, and even to verse experimentation, skilfully phrase your material so that it shall appeal to all these interests even as it tells the slight story we have just been analyzing, and, presto! you have *Love's Labour's Lost*. Just in this appears one of the chief significances of this play in a study of Shakespeare's technique; it reveals the fact that very early in his career, and even before he was an adequate technician, instinctively or consciously he brought into his plays, as into his two early poems, elements of strong popular appeal.

Certainly from the side of plot *Love's Labour's Lost* shows that the young Shakespeare, as is to be expected, was weak. He starts the play with relative swiftness in the two scenes of Act I by making us understand the Quixotic agreement of the king and his nobles, the seizure of Costard and Jaquenetta by Armado for breach of the proclamation forbidding a youth to be "taken with a wench," and Armado's confession that he is smitten with sudden love for Jaquenetta. Act II gives us the meeting of the King and his nobles, on the one hand, with the Princess and her ladies on the other, and the prompt dissipation of the determination of the men not to look on women for a year. We are now ready, at the beginning of Act III, for some dramatic results of the complications in the two groups, — from the love of Costard and Armado for Jaquenetta and of the foresworn nobles and King for the Princess and her ladies, — but this act does not advance the story a particle except in some eight or ten lines near the end, when Biron arranges with Costard to carry his love-letter to Rosaline. Though that commission keeps us in suspense, it can hardly prevent an act, otherwise given over to mere fooling and amusing characterization that approaches caricature, from becoming something like a dead centre. Act IV goes somewhat better, but in Scenes 1 and 2 the handling is not strongly dramatic. Graceful and ingenious talk leads in Scene 1 to the lines in which Costard presents the Princess by mistake with the letter of Don Armado to Jaquenetta. The comic possibilities of this mistake are taken rather rapidly, and the scene closes with quite as much emphasis given to mere badinage on totally different subjects. Scene 2 shows somewhat similar proportions between the time spent on the letter of Biron which has been handed to Jaquenetta and on the quibbling and pedantry of Holofernes, Sir Nathaniel, and Dull both before the letter is read and thereafter. Scene 3, of course, is admirable dramatically up to the point when Jaquenetta's coming with the letter of Biron forces him to admit his hypocrisy in scoffing at his fellow-lovers. There is admirable comic climax as the King, Longaville, and Dumain enter in succession, thinking to pour out their love in secret, only to be overheard by each of the men who has preceded him, all of them except Biron totally unaware of the presence of the others. Climactic, too, is the successive revelation by each man of his real condition. Doubtless for the special audience of the time the contest of all four, after Biron's confession, in praising the excellencies of their mistresses, closing as it does with a splendid poetic outburst of Biron, had climactic value. There seems, however, to be but little left for the fifth act except such comedy as may be extracted from the presence of Don Armado's letter in the hand of the Princess. Consequently in Scene 1 of Act V, just at the end of Act IV, we are promised possible fresh complications from a masquerading visit to the Princess and her ladies, and we take an entirely fresh start in the announcement that Holofernes and his friends are to act *The Nine Worthies* before the Princess and her attendants. The interests in the final act have been, so to speak, thrust in from the outside rather than developed from elements of story started in the earlier acts. Yet the crowding incident, the variety, the surprise arising from the sad news Mercade announces, and from the curious postponing of the complete settlement of the love affairs, must have brought the audience to the graceful and lyric close in a state of great delight. That, however, does not dispose of the facts that technically the thin story has been developed very slowly till the fourth act; that in Scenes 1 and 2 of Act IV little skill is shown in holding the dramatic situation provided by the wrongly delivered letters; that the story halts badly toward the end of Act IV; and that Act V is a patchwork rather than a presentation of situations developing inevitably from the earlier parts of the story. The promised complication from the infatuation of Don Armado for Jaquenetta has provided nothing except the opportunity for the wrong delivery of the two letters. The only really strong situation resulting from this confusion of the letters is in Act IV, Scene 3, when it leads to the unmasking of Biron. Certainly in this play either Shakespeare did not desire much well-ordered story or else his power of plotting, both in the sense of finding a rich and promising fable and moulding it into orderly and sequential dramatic narrative, was yet to be developed.

When, too, one looks at the characterization it is again clear that either the special conditions under which the play was written made the dramatist feel only superficial characterization was desirable, or else he was not as yet able to present his people strongly. The comic figures, except Costard and Jaquenetta, owe much both in the content and the phrasing of their speech to John Lyly. That Shakespeare had read his plays or had followed them in the theatre till they had become so much a part of his intellectual equipment that he often transmuted their situations, lines, and very phrases into his own work, no one can for a moment deny who has read the plays of Lyly and the earlier work of Shakespeare, especially his comedy. Here, in *Love's Labour's Lost*, the chief comic figures show the same caricature, the same quibbling, and the same torturing of a phrase or an idea to the point of complete exhaustion of any comic possibility. Are the figures of the lords and ladies and the King and the Princess more than graceful puppets of the situation or mere utterers of the facile poetic imaginings of the dramatist? To the women of the play love is a mere game, every move of which is known to them and which they play with easy grace and charm, sure of themselves and of their victory the moment they wish to seize it. Let these lovers protest as they may, here is none of the passion of love. It is the very playfulness of the whole treatment of love throughout four acts and a half which makes the grave note of service struck at the end of the play seem incongruous.

The dialogue, however, reveals the secret of the play. Its relative proportions, as compared with incident,

I

show clearly it was of prime importance. Acts I and II are simply talk. So, too, is Act III. The action in Act II is slight enough, merely the meeting of the King, the Princess, and their followers; what gives it value is not what happens, but what is said. Indeed, as I have already pointed out, the action of the play is really centred in Scene 3 of Act IV and the last scene of Act V. The rest is clever or beautiful talk, or characterization that runs from something close to caricature, through the lovers chiefly significant as phrase-makers, to the few but sure and convincing strokes in Costard. That is, we have here a play on the model of John Lyly's works. In those plot was thin. So, too, was characterization, except in the comic figures, where it tended to run to caricature. Emphasis went to the graceful or the ingenious dialogue. In turn, Shakespeare, working as a disciple of John Lyly, — between 1585 and 1592, the most admired as well as the most literary of the workers in comedy, — in this play substitutes highborn men and women of the land of romance for the mythical figures of Lyly and presents somewhat caricatured figures of the day in place of Lyly's exaggerations of classic comic figures. Moreover, he releases the love story which Lyly had so rigorously repressed. That is what seems to me of prime significance in this play for any one studying the development of Shakespeare's technique. Though *Love's Labour's Lost* is technically weak, though it lacks originality in its elements of story, and though it is closely modelled on

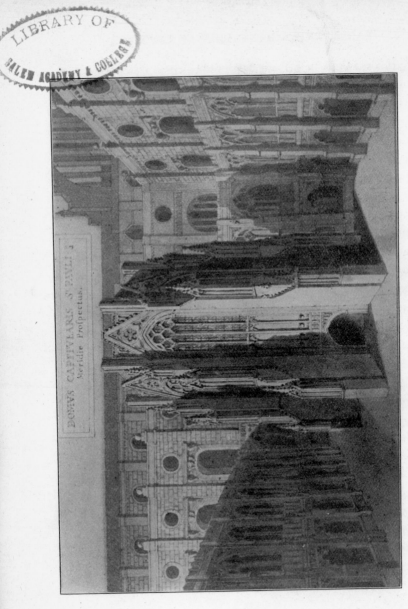

BONVS CAPITVLARIS S^{TI} PAVLI
Sterilis Prospectus.

THE CHAPTER HOUSE YARD, ST. PAUL'S CATHEDRAL
(Possibly the place where the "Children of Powles" acted)

Lyly's method in his court comedies, it is independent and contributive in that modern English comedy first sees the light in it. The play of romantic story in the rough already existed, as in *Common Conditions;* in a sense, the tragedy of love had already appeared in Kyd's *Spanish Tragedy;* a mere change in emphasis would turn almost any play of Lyly's into a comedy of love, but he preferred to make his work comedies of literary expression which rigidly repressed the human passion that at times almost eluded his watchfulness; in Robert Greene we have the story of wifely love in *James IV*, but the play is rather one of adventures than merely a love story; and though in *Friar Bacon and Friar Bungay* Greene charmingly develops the story of Margaret of Fressingfield and her love for Lacy, it is merely an element in the whole plot. Here, in *Love's Labour's Lost*, we have our first specimen of a play in which the love story is of prime importance and all else is arranged merely to set it off or make it more appealing to the public. Before, however, this comedy of love can attain its full dramatic possibilities, Shakespeare must make great advances in his technique. It is certainly striking, however, that when this comedy of love first appears, it is written with a keen sense of literary effect and much poetic vigor. This is not the place for a discussion of high comedy; that will come later; but in *Love's Labour's Lost* Shakespeare has constructed the footbridge by which one may cross from John Lyly's over-ingenious comedies of fantasy to his own superb accomplishment in high comedy. It is not, however, so much a creation as an unmasking.

In *The Two Gentlemen of Verona*, first printed in the folio of 1623, but mentioned by Meres in his *Palladis Tamia* in 1598, we have a play evidently written for the public stage. It is placed by the critics at various dates between 1591 and 1595, with a preference for 1591–1593. What makes it likely that *The Two Gentlemen of Verona* is, in date of composition, closely related to *Love's Labour's Lost*, is that in it, too, the love story is both the chief interest and the thread which binds all the incidents together, and that, as we shall see in a moment, its advance beyond *Love's Labour's Lost* in technique is not great. The slight advance, however, and the decrease in the tendency to quibble and to overemphasize speech at the expense of action show that *The Two Gentlemen of Verona* followed *Love's Labour's Lost*.

The Two Gentlemen of Verona is indebted to the story of Felismena as told in the *Diana Enamorada* of Jorge de Montemayor. This book was not printed in English till 1598, but an English manuscript was in circulation from 1582. Possibly, too, Shakespeare knew and used a play acted before the Queen in 1584 entitled *Felix and Philiomena*. In the *Diana* Felismena is a maiden destined by Venus and Minerva to be unfortunate in love, but successful in war. She was wooed by a neighbor, Don Felix, and gave him her love after much affected scorn. His father discovered their love and sent Felix to Court to prevent the match. Thither Felismena followed him disguised as a page. On her first night in the city and before she has sought Felix out, she hears him passionately serenading some Court lady in the same street in which she lodges, and learns from her hostess that he is openly paying his addresses to this lady. Next day she sees him at Court, a splendid figure in white and yellow, the colors of the lady Celia. Felismena maintains her disguise as the page Valerius, enters the service of Felix in order to be near him, and carries his tokens and messages to Celia with earnest pleadings of her own for the happiness of her false lover. Celia, still cold to Felix, waxes warm to Valerius, and when she cannot move him dies of unrequited love. Then Felix disappears and people suppose him dead of grief. Felismena in despair becomes a shepherdess. After a time she chances upon a knight in the forest, hard pressed by three foes. She delivers him by her skill in archery and discovers that he is Don Felix. His old love for her returns, and she forgives the past.

This outline of the original story shows that when Shakespeare wrote *The Two Gentlemen of Verona* he had waked to a fact constantly demonstrated by his later plays, namely, that the Elizabethan audience of the public theatres liked a crowded and complicated story. To meet this desire, Shakespeare provides not only the figures of the purely comic scenes, but also Valentine, Thurio, and Eglamour. Taking a hint from a portion of the story which he discards, he adds the outlaw scenes. But though he provides more material for his proposed plot, his whole treatment of it proves that he is yet at the beginning of the acquirement of his technique. He feels strongly now the value of contrast in drama, and therefore frankly opposes Valentine to Proteus, Silvia to Julia, as characters, and alternates his scenes of pure exposition or of emotion with scenes of comedy. Sometimes he even splits a scene midway, as in the first scene of Act I, to get this sort of contrast. He has discerned one of the permanent essentials of dramatic composition, contrast, but as yet his art is not sufficient to conceal his methods.

It is, however, in his exposition and plotting that he is weakest. It takes this dramatist, who by 1596 at latest has gained a wonderful combination of swiftness and clearness in opening his plays,[1] two acts, including some ten scenes, to state the relations of Proteus, Valentine, Silvia, and Julia; to bring the first three together at the Court; to prepare us for the coming of the fourth; and to introduce us to Launce and Speed. He would have done all this in at most three scenes a few years later: one, as now, showing the planning of Julia with Lucetta to leave Verona and go to the Court in search of Proteus; one preceding scene for Launce and Speed; and a longer scene, now Scene 4 of Act II, in Milan at the Duke's palace, where the coming of Proteus to the Court would bring out clearly his previous relations with Valentine and Julia, the love of Valentine for

[1] See the opening scene of *Romeo and Juliet*.

Silvia, the sudden infatuation of Proteus for her, and the place of Thurio in the story. The movement in these two acts is still closely akin to the slow movement of *Love's Labour's Lost*.

From the beginning of Act III the play moves with constantly increasing suspense for the spectator, but the use of this suspense proves that Shakespeare could not yet handle it perfectly. In Act III, Scene 1, Proteus basely betrays to the Duke the secret of Valentine's love for Silvia. There follow the dramatic banishment of Valentine by the Duke, the perfidy of Proteus as he counsels Valentine to flee, and the amusing dialogue of Speed and Launce. Act III, then, contains at least one good dramatic situation, moves with relative swiftness, and shows especially well the sharp contrasting of serious and comic which Shakespeare delighted in at this time. Moreover, it urges us on to the other acts in order that we may know the outcome of the complications for Valentine and of the perfidy of Proteus. The second scene of this act shows us more perfidy on the part of Proteus when, agreeing to be false to Valentine, he seems to favor Sir Thurio's plan in regard to Silvia, but really schemes only for his own ends. It is, however, a transitional scene preparing us for complications to follow. In the fourth act the first scene simply shows us the taking of Valentine by the outlaws and their choice of him as captain. Scene 2 is probably the most human and charming of the play. It is the serenade of Silvia by Thurio, Proteus, and the musicians which the love-lorn Julia watches from her hiding-place. Even it, however, points forward to scenes seemingly sure to result because Julia now knows that Proteus is false to her. Scene 3, again transitional, shows us Silvia arranging with Eglamour to aid her escape from Milan in search of Valentine. Scene 4, after the opening between Launce and his dog, gives us the second strongly human scene of the play in the talk between Proteus and Julia, still disguised as a page, and her charming interview with Silvia, the latter a kind of preliminary sketch for the scene of Viola and Olivia in *Twelfth Night*. Yet this complication of the relations of Silvia, Julia, and Proteus reaches no settlement in the act and we turn to the fifth, sure that there, in a series of dramatic scenes or in one long scene, the very complicated relations of the four young people will be worked out. Scene 1, merely transitional, only shows us Eglamour and Silvia leaving Milan. In Scene 2 the Duke, discovering the flight, starts with Proteus and Thurio in pursuit. The very brief third scene shows the capture of Silvia by the outlaws. Now but one scene is left in which to unravel all the complications and satisfy at last our long suspense.

Could there be a more complete confession of dramatic ineptitude than that last scene? It fails to do everything for which we have been looking. Valentine, after communing with himself in a way that foreshadows the banished Duke in *As You Like It*, withdraws as he sees strangers coming through the forest. Proteus, who is accompanied by the faithful Julia, still disguised as a page, has found Silvia and is trying to force his love upon her. Valentine, overhearing, bursts forth and denounces his friend. If Shakespeare did not wish to "hold" the scene of the avowal of his love by Proteus through letting Julia take some part in it, or by prolonging the play of emotion between Proteus and Silvia, he had, on the reappearance of Valentine, an opportunity for a strong scene in which the play and interplay of the feelings of the four characters might lead at last to a happy solution. Yet this is his weak handling of the situation : —

 Valentine. Now I dare not say
I have one friend alive; thou would'st disprove me.
Who should be trusted now, when one's right hand
Is perjured to the bosom? Proteus,
I am sorry I must never trust thee more,
But count the world a stranger for thy sake.
The private wound is deepest; O time most accursed,
'Mongst all foes that friends should be the worst!
 Proteus. My shame and guilt confounds me.
Forgive me, Valentine : if hearty sorrow
Be a sufficient ransom for an offence,
I tender 't here : I do as truly suffer
As e'er I did commit.
 Valentine. Then I am paid;
And once again I do receive thee honest
Who by repentance is not satisfied,
Is nor of heaven nor earth, for these are pleased.
By penitence the Eternal wrath's appeased :
And, that my love may appear plain and free,
All that was mine in Silvia, I give thee.

It is hard enough to believe that Valentine would forgive so promptly, but that he would go as far as to offer to yield up Silvia is preposterous. That touch came simply to motivate the sudden swooning of Julia at the news. Only a little less absurd is the sudden swerve into rightmindedness of Proteus when Julia has revealed herself. After all these startling surprises, however, perhaps one is ready to agree to Julia's glad acceptance of the changeable affections of so worthless a person as Proteus. Is it not clear that in this scene the momentary effect, the start of surprise, mean far more to the dramatist than truth to life and probability? Having lured his audience on by writing scenes which constantly promised complicated action ahead, when the closing in of the afternoon at last drives him to bay, he gets out of his difficulties in the swiftest possible fashion, but with complete sacrifice of good dramatic art, the rich possibilities of his material, and truth to life.

Here, then, is a play which shows in Julia and Launce, and in Scenes 2 and 4 of Act IV, that Shakespeare can now do far more in characterization than he had in *Love's Labour's Lost*. In it, too, his medium of expression is gradually changing its mannered literary quality for genuine dramatic effectiveness. Yet the same play proves that, though he now recognizes the value of complicated plot and of creating suspense in the minds of his hearers, he can neither proportion nor develop firmly the story he has complicated nor properly satisfy the suspense which he has created.

Does not the young Shakespeare's omission of Celia's fatal love for the disguised Felismena suggest that, feeling sure comedy must end pleasantly, he did not as yet see how to keep the amusing complication without letting it strike far too serious a note and end fatally? A few years later, in *Twelfth Night*, Shakespeare finds in just this complication not only the cause for much amusement, but much poetry, and a delicate contrast of grave and gay. In *The Two Gentlemen of Verona*, as in *Love's Labour's Lost*, Shakespeare passes swiftly over the graver suggestions of his story. As yet he did not know how to throw his comedy into the finest relief by letting the serious cast slight shadows here and there.

Does not this comparison of his accomplishment in these two plays with what he had done in *Venus and Adonis* and *The Rape of Lucrece* demonstrate that his superiority at first was poetic and literary rather than dramatic; and that the distinction between dramatic ability, in the sense of projecting character by means of dialogue, and theatrical ability, the power of deriving for a special audience from particular material the largest amount of emotional result, was an art which must be learned even in Shakespeare's day?

This technical analysis of these two plays gives results so sharply in contrast with those to be gained from a similar analysis of the two remaining plays, *Titus Andronicus* and *The Comedy of Errors*, that it is hard to understand how Shakespeare could have stepped swiftly

and surely from one group to the other with no intermediate dramatic experience. On technical grounds
I am disposed to date *Love's Labour's Lost* and *The Two
Gentlemen of Verona* as early as possible, that is, rather
circa 1591 than *circa* 1593.

Titus Andronicus has long been a great puzzle to students of Shakespeare, chiefly, I think, because they
have exacted too high a standard from Shakespeare in
the days of his apprenticeship and because they have
often misunderstood his purpose in this particular play.
Of course, its horror is undeniable, and this horror is
for us so great that many parts of the play are revolting
simply. Now, in the first place, the Elizabethans had
stronger tastes and tougher nerves than ours. In the
second place, they did not come to this play, as our
critics too often have, as to a tragedy, but as to a melodrama. Even the audiences which to-day are filled
with delight over the horrors of our modern melodrama
would find the same material unendurable were it lifted
from the plane of melodrama to the level of tragedy;
for the Elizabethan melodrama meant just what it
means to us to-day, — "only a play." In the third
place, Dr. H. de W. Fuller has shown that probably
Titus Andronicus is merely a combination by Shakespeare, in 1594, of two old plays which had come into
the possession of his company: *Titus and Vespasian*
and *Titus Andronicus*.[1] One survives in a Dutch, the

[1] *Publications of the Modern Language Association*, Vol. XVI,
No. 1, pp. 1–65.

THE FIRST FORTUNE THEATRE, 1600

(See Ryther's Map, p. 36.)

THE SECOND FORTUNE THEATRE

(Built in 1621)

other in a German play. If the English originals were
only extant, we should have an admirable opportunity
to watch Shakespeare moulding a play from the most
popular scenes in two allied dramatic narratives. He
must condense ten acts into five, and bring into relation
with one group of persons a number of episodes which
really happened to two sets of people. Here, certainly,
was a very difficult problem in condensation, and if
this play were to prove successful with his immediate
audience, a difficult problem in adapting once popular
old material to new conditions. There was the possibility in this material of two other difficult problems.
If originally it was highly melodramatic, it might by
convincing characterization and consistent motivation
be lifted to the level of reality. It might, too, in the
hands of a dramatist of poetic instincts and attain-
ments, be given a fine literary setting. We shall see,
on analyzing the play, that Shakespeare gave his chief
attention to the first and the second possibility; that
he did much, even if somewhat spottily, for the fourth;
and that he did what the peculiar nature of his task
permitted for the third.

What must first strike any one who turns directly
from the two plays just considered to *Titus Andronicus* is the knowledge of essentials in theatrical narrative which the whole play, particularly the first act,
shows. Here is no slow and colorless opening.
Instead, a spectacle greets us at the start: "The
tomb of the Andronici appearing; the Tribunes and

Senators aloft as in the Senate. Enter below Saturninus and his Followers, on one side; and Bassianus and his Followers on the other; with Drum and Colors."

The two brief opening speeches take us at once into the contention between the brothers, Saturninus and Bassianus, for the crown of their father. Immediately there is surprise, when Marcus Andronicus appears aloft with the crown only to announce that the Senate has conferred it upon the victorious general, Titus Andronicus, now returning to Rome. Somewhat surprising, too, is the readiness with which both Saturninus and Bassianus agree to submit their cause to the judgment of the people. Again spectacle is with us in the next scene, in the entry of Titus Andronicus, with his soldiers and prisoners, bearing with him the bodies of his sons. On the opening speech of Titus, however, Shakespeare spends the best dramatic poetry of which he is capable at the moment. Compare its simplicity and dignity, its subtle characterizing quality with the verse of the two plays already considered. Instantly we pass from this speech to a strongly dramatic moment of large significance in the motivation of all that follows. The sons of Titus tear from the arms of the fiercely protesting Tamora her first-born son as a sacrifice to the *manes* of their departed brothers. As the sons of Titus return with bloody swords, the coffin is laid in the tomb, while the trumpet sounds and Titus chants his splendid requiem: —

"In peace and honor rest you here, my sons;
Rome's readiest champions, repose you here in rest,
Secure from worldly chances and mishaps;
Here lurks no treason, here no envy swells,
Here grow no damned grudges, here are no storms,
No noise but silence and eternal sleep.
In peace and honor rest you here, my sons."

As soon as Lavinia has welcomed her father Titus,
Marcus Andronicus, Saturninus, and Bassianus enter
to welcome the conqueror, and there is again surprise
in the unwillingness of Titus to accept the crown.
There is also suspense, as we wait to see for which of
the candidates Titus will decide. Again there is a surprising turn in the narrative when Saturninus announces
his sudden decision to choose Lavinia as his empress,
for in the first scene we heard Bassianus admit that a
reason for yielding to the decision of the Tribunes as
to Titus was his love for Lavinia. How, then, will he
take this sudden choice of his brother? Clearly, too,
the action which would accompany the words of Saturninus as he speaks admiringly to Tamora would make
an audience wonder as to the genuineness of his feeling
for Lavinia and suspect complications ahead because
of this admiration for the captured queen. Suddenly
Bassianus seizes Lavinia and makes off with her. Now
the dramatic incident comes thick and fast. While
the Emperor courts Tamora in dumb show, the sons of
Titus take sides for and against him as regards Bassianus; the angry father strikes down his son Mutius,
who bars his way; and Saturninus announces his deter-

mination to make Tamora his empress. Hard upon
all this follows the strongly emotional scene in which the
sons of Titus coax him to bury Mutius with his brothers.
Saturninus returns with Tamora, and Bassianus with
Lavinia. The dialogue makes it clear that feeling runs
high between the brothers, and that Titus is at odds
with both. Tamora at once assumes the right of her
new position and, while she apparently labors for harmony, lets us by her aside to Saturninus see that she is
bent upon revenge for the death of her son. After all
this crowding incident, this constant playing upon our
emotions, the act ends in promises of friendship and
harmony which we know from Tamora's aside will
amount to nothing. Is not ample suspense to carry
us over into the second act provided? Compare this
first act in all its richness of incident and its climactic
use of suspense with the thin plot and the slow development of *Love's Labour's Lost* and *The Two Gentlemen
of Verona.*

Surprise awaits us again in the opening speech by
Aaron in Act II, for he tells us that as the long-time
lover of Tamora he is completely bound to her interests and is ready to do all manner of evil to her enemies.
There follows the scene in which, by the advice of Aaron,
Demetrius and Chiron change their rivalry for Lavinia
to united scheming against her. Here is a new, if
disagreeable, element of interest and suspense. Scene
2 merely provides the coming of all the necessary figures to the hunt. Scene 3, however, is so crowded

with happenings, as is Scene 4, that they are hard to follow in the reading. First we have Aaron mysteriously hiding his gold and openly gloating over a villany which he does not explain. Then comes the strong love scene of Tamora and Aaron in which they plot against Bassianus and Lavinia; Bassianus and Lavinia discover them and taunt them. Demetrius and Chiron, entering, are led by Tamora to believe that her life has been in danger and that she has been unforgivably insulted. Thereupon they stab Bassianus, throw him into the pit, and drag off Lavinia. Scene 4 shows us Aaron luring Martius and Quintus to the pit so that they may fall in and when found be held to have murdered Bassianus. Aaron brings Saturninus, too, that he may discover his dead brother with the trapped Martius and Quintus. Tamora, entering with Titus Andronicus and Lucius, completes the chain of evidence by producing the forged letter inculpating Martius and Quintus. The sons of Titus are led off to execution. Scene 5 simply emphasizes the horrors of the ravished Lavinia. Surely the complications hinted at in Act I have come thick and fast in Act II — in the death of Bassianus, the rape of Lavinia, and the arrest of the sons of Andronicus. Moreover, all that has resulted can directly or indirectly be traced to the refusal of Titus to listen to Tamora's prayer in her son's behalf. Yet here is no dead centre. Still we want to know whether the sons of Titus die, whether Lavinia is revenged, and what Titus does in behalf of his sons.

In Act III Shakespeare moves with somewhat less complication because he makes the act, as a whole, centre around Titus and brings out the effect of all the griefs that have come upon him. The dramatist looks at the possibilities of his material, however, more from the point of view of situation and crude emotion than of characterization. Even as Titus begs in vain that the Tribunes will spare his sons, Lucius comes saying that he has been banished for attempting to rescue his brothers and is going to the Goths. Now, when it seems as if nothing worse could happen, Marcus enters with the maimed Lavinia, and the cup of bitterness for Titus seems full. But there is more to come. Aaron enters to say that if Titus Andronicus will send the Emperor his hand, his sons will be sent to him alive. No wonder, when a messenger returns with the severed hand and with the heads of his sons, that Titus cries, "When will this fearful slumber have an end?" He rouses only to think of revenge. Even if climax be gained by crudely melodramatic circumstance, here is swift, climactic movement and intense emotion. Undoubtedly the next scene, first printed in the first folio and perhaps not Shakespeare's, seems trivial and crude to-day, but when acted it would undoubtedly show a man, whose mind is breaking under the agony of his grief, and so would give a certain climax to the act.

Scene 1 of Act IV belongs to Lavinia, for in it, with a staff in her mouth which she guides by the stumps of her arms, she writes in the sand the names of her be-trayers. Scene 2 brings the episode of the Blackamoor child of Aaron and his departure to place it in hiding among the Goths. In Scene 3 Titus is mad from grief. Scene 4 shows us the way in which the letters Titus fastened to the arrows he has been madly shoot-ing into the air, or has delivered to the clown as mes-senger, turn up to annoy Saturninus. It brings news, too, that Lucius, who fled to the Goths, is coming on Rome as their leader. There is much variety and much emotional appeal in these four scenes, though the act, as a whole, is not so unified as some of the preceding. It, however, points steadily ahead to complications in the fifth act.

In the first scene of Act V, Aaron becomes the pris-oner of Lucius and reveals the responsibility for all the deviltry which has taken place. Scene 2 shows us the curious masquerading of Tamora and her sons before the house of Titus, doubtless far more interest-ing to an audience of the time than to-day, though even now the fact that the audience would know both Tamora and Titus are playing double would make it exciting. Its close in the sudden seizure and binding of Chiron and Demetrius and their murder by Titus and Lavinia would make it thrilling. In Scene 3 the swift killing of Lavinia, Tamora, Titus and Saturninus must have made a very climax of horror. Then the play slowly closes with one of those general summaries of the plot, here by Lucius and Marcus, of which the

Elizabethan audience in 1590–1595 seemed to be fond.[1]

I have gone into this rather detailed analysis because in no other way could I show the extremely large amount of incident, the constant use of suspense, the strong feeling for climax, and the relative unity of the plot which the play shows. Up to the end of the third act all moves not only swiftly, but compactly. Thereafter, it is as if the large amount of incident which the two old plays provided made it necessary for Shakespeare to use more scenes and to lose a little of his unity. But when one remembers that probably incidents originally not at all connected have here been brought together, is not this a somewhat remarkable piece of plotting for the man who could scarcely plot at all in *Love's Labour's Lost* and who was unable to fulfil the promise of the suspense he created in the *Two Gentlemen of Verona?*

What makes the play repellent to us to-day is its combined extreme impossibility and its brutal horror. We must remember, however, that Shakespeare was not writing at all for posterity, but for a very immediate public which had shown the highest enthusiasm over the horrors of Kyd's *Spanish Tragedy*. In their past enthusiasm for certain details and scenes of the two old plays he saw the strongest reason for reproducing them in his condensation and adaptation. Were he to make them less brutal than in the original, they would be less

[1] See comments on the Friar's speech at end of *Romeo and Juliet*, p. 209.

effective. Nor, on the other hand, could he, even if he wished, go very far in characterization. To make these people real, would be merely to emphasize the improbability of their doings. The only road to success lay in treating the drama frankly as a drama of blood — what to-day we should call melodrama — and compressing ten acts into five with as much technical skill in the creation of suspense and climax and in necessary motivation as he then possessed. Yet he did try for motivation whenever his crowding incident permitted it. Dr. Fuller has listed some ten points in which Shakespeare finds no original in the Dutch and the German survivals of the two old English plays. Putting aside the natural question whether the foreign plays are strict translations of their originals or adaptations which may have omitted some details, the significant differences show that Shakespeare was endeavoring better to motivate the story or to provide strong dramatic or spectacular effect. Apparently he added the preliminary dispute between Bassianus and Saturninus, which shows us in action the cause for their later bad feeling. The burial of the sons of Titus brought back from the war provides a spectacle and a strong emotional appeal. In naming Alarbus, the eldest born of Tamora, as the sacrifice, instead of merely proposing to sacrifice her lover Aaron, he makes the act seem more cruel to his audience and leaves Tamora a figure not wholly unsympathetic. The kidnapping of Lavinia offers a striking episode in itself, leads to the touching death of Mutius, does much to aid the characterization of Bassianus, Titus, and Saturninus, and critically motivates the hard feeling between the brothers, and to some extent accounts for the swift turning of the outraged Saturninus to Tamora.[1]

In the main, however, he contented himself with enriching the poetic expression where he could, and with getting what he had not yet gained before in the plays left to us — swift, climactic exposition of a story which grips the attention from start to finish. Viewed rightly, *Titus Andronicus* shows that by 1594 Shakespeare was a competent dramatist in one of the two rudimentary dramatic forms — melodrama.

Like *Titus Andronicus, The Comedy of Errors* affords an interesting study in adaptation. In all probability it was originally acted on December 28, 1594, at Gray's Inn, when a *"Comedy of Errors* (like to Plautus his *Menæchmus)"* was given. Certainly the play was reproduced before King James in 1604. It may then, of course, have been somewhat made over, though the verse is not supposed to justify the conclusion that any elaborate making over took place. Usually it is

---

[1] The remaining differences are slight except for Scene 2 of Act III, which as I have already shown is a late addition and possibly not Shakespeare's: the hand of Titus, Marcus, or Lucius is demanded instead of that of Titus only; young Lucius carries presents from Titus to Chiron and Demetrius; the arrow-shooting occurs on the stage; the sentence imposed on Aaron differs a little, and the farewell speeches to the dead in the last act are formal additions. *Publications of the Modern Language Association*, Vol. XVI, No. 1, p. 41.

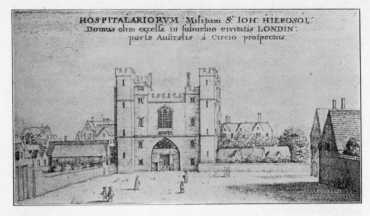

ST. JOHN'S GATE

(Office of the Master of the Revels)

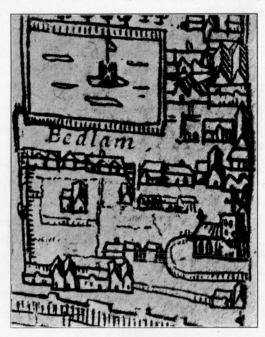

THE THEATRE, 1576

(See Ryther's Map, p. 36)

held that *The Comedy of Errors* is one of the earliest, if
not the earliest, of Shakespeare's comedies; but, as we
shall see, the technical accomplishment in it shows that
if written very early it must at least have been revised
carefully at a time after the writing of *Love's Labour's
Lost* and *The Two Gentlemen of Verona*, and not remote
from the date of the adaptation, *Titus Andronicus*.
The ultimate sources of the play are the *Menechmi* of
Plautus and his *Amphitruo;* but whether Shakespeare
worked from intermediary English versions is an open
question. Certainly a non-extant *Historie of Error*,
which may have been founded on Plautus, was acted
by the Children of Paul's on New Year's night, 1576–
1577. To this Shakespeare's play may possibly be
indebted. Though no English translation of the
Menechmi was published before that of W. W. in
1595, the manuscript of this had been in circulation
among the friends of the translator before it appeared
in print, and Shakespeare may have seen it. Certainly
he does not follow it closely.

Three things are especially noteworthy in Shakespeare's adaptation: the far greater complication in
story than in the Latin originals; the skill with which
the story is adapted to the tastes of the immediate
public; and the ingenuity combined with sureness
with which Shakespeare handles his many threads of
plot. In the first place, the story of the *Menechmi*
is at once complicated by creating a twin for the
servant. In the second place, Scene 1 of Act III,

in which Antipholus of Ephesus and his servant are kept out of their house because the twin Antipholus and the twin Dromio are within, is added from the *Amphitruo*, from which may also be borrowed the idea of the twin servant. There is added, too, the love of Antipholus of Syracuse for Luciana. Finally, the father and mother, of whom we only hear in the Latin, appear at the beginning and end of the play as Ægeon and Æmilia. Here again, as in *Titus Andronicus*, we have evidence of a fact which will confront us often in our examination of Shakespeare's plays, namely, that the Elizabethan audience liked a play crowded to the utmost with incident and complication. From the comic side *The Comedy of Errors* is as strong proof of this as is *Titus Andronicus* on the tragic. Here, then, is proof of two things: that in farce-comedy, as well as in melodrama, Shakespeare could by 1594 provide the complicated story which he certainly did not offer in his *Love's Labour's Lost* and apparently could not offer in *The Two Gentlemen of Verona;* and that consequently he now well understood one of the chief essentials of dramatic narrative for the audience of his time.

Moreover, the addition of the love scenes between Antipholus of Syracuse and Luciana and of the scenes of Ægeon and Æmilia shows his sensitiveness to his audience and at the same time his growing literary skill. The whole development of the English drama between 1590 and 1600 proves how hearty and instant must have been the response of the public to the love element the moment it was strongly emphasized. As we have seen, Shakespeare instinctively, or it may be with good judgment, had developed in *Love's Labour's Lost* and *The Two Gentlemen of Verona* what had been but an element in the plays of his immediate predecessors, the love story, into his central theme. Thereafter, he rarely fails to keep it before his public as main or as minor interest. Here he creates it out of whole cloth, evidently primarily because he felt sure of its additional appeal for his audience. In the second place, those scenes of Ægeon and Æmilia at the beginning and at the end of the play are in part, I believe, Shakespeare's response to the delight of the Elizabethans in strong contrasts. Always the delight of the English in blending in their drama the comic and the tragic has been a puzzle to the more civilized of the Continental nations, especially the French. Whatever its psychological cause, no careful reader of the Elizabethan drama will for a moment deny that the sharpest possible contrasts are common in it. There would seem to be a regard for the tastes of his public, too, in allowing the wife, Adriana, to have more prominence and more characterization in the adaptation than in the original and, above all, in the substitution of Luciana, as confidant, for the father of the wife in the *Menechmi*. Even for the Elizabethans the mere cheating of a wife in behalf of a courtesan was not as funny as it had been for the Latin audience, and to them the sister would seem the much more natural confidant.

Not only is Shakespeare keenly alive, in retelling his story, to the habits of mind and the prejudices of his audience, but he is master of his material. For instance, he finds no difficulty in handling the new people made necessary by his additions to the story of the *Menechmi* or his different emphasizing of it, namely, the Duke Solinus, Balthazar, Angelo, Luciana, Ægeon, Æmilia, and above all the second Dromio. It is common to decry the characterization of the play as slight, but it must be remembered that in all dramatic composition the amount of characterization we have a right to expect from a dramatist depends upon the aim he has in view. His is no indefinite stretch of canvas. A play must not take more than two and a half or three hours even in the days of Shakespeare; consequently if he crowds it with incident, the characterization must necessarily be faint or must be given in swift and masterly strokes. But do we ask in a farce of incident for any strong characterization? Are we not, and ought we not, to be satisfied with such characterization as makes the situations for the moment plausible? Study the scenes of this play carefully and I believe you will see there is a dramatic rightness of feeling in the amount of characterization given each which we have not noted before. In the scenes of farcical situation the characterization is either subordinated to the development of the complications, though it remains adequate, or it comes in swift revealing strokes. On the other hand, in the sisterly talk of Luciana and Adriana, and in the love making of Antipholus of Syracuse, characterization comes properly into greater prominence. Let any one who doubts the greater sureness of Shakespeare here in characterization contrast his treatment of Sir Eglamour or Thurio in *The Two Gentlemen of Verona* with his development of Angelo in the first scene of Act IV of this play. Again his great gain in control of his material appears in his sure-footed movement as he threads his way through the confusion worse confounded of the last scene of Act IV and in his development of the last act. All that he was unable to do in closing *The Two Gentlemen of Verona* he is competent for in this play. Making us feel every minute that the conclusion must be upon us, he draws all the people necessary to his dénouement naturally upon the stage, meantime piling up amusing complications until we are nearly ready to cry with the Duke himself, "I think you are all mated or stark mad." Then, and only then, he lets the abbess enter with Antipholus of Syracuse and Dromio his servant, and all the confusion is cleared away.

Shakespeare shows in this play, too, a marked sense of dramatic economy, which is one of the sure signs of the experienced playwright. The appearance of Ægeon at the beginning of the play not only provides an element of surprise when the hearer finds this grave opening turning suddenly into a roaring farce-comedy, but it is a device for badly needed exposition which gets rid of a chorus and also does away with the necessarily less dramatic recounting of the story by Menechmus Sosicles in the original. Moreover, the opening scene of Ægeon makes possible the neat adjustment of the story in the last scene. We see something of the same economy in the way in which the figure of Luciana, substituted for the wife's father, is made in her love story to provide a new thread of interest. Indeed, so wise and so firm is the handling of the material in this adaptation that one would almost be inclined to say a large part of its merit must date from the performance at Court in 1604, when Shakespeare had acquired his technique, were it not that the plays we are to consider next, *Romeo and Juliet* and *The Merchant of Venice*, give proof that shortly before their composition such work as this must have been possible for Shakespeare.

Usually *The Comedy of Errors* is called comedy; sometimes, frankly, farce. But is it exclusively either? Is it not rather a farce-comedy? As I am to consider in a later chapter Shakespeare's treatment of the forms of comedy, I wish here only to point out that in *The Comedy of Errors* farce-comedy of literary value first appears in our drama. Is it not striking that even in these experimental plays the young dramatist is well on his way toward high comedy, and in adaptation has mastered farce-comedy, a form heretofore unknown?

It is evidence of the fine normality of Shakespeare's development that his highest technical attainment before 1595 came in adaptations of preceding plays — in *Titus Andronicus* and *The Comedy of Errors*. Of course, it is easier to adapt for an audience of your own time a play or plays of a preceding decade, or even of a different age and language, than it is to create your story and build your play therefrom or even to transmute the narrative of a novel into successful theatrical narrative. But as adapter and as worker in melodrama and farce-comedy, Shakespeare had demonstrated by 1594 knowledge of his audience, a growing sense of technique, and the power to make that technique so mould a story as to conform with the prejudices and tastes of his public. Note that he gains his technique first where the heaviest demands in characterization are not made upon him, in melodrama and farce-comedy. He has yet to learn, on the one hand, how to metamorphose the stilted stories of his day into vivid portrayal of human conduct and how to make historic scenes live again. Inasmuch as he tried his hand very early at the chronicle history plays, let us next consider his development in that so-called form.

CHAPTER IV

THE CHRONICLE PLAYS

TEN of Shakespeare's thirty-seven plays are chronicle histories in the strict sense of the word. Three more, *Macbeth*, *Lear*, and *Cymbeline*, are drawn from English legendary history. Three others, *Julius Cæsar*, *Hamlet*, and *Anthony and Cleopatra*, are founded on the history of two other nations. That is, roughly speaking, one-quarter of Shakespeare's work is chronicle play, and nearly one-half of it has its source in the histories. The chronicle play is, however, so unstable, so transitional, that it cannot be defined by its differentia as a form, but is best distinguished from farce, melodrama, comedy, and tragedy by its material. Indeed, one can hardly distinguish it more than to say it was, in strict Elizabethan usage, a play which drew its material from national history. It mattered not whether this material was veracious or legendary, whether it dealt with Richard III or Lear, but, in the strict use of the term, if it did not deal with British history it was not a genuine chronicle play. Of course, as *James the Fourth* of Robert Greene shows, a play founded on an Italian romance [1] could easily be foisted on this none

---

[1] *James the Fourth* is founded on the story of Astatio and Arrenopia; cf. Giraldi Cinthio's *Hecatommithi*.

too discriminating public as a genuine chronicle play, merely by giving some of the figures well-known historical Scotch names.

In form, too, as well as in substance, nothing could be dramatically freer than the chronicle play of the sixteenth century. Its form was free because it simply applied to lay history the methods of dramatic narration already practised by the miracle plays for some centuries with secular material. The chronicle play, before an audience just as curious and at first little better informed historically than the people who had watched the miracle plays, recounted what had happened in the reign of a particular king, what incidents led to his accession, what episodes marked his fall or death. Particularly in the earlier stages of the miracle play, events as compared with characterization or dialogue, were of prime importance. If each of the great cycles may be called one great play, every division was, as it were, an act in a drama of twenty-five to forty acts. For two reasons at least, each special scene was sufficient unto itself. First, it was represented by a different company, one of the gilds, which naturally was interested in its play only as a unit and cared not at all to link its performance with what followed. Secondly, the prime duty of the writer was to reproduce the historical situation and to emphasize its moral purport, rather than to aim at perfect characterization or dialogue attractive in itself. Recall that in 1590 the miracle play still lingered in out-of-the-way parts of

England; that it had fallen into a decline only in the first quarter of the century; and it becomes clear that the early chronicle play could hardly avoid treating lay history even as the miracle play had presented Biblical history. Five acts of *Henry VI* are like five successive gild plays in their loose, discursive development, and their emphasis on situation as contrasted with character and dialogue. They are not unlike them in that, though they do not emphasize the moral significance of the material, they stress, by genealogies and expositions such as Shakespeare's of the Salic Law, education in history.

It is striking that before 1585–1590 the chronicle play had no real prominence. Though there were a few, such as Bale's *Kynge Johan*, the famous *Gorboduc*, and *The Misfortunes of Arthur*, the first was half morality, and the other two, like most of their fellows, were strongly influenced by Seneca's plays, and were at best, therefore, hybrids. The genuine English chronicle play — that is, English history treated in the method, or perhaps better with the absence of method, of the old miracle plays — rose to prominence with that sudden upswelling of English patriotism which burst forth after the death of Mary Queen of Scots and the defeat of the Armada gave promise of a time of peace from internal dissension and outer attack in which England could wax glorious as she had never been before. It is suggestive, as the special historian of this so-called form, Professor Schelling, has pointed out,[1] that this growth of the chronicle play accompanied the rapid multiplying between 1590 and 1600 of poems on historical subjects, and was itself doubtless due in part to the rapid publication between 1550 and 1590 of a succession of books dealing with English history. About a dozen of these plays belonging before 1590 exist, and even this number includes three plays in Latin, and two strongly influenced by Seneca, as well as two which are but pseudo-historical. That is, there are extant but three undoubted chronicle plays written before 1590. Yet the next decade leaves us some eighty out of a very much larger production. Indeed, I think it may be said that between 1588 and 1598 the chronicle play was the most popular kind of play in England. The pages of Henslowe's *Diary* certainly show that all the leading dramatists, at one time or another within that decade, tried their hands at this kind of work — Greene, Peele, Marlowe, Dekker, Jonson, Shakespeare. It was the child of the universal instinct for dramatic expression quickened by the youthful and vigorous spirit of nationalism, and it was trained in the freest of all schools, that of the only national drama England then had, — the miracle plays and moralities. Yet English through and through as it was, it gave way, about 1600, to the comedy of manners and to tragedy. And when both of those went out of vogue about 1608, in spite of scattered plays, like *Henry VIII* and Ford's *Perkin Warbeck*, it never

---

[1] *The English Chronicle Play*, F. E. Schelling, ch. II.

regained its old popularity. Why? It is easy enough to say that this was because, after the accession of James I, the just foundations of national pride rapidly crumbled, sapped by the base influences of his court; but that is not adequate. From its very essence, the chronicle play is transitional; not even the genius of a Shakespeare could have prevented its developing, when perfected, into some one of the three forms, — the comedy of manners, the play of romantic story, or tragedy.

I shall exclude *Henry VIII* from my consideration of the development of the chronicle play with Shakespeare, because, as it stands, it is a play on which not only Shakespeare, but also John Fletcher worked; because we are not sure when the form we possess was written; and because we do not know whether there was genuine collaboration or merely a making over by Fletcher after Shakespeare's death. Indeed, in spite of its purple patches of poetry and its dramatic moments, it is at best to be classed with the earlier chronicle plays, for, as Dr. Hertzberg has not unfairly said, it is "a chronicle history with three and a half catastrophes, varied by a marriage and a coronation pageant, ending abruptly in the baptism of a child." Enough evidence for my purposes can certainly be derived from the three parts of *Henry VI*, from *Richard III*, *Richard II*, *King John*, *Henry V*, and the two parts of *Henry IV*. Tracing rapidly the dramatic accomplishment in these plays, I hope to show that genius itself, even when as ready to learn and to submit to basic principles of dramatic composition as Shakespeare shows himself in *The Comedy of Errors* and *Titus Andronicus*, could not make the chronicle play a form by itself. Instead, it must be forced by the very nature of dramatic composition and the eternal interests of the public in drama to aid an inevitable evolution rather than to create or even to establish a separate form. Let us recall at the outset the axiom that the aim of drama is to give rise within the space of no more than five acts to the greatest possible amount of emotional effect, be it laughter, tears, or the many intermediate states. What we shall watch is the gradual recognition by Shakespeare of the ways in which he may get the largest emotional returns in telling his public of days of the past in terms of their own experience, and the consequent resolution of the chronicle history into comedy of manners, tragedy, and even mere romance.

I do not need to go into the complicated question of the relative authorship of the three parts of *Henry VI* or their exact relation to the two plays which the second and third parts much resemble: *The Famous Contention between the Two Houses of York and Lancaster* and *The True Tragedy of Richard Duke of York*.[1] It is enough here that the three parts must belong

---

[1] See especially *On the Authorship of the Second and Third Parts of Henry VI and their originals*, Jane Lee (*New Shaks. So. Transactions*, 1875–76).

between 1589 and 1592; that Shakespeare was probably making over old material in all three parts;
and that he may have had Christopher Marlowe as
a collaborator in the second and third parts. No
doubt some readers have wondered why of all the plays
I have in mind only *Richard III* is often seen, and why
it is that the others, when rarely performed, are
somehow less satisfactory than when read, — a curious
result for plays which surely no one would denominate
closet drama. All this results, I believe, because
certain great principles of dramatic composition which
spring from the relation of the public to this imitative
art — the drama — are not observed in this group
of plays. Not even genius can neglect these few
underlying principles and hope that his play will have
lasting popularity, or, often, even temporary success,
except with some coterie his own leadership has formed.
The first principle of all is that a play must have unity,
not because the rhetorics call for that in composition,
but because the great public does not permanently
care for story-telling which leaves no clear, final impression. It may be helpful to remember that these
historical plays are the Elizabethan prototype of
our plays of the Civil War. We, too, not long since,
were satisfied with a succession of ununified scenes
so long as they thrilled us with camp-fire scenes, the
marching and counter-marching of mimic forces, or
the horrors of Libby prison. But those plays we are
considering have gone into the oblivion where even

these Elizabethan plays would have dropped if characterization of distinct power and much rich if irregularly appearing poetry had not been present in these nine chronicle histories. The fact is, the three parts of *Henry VI, Richard II,* and even to some extent *King John,* fail as plays in two fundamental respects.

In the first place, in spite of characterization and poetry, occasional or frequent, these plays leave us in the theatre far less clear, and therefore less satisfied, than does *Richard III,* in which every scene is but one more light thrown on the facets of Richard's character. Say, if you like, that it is a very simple form of unity to keep one figure almost constantly before your audience and to show him not as a mixture of good and evil, but as unqualifiedly malevolent. Add, if you will, in derogation, that in *Richard III* Shakespeare was merely imitating the method of Christopher Marlowe in *Tamburlaine.* The fact remains, nevertheless, that *Richard III* responds to a permanent instinct of the public: an instinct that delights in a central figure or at least a group of figures which grip its attention at the start and which hold that attention to the end. Recall the curious effect of an evening of one-act plays. Some years ago the late Felix Morris tried the experiment — usually to half-empty houses. He told the writer that the audience when interested in one of his creations clearly disliked to lose sight of it after one act, and evidently found it difficult to readjust itself repeatedly to new characters and new interests. I believe that to be psychologically sound and something that could have been foreseen. Is the devotion of the American public to a "star" anything but another manifestation of the same instinct? If story fail them, if there be no character in the play which really interests them, at least they can watch how the "star" does his work! Now in every one of the plays I have in mind, except *Richard III* and *Henry V*, there is not the unification of material which carries on a reader or hearer with increasing interest from stage to stage, leaving him clear at the end as to the meaning of the whole play. Nor is there in any other play than these two a unification so complete, even if crude, by means of a central figure.

Lest there be any doubt as to this, let us run over the other plays rapidly. What is the real subject of the first part of *Henry VI*? Count Talbot and his brave deeds? He dies in the first scene of the fourth act. Is it the wars with France? If so, the play should end with the last scene of Act IV of the Folio. Is it the plottings of the barons? That is the only interest which holds out to the end of the play; but if so, it certainly has not compelled attention throughout. Indeed, what avails it if in the mind of the author a particular interest in his play is of prime importance when the public selects another which ends before the close of the play? The contemporary testimony of Thomas Nash shows us that to the public the Talbot scenes were the cause for enthusiasm.[1] It is true that the Second Part, which treats throughout of internal dissensions in the kingdom and the rise to power of York and his sons, splits up the interest less, and that in Part Three there is an approach toward unity in the rise of Richard and the passing of the crown to the party of York; but in each part we are hurried from one scene to another without any central figure on which to fasten our attention, without anything which, in the ordinary sense of the word, can be called plot, — if we mean by that word a related set of incidents with distinctly a beginning, a middle, and an end. Part I is incomplete without Part II; Part II without Part III; and even Part III without *Richard III*. That is, we have a great tetralogy of twenty acts in which no one of the quarters, except possibly the last, is conceived as a unit. Rather what should have been reduced by careful selective compression to two plays of five acts — one dealing with Henry and one with Richard — has been diffusively narrated. Even if some promising characterization and much poetry mark the narration, we have in *Henry VI* blocks of history rather than beads strung by a central dominating character or a unifying idea.

[1] *Piers Penniless* (entered August 8, 1592) contains the following: "How it would have joyed brave Talbot, the terror of the French, to think that after he had lain two hundred years in his tomb, he should triumph again on the stage, and have his bones embalmed again with the tears of ten thousand spectators." For a discussion of the significance of the reference at the moment, see *Life of Shakespeare*, F. G. Fleay, pp. 259–260.

A second dramatic flaw in *Henry VI, King John,* and *Richard II* is best illustrated by the third play. There are many who much admire what they feel to be the reserve and the artistic restraint of *Richard II,* and with those who talk of it as poetry or as narrative there can be no quarrel; but as drama the play has a fatal fault. Notice how little the actors care for this play. It is easy enough to say scoffingly that they see no star part in it, but there is no one star part in *Julius Cæsar,* yet the actors seem reasonably fond of that play. The truth is, here in *Richard II* is a play without a hero. Richard is constantly represented in an unfavorable light — as weak, dilatory, and selfish. The character with elements of popularity, who might easily have been made the central figure of the play, is Bolingbroke, yet, only lightly sketched in as compared with Richard, he is evidently deliberately subordinated to the latter. Once more we face a curious situation: like the child, an audience, loving story-telling for its own sake, craves some compelling central figure whom it can follow sympathetically or even with fascinated abhorrence. The least experienced story-teller for children knows that mere incident with no central figure can never compete with Jack the Giant-killer or the Ugly Duckling. Nor does the childish listener, no matter what his years, care for a weakling as the central figure. When he finds a weakling in that position, he falls back on either the incidents of the story itself or on some secondary person in the play. Iago and Macbeth compel attention quite as much as Othello or Lear, but Hamlet and Coriolanus as central figures do not command the unwavering attention of the uncritical. How much has the great public cared for attempts like Mr. G. B. Shaw's to interest them in the temperament of such a figure as the hero of *Arms and the Man?* On the other hand, to fall back on a secondary character is to shift interest midway, something which Marlowe, with his sure theatrical instinct, worked hard to prevent in *Edward II.* To-day, all these warring factions about Richard have for us no special interest in themselves. Worst of all, from the side of the actor, the great cause of disaster in the play — the vacillation and dilatoriness of Richard — are merely talked of or illustrated in their results rather than strikingly presented in action. That is, the actor's instinct tells him there is no good acting part in the play either in the sense that he can carry the sympathy of the house with him in ever-increasing attention from start to finish or that he can hold it fascinated, even with disgust or horror, as in *Richard III.* What tells in *Richard II* to-day is what relates it to *Love's Labour's Lost*, the fertility of its poetic imagination, and its verse. Listen to Richard giving up his crown in these beautiful but exceedingly self-conscious lines: —

> " Now is this golden crown like a deep well;
> It owes two buckets, filling one another:
> The emptier ever dancing in the air,
> The other down, unseen, and full of water:

That bucket down, and full of tears am I,
Drinking my grief, whilst you mount up on high."

Remembering that a few years later Shakespeare had learned that in the great crises in our lives a gesture, a glance, a monosyllable, are far more probable than any long speech, however fine, one is disposed to quote James Shirley's words, "Sir, your phrase has too much landscape."

In *King John*, though Shakespeare gains decidedly in dramatic skill, some of the old weaknesses persist. Again we face in John a weakling who can only slightly command our sympathy and whose death is far less touching than it would be had he in the earlier scenes been of larger mould. There can be no question that Falconbridge is the strength of the play as a play. As any reader knows who has compared Shakespeare's *John* with the earlier play in two parts, from which he skilfully condensed it, *The Troublesome Raigne of King John,* and with the historical material in Holinshed,[1] Falconbridge is Shakespeare's creation from vague and indequate suggestions. But it is not merely the courage, resourcefulness, and wit of Falconbridge,—in a word his characterization — which make him memorable: it is he who passes straight through the play, carrying our sympathies and affection with him and giving to it a kind of unity. But he cannot give it that essen-

[1] For a probable source of the dispute of the Bastard and his brother in *The Troublesome Raigne of King John,* see Halle's account of the reign of Henry VI, *Shakspere's Holinshed,* W. Boswell-Stone, pp. 48-50.

THE BANKSIDE THEATRES CIRCA 1600

(From the so-called 1657 map. The theatres from left to right are the Swan, the Hope, the Rose, the Globe.)

tial unity which would come from a compelling central figure indispensable to all the important scenes, without whom the play could have no being.

Particularly noticeable is the development of the comic in this play. Part I of *Henry VI* showed only touches, and those coarse; Part III lacked it; and in Part II Cade's followers provided comic relief. *Richard II* lacks it, and in *Richard III* its place is taken by the sardonic irony of the king himself. In *Henry V*, as it stands, the comic alternates with the graver scenes. Thus far, then, the really comic has come almost entirely, if present at all, from people not closely involved with the main plot. In *King John* it is Falconbridge himself, an important person in nearly all the main scenes, who brings the comic relief. This recognition that the comic is desirable for contrast and that it may relax tense emotion till a hearer may again be wrought upon with effect, Shakespeare, in part, owes the author of *The Troublesome Raigne;* but a few years later in *The Merchant of Venice* he will show us in the trial scene that the comic and the tragic depend not upon the person who is looked at, but the sympathies of the person who looks at him.

Growing maturity is seen also in *King John* in the scene of Arthur and Hubert, by the subordination of mere physical horror to working upon us through sympathies with the lad himself. There are, too, repeated instances which show increasing sureness of theatrical knowledge. In the original of the Hubert-

Arthur scene, the murderers enter shortly after Hubert begins to speak with the lad and seize upon the boy. Shakespeare holds them back till just as Hubert is beginning to yield. Their coming fills an audience with dread lest it strengthen Hubert's weakening purpose. Our eager watching of Hubert relaxes only when he orders out the murderers, for then we know that he will yield. In the first chapter I pointed out that the earlier dramatists seem not to have understood how to make an entrance or an exit dramatically effective. Here Shakespeare proves that he knows how to make both significant for their scene. In this play, too, Shakespeare shows marked alertness to motivate the details of his story; for example, when Philip breaks his bond with John. In the original Philip breaks it promptly and with no conscience; in Shakespeare he yields only after appeals to him from all his friends and followers. This care for motivation in characters other than the title part is noteworthy because unusual in the preceding work both of Shakespeare and his contemporaries. In brief, *King John*, except in not providing for the title part a person who holds us to the end thoroughly sympathetic or fascinated by his evil doing, and in the momentary abeyance of rich poetic expression, shows dramatic gain by Shakespeare.

Even when one comes to the two parts of *Henry IV*, which one can praise unreservedly for humor, humanity, and general characterization, it is not difficult to see why the play is rarely acted to-day. Every one admits that the Second Part is episodic; that the scenes of the barons are largely repetitive of Part I, and that the warring of the king with his barons lacks the interest which the fascinating Hotspur gave similar scenes in the First Part. Delightful, too, as are the Falstaff scenes, they mingle midway in Part II with the almost equally delightful scenes of Shallow and Slender. That is, even in the Falstaff scenes of this Part — and it is also true of Part I — we have a group of perfect character scenes appearing as episodes rather than as a story. Moreover, he who does not care for Falstaff, if such there be, will find in the strictly historical portion neither central figure nor absorbing story to interest him. Perhaps that explains why the play to-day reads better than it acts: in reading, it is characterization which tells most; but on the stage, it is a story in action. Even in Part I, though it is Hotspur who carries our sympathies with him, no matter how much the dramatist himself may have favored the prince, we are doomed to see our hero fall sometime ere the close of the play. Evidently, then, the moment you consider the relation of an audience to story-telling upon the stage, you see easily why it is that of all these plays *Richard III* — even if its motivation is by no means equal to some of the others, and the characters, except Richard, are little more than types in an essentially melodramatic presentation of history — holds its public to-day by its characterizing action for a central figure. Perhaps, too, you see why *Henry V*, with that fascinating portrait presented in memorable verse, holds us better in reading than in acting, depending as it does not so much on action as on characterization in poetry. In other words, even in the best of these chronicle plays, it is not plot which tells, as was the case with *Titus Andronicus* and *The Comedy of Errors*, but episode, and such unity as there is comes through such figures as Falconbridge, Hotspur, Henry V, and Richard III. The art of developing a well-unified plot out of historical material had not, in this form, been attained by Shakespeare even four years later than he had acquired it in melodrama and farce. The reason for this striking difference bears on the point I made in opening this chapter as to the impossibility of treating the chronicle play as a form by itself.

In the first place, it cannot be shown that this episodic nature of the so-called form resulted because the Elizabethan public remained permanently indifferent to a well-unified recounting of history. At first they were undoubtedly such avid hearers of dramatic narration of their historic past that, for the moment, if the dramatist made past scenes and figures live again, they were so absorbed and grateful that they took what came even as it was offered. Yet after 1598 the chronicle play gave way to high comedy, to the comedy of manners, and to tragedy. Would this have happened if mere reproduction of the past could permanently delight the Elizabethan public? Why, too, since they responded to the increasing unity and technique in such plays as *Titus Andronicus, The Comedy of Errors, The Merchant of Venice,* and *Romeo and Juliet,* should they have made an exception with this one kind of material, — from national history? Does it not look as if some different theory of composition for historical and non-historical subjects existed in the mind of the dramatist?

Again, it may be said that the material, since it was largely a matter of common knowledge, hampered the dramatist through his sense of fact, and that the technique of Shakespeare before 1600 was not equal to surmounting the difficulties resulting. This is at best a half truth. I have shown that, even before Shakespeare wrote, some of the chief essentials of dramatic composition were well understood. In *Titus* and *The Comedy of Errors* we see that by 1594 he knew how to weld the work of another, complicated by new elements, into an admirably constructed and empha-sized play. Moreover, even in these very chronicle plays there are in small matters signs of conscious technique. More than once one notes a striking but somewhat puzzling action at the opening of a play, not fully explained for some time thereafter. For example, in Part I of *Henry VI*, the genealogy which accounts for all the plotting and fighting of the preced-ing scenes is given by the dying Mortimer just at the end of Act II. To-day we should be likely to state or to hint in the first act the causes for the scenes sur-rounding this exposition or immediately succeeding it. Such combination of exposition with action is, however, difficult, and these men of 1590–1595 had the sense to see that a good exciting incident, the causes of which the audience did not quite understand, made it willing and eager to listen later to exposition which would be boresome if stated at the outset and which the dramatists had not art enough as yet to present in any other way than baldly. One finds also in these earlier plays a curious use of suspense. Apparently Shakespeare outgrew it, but it is evident in plays of Ben Jonson as late as 1610. We create suspense to-day by showing, as Shakespeare did later, the feud between the two houses of the Montagues and Capulets, and letting an audience know that the son of one house has fallen in love with the daughter of the other. That seems to us enough to set the imagination working in pleased anticipation of complications to follow. Not so some of these earlier dramatists. They break off the ends of their acts sharply in the middle of something that should immediately follow, as, for instance, at the end of the three parts of *Henry VI;* and sometimes at the end of a scene they introduce one or two new figures merely to start an interest which promptly goes over into the next. The reason for this lay in the nature of their stage : one scene was separated from another, not by our long waits, but merely by the opening of the curtains about the inner stage or the entrance from behind the arras of other persons. Yet both of these devices constitute technique. Moreover, the technique is conscious, for the devices could result only from care-

ful watching of the effect on audiences of plays presented.
Yet it is an ephemeral technique, for with more experience and a truer understanding of the art of the drama
came other and permanently successful methods of
gaining the same results. For us, however, it is enough
at the moment to show that even in the chronicle play
Shakespeare was working not blindly, but with an
increasing sense of methods and laws underlying his
art of playwright. Moreover, detailed comparison of
Richard III, *The True Tragedy of Richard, Duke of
York*, and Heywood's *Edward IV* with one another and
their sources, proves that Shakespeare successfully
used the historical sources more fully than either of
the other authors. Why, then, the contrast in technique between his chronicle plays and his other work
of 1593–1598?

For two reasons: first, the aim of the Elizabethan
dramatists, notably Shakespeare, in writing the chronicle play was different from their purpose in other kinds
of work; and, second, their sense of historical fact kept
them from handling this material with the perfect
freedom which marked their use of all other sources.
Slowly, since the days of the miracle plays, the English
dramatists, known and unknown, had been gaining the
art of telling stories on the stage. By the advent of
Shakespeare, as the work of Greene and Kyd proves,
especially in *James the Fourth* and *The Spanish Tragedy*,
they had practically mastered the essentials of the art.
But with the sudden rise into great popularity of the

M   [161]

chronicle play between 1585 and 1598, their purpose became by well-chosen illustrative scenes to exhibit the historical figures doing the deeds for which they were famous and uttering their equally famous words. Not story but character became central as the chronicle play developed. Nor was the character, as was the case with the plays developed from fiction or from observation of life about the author, chiefly the result of his imagination working either on a few hints in his sources or from close observation of life about him. Instead, from the rather bald accounts in the histories, the dramatist must re-create the historical figures, but without his usual freedom in his use of incident and dialogue from his sources. He was not to tell a story about Henry VI; instead, he was to represent as many as possible of the famous events in the reign of that king. He might tamper with chronology; he could much develop minor figures only suggested in the histories; he might add new figures; but the great personages of history he must represent in the main as history shows them. All this meant, in the first place, a much more difficult problem of characterization because of the dramatist's restricting sense of fact: he was called on to paint, not the type, but an individual. In the second place, this presented particular difficulty just where the Elizabethan was weakest: in devising a fable and constructing a plot around it. If all the illustrative incident used by these dramatists in the chronicle plays were to be wrought into as well unified a play as *The Comedy of Errors* or *Titus Andronicus*, these men must first discern in all the widely separated and dissimilar circumstances the thread of fable, story, which could be woven into a plot.

To watch the development technically of Shakespeare in these chronicle plays is to find constant proof of the truth of the foregoing statements. At the outset, his scenes depend for effect almost wholly on the contained incident. The figures speak the necessary words, but the phrases characterize only in the broadest fashion. There is no evidence that the young dramatist saw the full emotional possibilities of his situation. He rushes through the scene, giving all the striking moments contained in it, but without transition from part to part, and losing opportunity after opportunity for clash and contrast of character. By 1596–1597 Shakespeare had become a master of the art of creating and sustaining dramatic suspense. How he misses the evident and admirable opportunities for it in what follows! We suspect strongly that the Talbot scenes in *Henry VI* are Shakespeare's. Unfortunately the source of Act III, Sc. 2, between the French Countess and Talbot, is not known, so that it is impossible to tell whether the dramatist at all developed upon his original, but a reading of this scene from *Henry VI* should make clear to any one that its author was lacking in all the respects just named. Only his poetic power breaks free from the restraining force of his memory of the details of his scene.

Auvergne.   Court of the Castle.

Enter the COUNTESS *and her* Porter.

Countess. Porter, remember what I gave in charge;
And, when you have done so, bring the keys to me.

  Porter. Madam, I will.   [*Exit.*

  Count. The plot is laid: if all things fall out right,
I shall as famous be by this exploit,
As Scythian Thomyris by Cyrus' death.
Great is the rumor of this dreadful knight,
And his achievements of no less account:
Fain would mine eyes be witness with mine ears,
To give their censure of these rare reports.

Enter Messenger *and* TALBOT.

Messenger. Madam, according as your ladyship desir'd
By message crav'd, so is lord Talbot come.

  Count. And he is welcome.   What! is this the man?

  Mess. Madam, it is.

  Count.   Is this the scourge of France?
Is this the Talbot, so much fear'd abroad,
That with his name the mothers still their babes?
I see report is fabulous and false:
I thought I should have seen some Hercules,
A second Hector for his grim aspect,
And large proportion of his strong-knit limbs.
Alas! this is a child, a silly dwarf:
It cannot be, this weak and writhled shrimp
Should strike such terror to his enemies.

  Talbot. Madam, I have been bold to trouble you;
But, since your ladyship is not at leisure,
I'll sort some other time to visit you.

  Count. What means he now? — Go ask him, whither he goes.

  Mess. Stay, my lord Talbot; for my lady craves
To know the cause of your abrupt departure.

[164]

THE ROSE THEATRE?

(From Hollar's Map of London, 1640)

THE SWAN THEATRE

(From Visscher's Map of London, 1616)

Tal. Marry, for that she's in a wrong belief,
I go to certify her Talbot's here.

Re-enter Porter, *with keys.*

Count. If thou be he, then art thou prisoner.
Tal. Prisoner! to whom?
Count.   To me, blood-thirsty lord;
And for that cause I train'd thee to my house.
Long time thy shadow hath been thrall to me,
For in my gallery thy picture hangs;
But now the substance shall endure the like,
And I will chain these legs and arms of thine,
That hast by tyranny these many years,
Wasted our country, slain our citizens,
And sent our sons and husbands captivate.
Tal. Ha, ha, ha!
Count. Laughest thou, wretch? thy mirth shall turn to moan.
Tal. I laugh to see your ladyship so fond.
To think that you have aught but Talbot's shadow,
Whereon to practise your severity.
Count. Why, art not thou the man?
Tal.   I am indeed.
Count. Then have I substance too.
Tal. No, no, I am but shadow of myself:
You are deceiv'd, my substance is not here;
For what you see, is but the smallest part
And least proportion of humanity.
I tell you, madam, were the whole frame here,
It is of such a spacious lofty pitch,
Your roof were not sufficient to contain it.
Count. This is a riddling merchant for the nonce;
He will be here, and yet he is not here:
How can these contrarieties agree?
Tal. That will I show you presently.

*He winds his Horn. Drums strike up; a Peal of Ordnance. The
Gates being forced, enter Soldiers.*

[165]

How say you, madam? are you now persuaded,
That Talbot is but shadow of himself?
These are his substance, sinews, arms, and strength,
With which he yoketh your rebellious necks,
Razeth your cities, and subverts your towns,
And in a moment makes them desolate.
   Count. Victorious Talbot, pardon my abuse:
I find, thou art no less than fame hath bruited,
And more than may be gather'd by thy shape
Let my presumption not provoke thy wrath;
For I am sorry, that with reverence
I did not entertain thee as thou art.
   Tal. Be not dismay'd, fair lady; nor misconstrue
The mind of Talbot, as you did mistake
The outward composition of his body.
What you have done hath not offended me:
No other satisfaction do I crave,
But only, with your patience, that we may
Taste of your wine, and see what cates you have;
For soldiers' stomachs always serve them well.
   Count. With all my heart; and think me honored
To feast so great a warrior in my house.   *[Exeunt.*

Contrast with the dramatic ineptitude of this the scene in the last act of *Richard II*, when the young Aumerle, returning home to his father, the Duke of York, is found by the latter to be really involved in a conspiracy against Bolingbroke. Here is the original of the scene in Holinshed and also Shakespeare's development of it.

"For this earle of Rutland departing before from Westminster to see his father the duke of York, as he sat at dinner, had his counterpane of the indenture of the confederacie [made at Oxford] in his bosome.

"The father, espieing it, would needs see what it was: and, though the sonne humblie denied to show it, the father, being more earnest to see it, by force broke it out of his bosome: and percieuing the contents therof, in a great rage caused his horses to be saddled out of hand, and spitefullie reprooving his sonne of treason, for whome he was become suretie and mainpernour for his good abearing in open parlement, he incontinentlie mounted on horseback to ride towards Windsore to the king to declare vnto him the malicious intent of his complices." [1] In Shakespeare's version the Duke and the Duchess have been talking of the triumphal entry of Bolingbroke into London and the contemptuous feeling of the people for Richard, when the Duchess cries: —

Duchess. Here comes my son Aumerle.
York. Aumerle that was;
But that is lost for being Richard's friend,
And, madam, you must call him Rutland now:
I am in parliament pledge for his truth
And lasting fealty to the new-made king.

Enter AUMERLE.

Duch. Welcome, my son: who are the violets now
That strew the green lap of the new-come spring?
Aumerle. Madam, I know not, nor I greatly care not:
God knows I had as lief be none as one.
York. Well, bear you well in this new spring of time,
Lest you be cropp'd before you come to prime.
What news from Oxford? hold those justs and triumphs?

[1] R. Holinshed, *Chronicles*, III. 514.

[167]

Aum. For aught I know, my lord, they do.

York. You will be there, I know.

Aum. If God prevent it not, I purpose so.

York. What seal is that that hangs without thy bosom?
Yea, look'st thou pale, sir? let me see the writing.

Aum. My lord, 'tis nothing.

York.   No matter, then, who sees it:
I will be satisfied; let me see the writing.

Aum. I do beseech your grace to pardon me:
It is a matter of small consequence,
Which for some reasons I would not have seen.

York. Which for some reasons, sir, I mean to see.
I fear, I fear, —

Duch.   What should you fear? It is
Nothing but some bond that he's enter'd into
For gay apparel 'gainst the triumph-day.

York. Bound to himself! what doth he with a bond
That he is bound to? Wife, thou art a fool. —
Boy, let me see the writing.

Aum. Beseech you, pardon me; I may not show it.

York. I will be satisfied: let me see't, I say.

                                        [*Snatches it, and reads.*

Treason! foul treason! — Villain! traitor! slave!

Duch. What's the matter, my lord?

York. Ho! who's within there? ho!

Enter *a* Servant.

                                        Saddle my horse. —
God for his mercy, what treachery is here!

Duch. Why, what is't, my lord?

York. Give me my boots, I say; saddle my horse. —
Now, by mine honor, by my life, my troth,   [*Exit Servant.*
I will appeach the villain.

Duch.   What's the matter?

York. Peace, foolish woman.

Duch. I will not peace. — What is the matter, son?

[168]

Aum. Good mother, be content; it is no more
Than my poor life must answer.
  Duch.   Thy life answer!
  York   Bring me my boots: — I will unto the king.

Re-enter Servant *with boots.*

  Duch. Strike him, Aumerle. — Poor boy, thou art amaz'd. —
[*To the Servant*] Hence, villain! never more come in my sight.
  York. Give me my boots, I say.   [*Exit Servant.*
  Duch. Why, York, what wilt thou do?
Wilt thou not hide the trespass of thine own?
Have we more sons? or are we like to have?
Is not my teeming date drunk up with time?
And wilt thou pluck my fair son from mine age,
And rob me of a happy mother's name?
Is he not like thee? is he not thine own?
  York. Thou fond mad woman,
Wilt thou conceal this dark conspiracy?
A dozen of them here have ta'en the sacrament,
And interchangeably set down their hands,
To kill the king at Oxford.
  Duch.   He shall be none;
We'll keep him here: then what is that to him?
  York. Away, fond woman! were he twenty times
My son, I would appeach him.
  Duch.   Hadst thou groan'd for him
As I have done, thou'dst be more pitiful.
But now I know thy mind; thou dost suspect
That I have been disloyal to thy bed,
And that he is a bastard, not thy son:
Sweet York, sweet husband, be not of that mind:
He is as like thee as a man may be,
Not like to me, nor any of my kin,
And yet I love him.
  York.   Make way, unruly woman!   [*Exit.*
  Duch. After, Aumerle! mount thee upon his horse;

[169]

Spur post, and get before him to the king,
And beg thy pardon ere he do accuse thee.
I'll not be long behind; though I be old,
I doubt not but to ride as fast as York,
And never will I rise up from the ground
Till Bolingbroke have pardon'd thee. Away, begone!   [*Exeunt.*

There can be no doubt of the dramatic power of
that, for it portrays character by means of dialogue.
It shows, too, the way in which training an imagination
originally sympathetic may develop almost intuitive
powers. Shakespeare metamorphoses the dry lines
of the history into human documents, quickens them
into human figures. The scene shows, also, theatrical
as contrasted with mere dramatic skill. Note the sure
feeling for the emotional possibilities of the two incidents, the discovery of the indenture and the departure,
which leads Shakespeare to "hold" them, as the technical phrase runs, by looking at them through the eyes
and feelings of each participator. It shows, too, in
the swift contrasting of the doting mother and the
outraged, sternly loyal father. It is specially evident
in the climax gained by having York so long hold back
the exact nature of what he has read in the indenture,
and in the frenzied cry of the Duchess to Aumerle as
the servant enters to receive the orders of the infuriated
Duke: "Strike him, Aumerle!" But in this scene,
as elsewhere in these chronicle plays, when Shakespeare
is at his best, he is absorbed in the emotional content
of the scene rather than in portraying some figure so

well known that his sense of fact steadily restricts him. Nearly always one finds him at his best when freest from the shackles of historical fact. This extract from *Richard II* proves, then, that by 1592 or 1593 Shakespeare had gained the power, within a scene, of getting from his material that "peculiar emotional effect which is the chief end of the theatre." That is, within the scene, even in the historical play, he was theatrically competent. The lines just quoted show also what marks even these early plays in contrast with similar work of his contemporaries, — Shakespeare's marvellous understanding of the inmost feelings, not merely of a single figure but of a group.

Yet *Richard II* shares with the three parts of *Henry VI* and *Richard III* a decidedly undesirable characteristic, in that in them action is merely represented rather than explained in the representation. Many, many things happen, but the actions are related one to another rather because historically they did happen in that order or because they happen to the same person or group of persons, than casually. Recall the wooing of Lady Anne by Richard III. Is that, even when acted, ever wholly convincing? I can never see it without recalling these words: "What distinguishes melodrama is that it stops at nothing to attain its effects." It is undoubtedly true that in the group, namely, *King John*, the revision of *Henry V* made in 1598, and the two parts of *Henry IV*, there is a persistent effort to motivate action; and that is just why

[171]

all those plays are more convincing than the earlier group. But with the exception of the two parts of *Henry IV*, Shakespeare is ever ready to let his characters explain themselves in long speeches rather than by significant and connotative action. Recall the opening soliloquy of Richard III: —

> "Now is the winter of our discontent
> Made glorious summer by this sun of York."

Recall *Richard II* resigning his crown to Bolingbroke, or the many splendid declamatory speeches of Henry V. Shakespeare begins in *Henry VI* with mere action, unrelated and discursive; moves to illustrative action, too often subordinated to speech, in *Richard II* and *Henry V;* [1] to illustrative action that is not sufficiently motivated in *Richard III;* and then through *King John* and the two parts of *Henry IV* to a point where his motivation makes his characters at the moment thoroughly human, but is not searching enough to make us understand, instead of the single scene itself, the tragedy of their lives. Action resulting from character he grasps first in *Richard III*, but action resulting from an initial event of far-reaching significance he seems to understand less well. That there are such things as laws of human conduct whose puppets human beings are, apparently in these chronicle histories he either does not even suspect or does not

[1] I group these plays together in time because I believe that *Henry V*, though revised in 1598, was originally written before 1595.

care to illustrate. The fact is, these chronicle plays before *King John* may easily be grouped as follows: strictly experimental, three parts of *Henry VI;* experimental with literary feeling dominant, *Richard II* and *Henry V;* experimental with a growing sense of theatrical effectiveness, *Richard III.* I have already spoken of the resemblance between *Love's Labour's Lost* and *Richard II,* in the fact that each sacrifices the dramatic moment to ephemeral and essentially false standards of literary expression.

Surely there is no need to dwell on the poetic richness of *Henry V.* It is true also that Henry V declaims in character when he declaims, but, nevertheless, as a play this is a pageant and a character study rather than a story in which Henry V is the central figure or a play in which Henry reveals himself by significant and deftly correlated action. Does not all this analysis make clear Shakespeare's weakness up to 1595–1596, the date of *King John?* He could characterize perfectly within the scene; he could develop from the merest historical suggestion characters which fitted perfectly into the chief historical incidents of the play, he could even subordinate his literary instinct to his dramatic, but he could not bind, or did not care to bind, all this crowding incident together except through some one central figure like Richard III or Henry V; nor did he apparently as yet discern behind the historical events the great laws and forces for which these kings, queens, and nobles were but the puppets. That is, till *King John* he is, after all, producing from historical fact only a kind of sublimated melodrama. Even *King John* and the two parts of *Henry IV* bear out what has just been said, for though both show great gain in general characterization, in technical skill, and even in the creation of figures so real that they pass unchallenged side by side with the historical, neither play is as well unified as *The Comedy of Errors* or *Titus Andronicus*.

This singular contrast in unifying power resulted, as I have said, from two causes. To Shakespeare and his contemporaries of 1590–1600, except Marlowe, the chronicle play probably seemed as distinctly a form as comedy or tragedy. As yet all the forms as forms were little understood. Comedy meant dramatic story-telling for a pleasant ending; tragedy was story-telling with a grim conclusion. The developed chronicle play meant not story-telling, but characterization by means of illustrative scenes. As a rule, the characterization was not general, but confined to the central figure or a few of the *dramatis personæ*. As has just been stated, it was in the pervasive quality of good characterization that Shakespeare began to pass beyond his fellows. The other dramatists, except Marlowe, in their historical plays were at best satisfied with such unity as they could get from a central figure passing through most of the scenes. Marlowe, especially in his *Edward II*, had begun to lay the foundations of sound dramatic technique, but his untimely death checked its develop-

THE SECOND GLOBE THEATRE

(Enlarged from the Visscher Map of 1616. For the original Globe see Frontispiece.)

THE BEAR GARDEN AND HOPE THEATRE

(Enlarged from the Visscher Map of 1616)

ment. The second cause for the contrast in Shakespeare's unifying power is his restricting sense of historical fact, which kept him from seeing that till he could stand apart from the historical material and regard it with the same freedom with which he used other sources, he could not produce from it plays of so high an order as his own from non-historical material.

When we turn to closer study of the two parts of *Henry IV*, we may see, I think, why it is that the chronicle play could not be a form by itself. Look for a moment at the proportion in that play between the Falstaff material, which, let us remember, is purely fictitious, and the genuinely historical material. In the first act only the second scene deals with Falstaff; in Act II, three out of four scenes treat him, and the fourth scene is a decidedly imaginative development of the historical material. In Act III only the third scene belongs to Falstaff, but fully two-thirds of the first scene, while dealing with historical figures, is the result of Shakespeare's imagination. In Act IV only the second scene goes to Falstaff, but two of the others are treated very imaginatively by Shakespeare, and the third is a mere transitional scene. Naturally, now that we have reached the climax of the play, historical incident must dominate, and in Act V the Falstaff story is merely a part of three of the four scenes. When, however, one notices that six out of fourteen scenes go to Falstaff and that fully half of the others are almost wholly the product of Shakespeare's imagination, one sees why it is that critics have declared that in these plays historical fiction is born. Here the imagination of the dramatist revivifies historical facts both by making human and comprehensible details of scenes known at most to his audience only in outline and by adding figures who had no real historical existence. Moreover, when one turns to the Second Part one finds that the chronicle play, forced by the applause of a public delighted beyond measure by the Falstaff scenes of the First Part, is fairly turning into the comedy of manners. This part, like the first, gives in the first act only one scene to Falstaff, but freely develops historical material in the other two scenes. In the second act, it gives three scenes out of four, the last a very long one, to Falstaff. Act III divides its two scenes between the two interests, the historical and the fictitious. Thus far the proportions have been very much what they were in the First Part, but in the remaining two acts the emphasis is very different. All four scenes of the next act are given up to the historical material. In the fifth act, instead of putting the emphasis on this, as was the case in Part I, Shakespeare gave the first, the third, and the fourth scenes to Falstaff, Shallow, and their fellows, and only the second and the last to history. Indeed, the Second Part is memorable hardly at all for the history it revivifies, but rather for its comedy of manners. The public interest actually forced the fictitious, in this sequel, to the most prominent position, — the closing part of the play. That is, by 1598 we find comedy of manners emerging from these plays based on lay history just as centuries before comedy of manners had emerged from plays based on Biblical history. In each case the result came through an emphasis given the material because of the eager interest of the public in seeing figures like unto themselves moving amusingly amidst historical scenes. Clearly, then, the chronicle play might develop into the comedy of manners, and even give way to it, as ultimately the miracle play gave way to the interlude and its presentation of social conditions of the moment.

A faint foreshadowing of another form into which the chronicle play might turn appears in Part I of *Henry IV*, namely, the play of romantic story. Next to Falstaff is it not Hotspur whom we remember from that play, and remembering him do we not recall, quite as much as his scene with his colleagues in resisting King Henry, his parting with his wife and his admirable fooling with her in the scene of the music and dancing which follows that of the portents? In other words, we follow his fortunes not so much as a historical figure, but rather as the man and the lover. If, then, the love element in these plays were allowed to come into prominence, it would rapidly transform them into romance. Always this is waiting in history just behind or beside the facts these contemporaries of Shakespeare chose to treat, ready to spring forth at the call of the mind discerning enough to see it,

N   [177]

and competent to give unity to the material if so summoned forth. The studied indifference of John Lyly to human emotion with difficulty prevents the natural feeling of some of the scenes of his *Alexander and Campaspe* from sweeping aside the eccentricities of his style. Greene, in *James the Fourth*, recognized the romantic in history when he successfully palmed off on his public as a genuine chronicle play the pure romance of Giraldi Cinthio. Thomas Heywood midway in this decade in his *Edward IV* makes a sturdy step toward releasing this form from the restrictions of historical fact and turning it into romantic story. At the end of the next century the dramatists would, in Otway and Rowe, for instance, see little else in history but its romance. Witness especially *Venice Preserved* and *Jane Shore.*

But why not a development of the chronicle play into a form by itself? We have just seen what its material becomes when manners or story in it are specially emphasized. Look now at what happens if we continue the emphasis of the contemporaries of Shakespeare, — on character. First we find scattered uncorrelated incident in *Henry VI*, for instance, then correlation of it by one central figure, as in *Richard III;* next, we see an attempt to characterize more figures than the central one and to portray the results of a ruling passion, as in *Edward II*, or of a vacillating nature, as in *Richard II*. But the dramatist felt what his audience must have felt, that somehow this last development is for acting purposes less effective than unity by means of a central figure. What could he do? He could study character till he came to see that behind the individual lie greater forces of which the individual is but the sport or servant. Then he must recognize that any of these reigns he has been considering as merely illustrative of the weakness or the strength, the courage or the vacillation of a particular king, was but the history of a conflict within the individual, between the individual and his environment, or of the futile beating by the individual against the irresistible progress of some great force at work long before he took the reins of government. If the dramatist sees these facts, tragedy will be born, for the discovery will correlate his illustrative tragic incidents.

Is it not clear, then, that by 1596, in the two parts of *Henry IV*, Shakespeare had gone as far as he could go and not have that so-called form change under his very fingers into something quite different? It might be the play of mere story or what we commonly call the romantic play; it might be comedy of manners, and even that needs some story to bind its incidents together; or it could be tragedy, and that demands story most of all. That is, for development into its fullest possibilities as dramatic material the chronicle play constantly called on the playwrights to mould from its myriad details some central story. But this is just the task which the Elizabethan playwright shirked as far as he possibly could. He much preferred re-presentation to creation of story, even in modified form. It is true that Shakespeare by 1594 showed a technical skill outside of the chronicle plays which has made us wonder why he did not do better even with those; but the work we praise, in *The Comedy of Errors* and *Titus Andronicus,* is adaptation, not drama in which he had largely to create his story from scattered incident or suggestion. Since, in the chronicle play, Shakespeare faced this distasteful exaction, and since he could not meet it successfully, even if willing to make the attempt, unless he could come to regard the historical material as just as flexible, just as freely to be tampered with as any other source, is it surprising that the years from 1595–1600 in his production are given to steadily finer and stronger adaptation for his public of existing plays and stories rather than to drawing from the historical material the story elements it certainly contained? Is it not a striking fact, too, as bearing on what I have said of his restraining sense of fact, that Shakespeare's tragedies in every case deal either with non-English material or with mythical portions of English history?

In the next chapter we shall examine a group of plays which show Shakespeare completely awake to the importance of story in play-writing and acquiring the art of moulding story from manifold details.

THREE UNRELIABLE VIEWS OF THE GLOBE THEATRE
(For comments see List of Illustrations.)

CHAPTER V

THE ART OF PLOTTING MASTERED

IN this chapter I shall consider a play of fantasy, *A Midsummer Night's Dream;* a romance that is usually called a tragedy, *Romeo and Juliet;* and a third romantic story in which the grave and the gay are adjusted with a niceness which shows the hand of a master, *The Merchant of Venice.* In all of these plays what is instantly noteworthy on the technical side is the amount of incident, and that the incident is so related that one unhesitatingly denominates it plot. But what does "plot" mean? Has not all the earlier analysis proved that it is simply design, "the means by which the artist, out of a chaos of characters, actions, passions, evolves order"?[1] He may have only the purpose to tell within the limited space of five acts a simple story, but even that story must have a beginning and an end, related incident, sequence, and climax — in a word, an orderly telling. Or it may be that the dramatist, before he writes, threads his way amid an almost infinite number of incidents, guided in his selecting by some central purpose. That central

[1] W. H. Fleming, *Shakespeare's Plots,* p. 15.

purpose may be to illustrate a many-sided character by selecting, not simply scenes which show this or that aspect of it, but the scenes which, first, represent it dramatically, and, secondly, represent it in the shortest space of time. Or the guide of a dramatist in selection and arrangement may be a central idea which each of his scenes or groups of scenes is to enforce. Or it may be that the special conditions under which the play is to be given — a Christmas merrymaking, a wedding, festivities to welcome some foreign prince — determine the selection and the adjustment of the material. It is the first purpose, storytelling, which underlies such a play as *Titus Andronicus;* the second purpose, characterization, marks *Richard III* and *Henry V;* it is the third, a central idea, which unifies *Hamlet;* and the fourth method, selection determined by special conditions of presentation, is exemplified in *A Midsummer Night's Dream.*

In any case there must in good plotting be some central purpose to act as a kind of magnet to draw to itself unerringly and swiftly the filaments of illustrative incident. That is, plot rests primarily on selection of incident, which in turn is determined by the dramatic purpose of the author. Yet when these incidents have been selected, there is as yet only a primary sort of plot — what may be denominated fable or story as contrasted with real plot. If this distinction did not hold, we should not call the chronicle histories poorly plotted. The dramatic artist who is capable of real design sees instantly that some of his incidents should fill only brief, transitional scenes; that others should be developed till they have yielded all their capacity of serious or comic results; and that between, treated with just the amount of detail the dramatist's artistic purpose in the whole play requires, should lie the bulk of the incident. It is when the incidents selected for some definite purpose, whether mere story-telling, study of character, or tragic import, have been thus proportioned and moulded till they tell a unified story with perfect clearness and with just the emphasis on each part which the artistic purpose of the author requires that we have in the strict sense of the word plot. Clearly, then, — and this is the first point I wish to stress, — plot is neither simply a matter of selection nor of sequential incident. It is as well a matter of proportion and emphasis. All these characteristics can exist in perfection only when a dramatic author knows just what he wishes to do, has all the resources of the technique of his time at his disposal, and consequently, as I have already tried to show, understands perfectly the relation of the public of that time to story-telling on the stage. Plot is, then, fable or story so proportioned and emphasized as to produce in the number of acts chosen the greatest possible amount of emotional effect. In the three plays under consideration all the named requisites of good plotting are fulfilled.

The date of *A Midsummer Night's Dream* is puzzling. Though we first find it mentioned in 1598 and it was not entered for publication till 1600, most critics agree that it belongs *circa* 1594–1595. It has often been pointed out that its nature suggests a play written for festivities attending some marriage, but it has not as yet been possible finally to determine whose marriage. If we may strictly interpret the lines of Titania in Scene 1 of Act II as to the season of floods and other disasters, we should place the play in 1593–1594, but unfortunately just such topical allusions we know must not always be taken literally, and, when they may, often belong to some revival rather than to the original production.

Any one who has experience in writing plays for special occasions knows the signs of that kind of composition. In some way its author must connect such work directly, or by suggestion, with the time and place for which it has been written. Yet if the play is to hold together, it must contain some story, and that story must unroll itself sequentially and clearly. Therefore, the writer gives it what nowadays we choose to call its local color, particularly at the beginning and at the end. That is, in the mid space he develops a story which he started in conditions giving the mask or play special fitness, and which he concludes in some way connected with the occasion. He strives also, now and again in the course of telling the story, to connect it with the special circumstances which have called forth the play, but if his fable does not permit this or his skill is not equal to the task, his audience will probably not note the omission if he has made, at the opening and at the close, an effective connection between his play and the special occasion.

Notice how completely this description fits the method used in *A Midsummer Night's Dream*. To Theseus and Hippolyta comes Egeus complaining that his daughter Hermia prefers Lysander to the man of his choice, Demetrius, and asking aid in forcing her to marry Demetrius. One wonders, on finding Shakespeare beginning a play, the purpose of which is chiefly amusement, as seriously as a tragedy, whether this play must not in date stand near *The Comedy of Errors* with its similar contrasts, and whether the Elizabethans may not have derived more satisfaction than we do from emotional contrasts so sharp as to be melodramatic. Theseus, bidding Hermia obey her father or else submit to the law of Athens for such disobedience, — death or a vow to live forever single, — goes out with all except Lysander and Hermia. Neither Theseus nor Hippolyta returns till the end of the fourth act, just as the story of the lovers reaches its solution. Entering at this point, they make a transition to the fifth act, which, as a reader will probably remember, deals no longer with the story of the lovers, but with the performance of *Pyramus and Thisbe* by Bottom and his friends, and, finally, with the blessing invoked on the marriage by the fairies. The relation of Theseus and Hippolyta to the other figures of the play, the closing of the story of the lovers in Act IV instead of

Act V, and the blessing invoked by the fairies in the last scene of all, should be enough to convince any one that the play was written for some special occasion. Here are all the earmarks of such plays.

Each group of the plot — the lovers, the rustics, the fairies — has its definite purpose in the work which the special conditions provided: the lovers make the main thread of story; Bottom and the rustics afford the low comedy which evokes steady laughter instead of the mere interest or the occasional laughter produced by the story of the lovers; and the fairies make the complicating element for each of the other two groups, bind them together, and, above all, give the graceful and fitting close which the dramatist for a special occasion must always find. Yet here are original strands of material as diverse as those which Shakespeare seemed to find it, in the chronicle plays, so difficult to weave into a perfect plot. Let us, therefore, watch for a moment Shakespeare's interweaving of the three groups and his exposition of the resulting plot. Any one must see, I think, that the interweaving is deft, concise, and always managed with a clear understanding of the relation of the public to any play given at such a festivity as a wedding. The order given Philostrate in the first few lines prepares for connection, whenever in the play it seems best to Shakespeare, of the country actors with the group surrounding Hippolyta and Theseus. This first scene sets us well ahead, too, in the story of the four lovers. We hear the agreement of Hermia and Lysander to meet and flee from Athens, as well as Helena's decision to warn Demetrius of the flight. As we have learned, also, that Helena is in love with Demetrius, who loves Hermia, the love chase is well started. Now that we are eager to know what complications will ensue in this, we are introduced to the amusing country players planning for a performance before the Duke, Theseus. The next scene, to-day called the first of the second act, shows us the quarrel between Oberon and Titania resulting in his order to Puck to place the magic juice upon her eyes as she sleeps. This is, of course, the means for amusing complication later, her sudden passion for Bottom. Yet even as Oberon gives his orders, Demetrius, pursued by Helena, enters in search of Hermia. Oberon, overhearing Helena's vain importunings of Demetrius, orders Puck, when the lovers have left the stage, to follow and anoint the eyes of the sleeping Demetrius at such a time that on waking he shall see Helena and fall madly in love with her. That is, by the end of the third scene of the play, interest has been aroused in the three groups of figures; the lovers and the fairies have been connected through Oberon; and a cause for complications in all three groups has been set working. Naturally we are eager to press on.

Note, as we proceed, Shakespeare's skill in the use of surprise that causes laughter. The very next scene has an element of surprise that must have greatly amused its audience, for after Oberon has anointed the eyes of Titania as she sleeps, there comes a wholly unexpected complication in the fact that the other two lovers, Lysander and Hermia, wander in and lie down to sleep. Conceive the delight of the auditors as it dawns on them when Puck enters, that by mistake he will anoint the eyes of Lysander, already devoted to Hermia, instead of the eyes of Demetrius. Conceive, too, their keen anticipation of some such complication as that which follows immediately, when Lysander wakens to see Helena hastening by and falls instantly in love with her. Nor, as any one must see who has visualized the action, was amusement lessened by the fact that by the end of the fourth scene the play shows a complete reversal of the original condition of two of the lovers. It is now Hermia, lovelorn and bereft, who follows Lysander, who in turn follows Helena, just as Helena had at the outset followed Demetrius who followed Hermia. Surely the first laughable working out of the complication of the magic juice leaves us eager for others which we suspect must ensue before peace can come to the four lovers. The next scene, through mischievous Puck, gives us the crowning of Bottom with an ass's head, and the sudden passion of Titania, when she wakes, for Bottom thus equipped. The scene following this one is the height of the complications in the story of the lovers, for Oberon, discovering the mistake of Puck, tries to set it right by having Puck anoint the eyes of Demetrius and bring Helena before him as he wakes. Conceive, again, the delight of the audience as it hears Oberon planning for this. They know, what neither Oberon nor Puck knows, of Lysander's sudden change to infatuation for Helena, and see that if she is brought before Demetrius as he wakes, there will only be confusion worse confounded. Then there will be two lovers for Helena and none for Hermia, where originally there had been none for her and two for Hermia. All this planning of Oberon must have been played to a ripple of laughter that became a roar when expectation was fulfilled by the waking Demetrius. Swiftly follows the quarrelling of the lovers, whose original relations are now completely reversed, and the tricking of the men by Puck as he leads them on by false calls and cries. At last, wearied out, the men lie down to sleep near together, though unwitting because of the fog. To them enter singly the two women, also wearied and lost in the fog. They in turn lie down to sleep. When Puck has squeezed the juice on Lysander's eyes the scene closes, and unless a new complication, a new surprise develops, the end of the troubles of the lovers is in sight, since Demetrius now cares for Helena, and Lysander, when he wakes, will once more love Hermia.

Shakespeare saw that to make space for the special application of his material in the fifth act, he must now swiftly bring the story part to a close. The strong feeling of Theseus in the first act that the laws of Athens must hold, cannot withstand the discovery that Demetrius now cares for Helena, and above all, his desire not to miss the hunt, so the fourth act is a swift presentation of the awakening of Titania from her illusion and the readjustment of the lovers, who wake at the right moment to find Theseus, Hippolyta, and Egeus beside them. Helena takes Demetrius, Hermia Lysander, and all is ready for the brief scene in which the restored Bottom arranges with his comrades for the performance which is to take place in the fifth act. The contents of that last act I have already noted. From this rapid summary it must be clear, I think, how much plotting there is in all this arrangement and adjustment of the three groups who make the incidents of the play, — the lovers, the rustics, and the fairies, — and even in the relating of the fourth group, Theseus and Hippolyta, to the other three. The skilful use of surprise also has been specially noteworthy. If we recall Shakespeare's inability in *The Two Gentlemen of Verona* to bring to a climax the suspense he created, we shall see how greatly he has gained by the time of writing *A Midsummer Night's Dream*. But successful dramatic surprise always implies an understanding of the audience for which it was planned. Clearly, then, Shakespeare in this play knows his audience better. Here is, too, just the masterly sense of dramatic values in originally separate groups of figures which was absent in the handling of the historical plays. But here imagination works unre-

AN EARLY TYPE OF STAGE

stricted by any sense of fact, and characterization is, because of the nature of the occasion, not of first importance, as in the chronicle plays, but subordinate to incident, to story.

Yet it is in the subordinated characterization that the deftness of Shakespeare's emphasis becomes apparent. Surely I need say nothing in praise of Bottom and his fellow-actors. Why they are so much better than our friends of *Love's Labour's Lost*, Costard, Jaquenetta, Don Armado, and Holofernes, is evident: they are real, and not caricatures as are Don Armado and Holofernes; they are amusing not only for what they say, but for what they do. Moreover, both what they say and what they do in every case adds to the clearness of their characterization. Of course, one does not expect the fairies to have much characterization. If Oberon is mildly jealous, Titania gently obstinate, and Puck always tricksy, that is enough for the story, and we should demand nothing more. But why is it that the middle group of the four lovers is so slightly characterized? Certainly, it is perfectly fair to say that they exist merely for the situations. Nor can one take refuge in the theory that Shakespeare was here not able to characterize them adequately; that is absurd in the face of characterization of far more difficult figures, in *The Comedy of Errors* and in the chronicle plays written by 1595. Besides, when Helena follows Demetrius in those early scenes, it is essentially only *Venus and Adonis* over again, and we know how comprehendingly Shakespeare could handle that situation by 1593. Why is this woman who cares for Demetrius so intensely that she scorns common report and pursues him from the city, little more than a puppet? I believe that the slightness of the characterization in this group, the emphasis on situation and on mannered dialogue rather than on the play of emotion which made these situations possible, arose from Shakespeare's perfect understanding of the task set him by his special occasion.

It was his business to provide for this wedding, or other festival, an amusing story ranging from light comedy of intrigue and situation to farce, and to give it all some special fitness for the occasion. To treat that group of lovers as the emotions they were experiencing would permit, to develop their characters as any adequate portrayal of their emotions would mean, would be to move his audience in sympathy with those characters, to make the audience serious when it wished to smile, to excite it when the spirit of the hour demanded laughter. Moreover, if these lovers had been painted with, we will not say the intensity of imagination that went into *Venus and Adonis*, but even with the adequacy that marks the figure of Adriana, the wife, in *The Comedy of Errors*, these people would have held us not by the situation, but by their own humanness, their reality. But was it wise to subject a group of realistically drawn figures to so improbable an experience as the magic juice? Has not dramatic practice shown that when mortals and fairies meet, it is best, if the proper illusion is to be produced, that the mortals shall be types, creatures of situation, rather than convincing studies of character? Is there not evident, then, a nice sense of values in these facts: of the rustics, the very real figures, only Bottom meets the fairies; and even he only when bewitched, and that to the group of lovers, standing between the very real group and the unreal, the fairies, belongs only the reality of the situations in which they appear? That is, the lovers make a bridge from the real to the unreal. Note, too, the care of the dramatist to make his fairies as real as possible, so that their intercourse with human beings may not seem too improbable. It is not simply that Oberon and Titania, in their jealousy and pique, show the failings of mortals, but that the references of Titania to conditions of flood and storm (Act II, Sc. 1), which the audience could remember, helped to mesmerize them into accepting the improbable as probable.

In *Love's Labour's Lost* and *The Two Gentlemen of Verona* Shakespeare stood, as it were, amidst his material, accumbered by it, sure neither of its dramatic values nor of the methods by which to give his material full dramatic effect. In *A Midsummer Night's Dream* one can see that Shakespeare has gained the power of looking at his material from outside; of selecting and arranging from it, not merely according to some controlling idea of his own, but in the light of his pre-

o   [193]

ceding experiences with audiences. He emerges triumphantly from the problems raised by the limitations of the special conditions under which the play was to be given and by the ordinary attitude of his audience toward his improbable plot. Once again, too, we have in this play proof that while he is as much of a poet as ever, his poetry serves, no longer dominates, his dramatic purpose. What is particularly noteworthy is that in this play he is no longer adapting, as in *The Comedy of Errors, Titus Andronicus*, and even *The Two Gentlemen of Verona*, but, as we suspect is the case in *Love's Labour's Lost*, is creating the fable which makes the core of his plot. But the difference in complication of narrative and in technical mastery between that last play and *A Midsummer Night's Dream!* If Shakespeare by 1595 could provide as ingenious and well-wrought plots as this, why his weakness in extracting equally good plots from the material of the chronicles, unless he felt that the purpose of the historical play was different? But thus far in the best accomplishment of Shakespeare outside of the chronicle play it is situation rather than characterization which has been of prime importance. Let us see how his growing technique stood the greater test put upon it when his plan called for characterization of subtler or more unusual figures.

Let us look now at a play which deals in human fact as much as *A Midsummer Night's Dream* deals in fancy, namely, *Romeo and Juliet*. The first quarto of it, in 1597, is probably from a stage copy condensed for acting purposes, and none too well printed. It is clear that the second quarto in 1599, though it has been revised in a few places for whole speeches, and has been touched up verbally throughout, represents, except in these respects, the play from which the first quarto was cut down. If the words of the nurse in Act I, Sc. 3,

" 'Tis since the earthquake now eleven years,"

may be trusted, a version of the play, probably the first, belonged to 1591. It is probably fair to say that it was first written by Shakespeare in 1591, but in its form of the 1599 quarto was revised about 1594 or 1595. It would be interesting, if space permitted, to trace the popularity of the story of *Romeo and Juliet* and its analogues upon the Continent, but it must suffice here to say that it was specially known in England through a poem of Arthur Broke, or Brooke, first printed in 1562, and Paynter's collections of stories, *The Palace of Pleasure*, first printed in 1566–1577. The verse and prose accounts show only slight differences. Broke in his dedication to the reader states that he "saw the same argument lately set forth upon the stage with more commendation than I can look for: (being there much better set forth than I have or can be) yet the same matter penned as it is, may serve to right good effect if the readers do bring with them like good minds to consider it." Indeed, knowing the dramatic economy of these Elizabethan dramatists, one is inclined to suspect that the resemblances between Broke and Shakespeare are largely resemblances due to a common origin and that both owed much to this lost play so complimented by Broke. If, however, Broke is Shakespeare's original, it provides him with all his characters, though by no means with all the details of these characters which we find deftly filled in by Shakespeare.

Surely it is hardly necessary, after all the plot analyses already given, to ask a reader to watch in detail Shakespeare's exposition in this play. I am sure all must have felt the swiftness of its movement, the crowding of exciting incident on exciting incident, and have recognized how deftly Shakespeare gets his comedy relief from figures very essential to the story, in particular Mercutio and the nurse. It is noteworthy, too, I think, that this play shows better than any we have thus far considered Shakespeare's skill in making a scene which aids the tragic movement of the story call up a lighter mood as it opens, or touch that lighter mood in skilful contrast even as the scene progresses.[1] That, however, in *Romeo and Juliet,* to which I wish to call attention especially, is its motivation.

In the first place, that opening scene of the quarrel in the streets is dramatically a model. In the original, if Broke be this, we merely hear that, because of repeated street brawls, the Prince had uttered por-

[1] See Act III, Sc. 1; Act IV. Sc. 5; Act III. Sc. 3.

tentous threats as to what he should do if more trouble came. In Broke we see him act only after the killing of Tybalt. The opening scene with Shakespeare, beginning amusingly, expounds immediately by action in the quarrel of the followers of the two houses; rushes to a climax of excitement in the entrance of the Prince; and gives us in his wrathful forbidding of all further outbreaks on pain of death the first complicating element in a play as yet hardly begun. What better motivation, too, than a mother's anxiety, could there be for the ensuing talk in regard to Romeo? Yet it masks information that must be ours before we can enter into the play understandingly. Notice, also, that Tybalt, who in the story appears first in the later street fight resulting in his death, is so characterized by this scene as to make all his later attitude toward Romeo consistent and natural. That Romeo and his friend should go to the house of Capulet is, considering the bitter feud between the two families, not at all well motived in the poem. In the play the chance meeting of Romeo and Benvolio with the stupid servant of Capulet who cannot read the directions which have been given him, aptly puts the idea into their heads. Moreover, Benvolio completely justifies the madcap adventure for us, as for Romeo, by pointing out that the fair Rosalind will be a guest at this feast. It is noteworthy, too, that while Juliet is sixteen in Broke and eighteen in Paynter, she is but fourteen in the play.

That change is, I believe, but one of several devices on the part of Shakespeare to overcome what must have seemed to him the chief problem the story presented. We are to watch the tragedy of a love at first sight, so intense and overmastering that it sweeps everything before it. Probably that was not very much more convincing in the days of Elizabeth than it is to-day, and its unusualness was increased by the fact that the five-act limit compelled Shakespeare to bring about his scenes much more rapidly than was the case in the poem. For instance, in the poem some weeks elapse between the scene of Romeo and Juliet at the Capulets, and their next meeting, so that their love was fostered inasmuch as they increasingly desired to meet yet could not. With Shakespeare, Juliet, when first we see her, is a mere child, whose mother and nurse are talking to her of marriage. Seeking to prepare her to love the County Paris, they succeed only in preparing her to fall in love with the man of her own choice. That motivation was carefully considered in this play is shown by this fact: in the condensed stage version, which the first quarto represents, the scene in which Benvolio and Romeo talk of the latter's love for Rosalind is cut only just at the end. Evidently artificial though that scene seems to-day, it was too important in the motivation of the later scenes to be sacrificed when the play was cut. Surely it was not kept for its verbal play, when scenes of crowding incident lay just ahead, but rather because its content is essential to an understanding of the story. And what does it signify? Just contrast its playing with sentiment, its delight in its own emotions, with the simplifying effect in phrase of real passion in the first balcony scene, and, above all, in the final parting the morning after the marriage. Those three scenes form the best text-book I know on the way in which phrase may connote as well as denote a state of mind. That first scene in which the two men talk of Rosalind shows a youth luxuriating in his own sense of dawning manhood, in love with being in love. Emotionally he is just where, in the rebound from the rebuffs of Rosalind, for whom he has never really deeply cared, he is likely to fall intensely and genuinely in love with the right person the moment she appears. Even in that balcony scene there are in its richness of imagery traces of a self-consciousness which fades as the emotion deepens. All consciousness of phrase for its own sake, however, is burned away in the absorbed intensity of that passionate parting at daybreak.

It is interesting, too, that, even before we meet Juliet, we learn that the County Paris is a suitor for her hand. How much more portentous becomes this sudden love between the daughter of the Capulets and the son of the Montagues than it was in the poem, where, when they meet, we have heard no edict of death in case of further fighting between the two houses; have not seen how ready Tybalt is to draw his sword against a Montague; and know of no rival suitor favored heartily by the father. The meeting in the play, especially after Tybalt has only with difficulty been restrained from attacking Romeo for his insolence in coming as a guest, means that this love affair must sooner or later bring drawn swords and that drawn swords must result in death for some and banishment for others. Such careful inworking early of figures who came late in the original story is just what makes possible the tragic significance for us of the first meeting which, to these two young lovers, is a moment of unqualified happiness. Shakespeare has had no tragic contrast like that before. Such a contrast, also, is possible not for him who merely has the dramatic instinct to see it, but only for him who has, too, the technical equipment which sends him straight to the details and characters which must be worked in early if this contrast, largely missed in the original, is to come out in the play.

Moreover, one of the most perfect pieces of artistry in the play is the way in which Mercutio, who does so much to lighten the necessary exposition of the early scenes, is made the cause of one of the most tragic moments, the banishment of Romeo. It is true that in Broke Romeo enters the fray only to quiet it and strike up the weapons, but there he is led into killing Tybalt, because of the latter's furious assault upon him as he tries to make peace. In the play Shakespeare does everything he can to heighten the tragic effect and the irony of the situation by relieving Romeo as far as possible of responsibility for his fight with

A TYPICAL ELIZABETHAN INN-YARD
(The Four Swans)

A PLAY AT ONE END OF AN INN-YARD

Tybalt. When Tybalt tries to draw him into a fight,
Romeo puts Tybalt aside, to the great wrath of Mercutio, who picks up the quarrel. It is only after news
is brought Romeo of Mercutio's death that, in grief
and anger, he loses his control and consents to fight.
Of course, the main purpose of all this is to keep us
wholly sympathetic with the lovers, but surely in some
part this is done to heighten the irony of the banishment.

The sureness of Shakespeare's dramatic instinct
in this play shows nowhere more clearly than in
making this fight occur not some weeks after the
marriage, as in the poem, but between the time of the
marriage morning and its evening. Even as happiness seems secured for the lovers, the family feud tears
them apart. Just conceive, on the Elizabethan stage,
the splendid irony and pathos of the contrast, when
that soliloquy of Juliet dreaming of her husband's
coming followed instantly the scene which closed with
his banishment to Mantua. The audience must have
been fairly aquiver with sympathy when the nurse
entered with her evil news, — an effect, as I have pointed
out, often lost for us because of our long stage waits.
Again, as illustrating the care with which all the little
details were so handled in this play as to make the
later situations convincing, notice Sc. 3 of Act II.
Here, when we first meet the friar, he is busied with his
herbs and simples, so that when the time comes for
the potion for Juliet, it will be perfectly natural to

us that he should provide it. Motivation, then, not merely within the scene but so as perfectly to relate part with part within a play, and so as cunningly to expound character, Shakespeare understands in *Romeo and Juliet.*

What marks this play, too, besides minute care in motivation is perfection of dramatic phrase. I say "dramatic phrase" because that may be quite distinct from poetic phrase. Power of poetic phrase we saw that Shakespeare possessed even in his earliest work. In it he has simply matured as the years have passed. Dramatic phrase means that whether the dialogue be narrating, describing, expounding character, or seemingly indulging in beauty for beauty's own sake, its phrase shall, first of all, be in character. It is not enough that it shall merely tell what we need to know, or be beautiful in itself, whether the statement fit the character or not; nor is it the highest form of dramatic phrase unless it shall be not merely what the character might have said, but what we feel the character must have said under the circumstances. That is, perfect dramatic phrase has the quality of definitiveness. Moreover, perfect dialogue creates a sympathetic mood in the hearer. Here, then, are the characteristics of perfect dialogue: it must definitively characterize; it may create a sympathetic mood in the hearer; and it may have a rich poetic beauty of its own. It is at its highest when it combines all these three qualities. What it rests on is a complete sympathetic under-

[202]

standing of the characters and an equally complete
visualization of the scene: the dramatist must feel
what his character is feeling and see exactly what, as
a consequence, he is doing.

The death of Mercutio — it takes but a few lines —
proves how completely by 1595 Shakespeare understood perfect dramatic dialogue. It is impossible to
read it without visualizing it, for the phrases grow out of
the movements of the figures, and even out of the physical pain which makes Mercutio writhe as he speaks, —

Romeo. Hold, Tybalt! good Mercutio!
[*Tybalt under Romeo's arm stabs Mercutio, and flies with his
    followers.*
Mercutio.   I am hurt.
A plague o' both your houses! I am sped.
Is he gone, and hath nothing?
Benvolio.   What, art thou hurt?
Mer. Ay, ay, a scratch, a scratch; marry, 'tis enough.
Where is my page? Go, villain, fetch a surgeon.   [*Exit Page.*
Rom. Courage, man; the hurt cannot be much.
Mer. No, 'tis not so deep as a well, nor so wide as a church-door;
but 'tis enough, 'twill serve: ask for me to-morrow, and you shall
find me a grave man. I am peppered, I warrant, for this world.
A plague o' both your houses! 'Zounds, a dog, a rat, a mouse, a
cat, to scratch a man to death! a braggart, a rogue, a villain, that
fights by the book of arithmetic! Why the devil came you between
us? I was hurt under your arm.
Rom. I thought all for the best.
Mer. Help me into some house, Benvolio,
Or I shall faint. A plague o' both your houses!
They have made worms' meat of me: I have it,
And soundly too: your houses!
                        [*Exeunt Mercutio and Benvolio.*
                            — Act III, Sc. 1.

How perfect in characterization, how impossible without complete visualization that last broken phrase: "Your houses!" That is character in action, definitively presented.

Notice, too, in the first balcony scene, the growth from somewhat conscious phrase in the opening lyricism, through a simpler phrasing as the thought deepens with the deepening feeling, to such absorption in feeling that the phrase is perfectly simple, and finally to such intensity of feeling as can find expression only in little commonplaces or in action rather than words. I think these four extracts taken in succession from this scene show what I mean.

I. Conscious phrasing:—

Romeo. The brightness of her cheek would shame those stars,
As daylight doth a lamp; her eyes in heaven
Would through the airy region stream so bright
That birds would sing and think it were not night.
See, how she leans her cheek upon her hand!
O, that I were a glove upon that hand,
That I might touch that cheek!

II, III. Deepening feeling that leads to simpler and simpler phrase:—

Romeo. Lady, by yonder blessed moon I swear
That tips with silver all these fruit-tree tops —
Juliet. O, swear not by the moon, the inconstant moon,
That monthly changes in her circled orb,
Lest that thy love prove likewise variable.
Rom. What shall I swear by?
Jul.   Do not swear at all;
Or, if thou wilt, swear by thy gracious self,

Which is the god of my idolatry,
And I'll believe thee.

 Rom.   If my heart's dear love —
 Jul. Well, do not swear: although I joy in thee,
I have no joy of this contract to-night:
It is too rash, too unadvised, too sudden;
Too like the lightning, which doth cease to be
Ere one can say "It lightens." Sweet, good night!
This bud of love, by summer's ripening breath,
May prove a beauteous flower when next we meet.
Good night, good night! as sweet repose and rest
Come to thy heart as that within my breast!

 Rom. O, wilt thou leave me so unsatisfied?

 Jul. What satisfaction canst thou have to-night?

 Rom. The exchange of thy love's faithful vow for mine.

 Jul. I gave thee mine before thou didst request it:
And yet I would it were to give again.

 Rom. Wouldst thou withdraw it? for what purpose, love?

 Jul. But to be frank, and give it thee again,
And yet I wish but for the thing I have:
My bounty is as boundless as the sea.
My love as deep; the more I give to thee,
The more I have, for both are infinite.   [*Nurse calls within.*
I hear some noise within; dear love, adieu!
Anon, good nurse! Sweet Montague, be true.
Stay but a little, I will come again.   [*Exit, above.*

 Rom. O blessed, blessed night! I am afeard,
Being in night all this is but a dream,
Too flattering-sweet to be substantial.

       Re-enter JULIET, *above.*

 Jul. Three words, dear Romeo, and good night indeed.
If that thy bent of love be honorable,
Thy purpose marriage, send me word to-morrow,
By one that I'll procure to come to thee,
Where and what time thou wilt perform the rite;
And all my fortunes at thy foot I'll lay
And follow thee my lord throughout the world.

Nurse. [*Within*] Madam!

Jul. I come, anon. — But if thou mean'st not well
I do beseech thee —

Nurse. [*Within*] Madam!

Jul.   By and by, I come: —
To cease thy suit, and leave me to my grief:
To-morrow will I send.

   Rom.   So thrive my soul —

   Jul. A thousand times good night!   [*Exit above.*

IV. Feeling so intense that it finds expression only in
the commonplace or in action rather than words: —

   Romeo. It is my soul that calls upon my name:
How silver-sweet sound lovers' tongues by night,
Like softest music to attending ears!

   Juliet. Romeo!

   Rom.   My dear?

   Jul.   At what o'clock to-morrow
Shall I send to thee?

   Rom.   At the hour of nine.

   Jul. I will not fail: 'tis twenty years till then.
I have forgot why I did call thee back.

   Rom. Let me stand here till thou remember it.

   Jul. I shall forget, to have thee still stand there,
Remembering how I love thy company.

   Rom. And I'll still stay, to have thee still forget,
Forgetting any other home but this.

                    —Act II, Sc. 2.

I should not be willing to say that that change in
vocabulary and method is the result of conscious plan;
rather I think it simply a proof that in *Romeo and
Juliet* Shakespeare, so far as insight into character
and phrase are concerned, had attained mastery in his
craft. For what does mastery in those respects mean

except this: that quick and well-trained sympathy have made it possible for the dramatist to lose himself in his characters; and that an instantly responsive vocabulary phrases with exactness just the feeling those sympathies have set astir in the dramatist? So perfectly responsive, too, is such a vocabulary that when the mood is less vital, because more conscious, the phrase shows this, and, as the feeling deepens, marks the change like some delicately adjusted instrument. Yet to say all this is to repeat the commonplace, that style, at its best, is only the perfect mirror of one's thought and feeling.

In the preceding chapters I complained that Shake-speare did not at first know how to hold a situation so as to get from it its full dramatic possibilities. Contrast that scene, in Part I of *Henry VI,* in which the French Countess tries to make a prisoner of Talbot with the balcony scene I have just been considering. As I have already said, a modern dramatist, for instance, Sardou, would have spun out the scene till every permutation of emotion in a battle of wits between these two figures had been worked up to a fine emotional climax. In Shakespeare there is little more than a mutual defiance before the soldiers enter and release Talbot. How inadequate that all seems when compared with these pages of *Romeo and Juliet,* in which nothing except the increasing intensity of youthful passion holds us enthralled as the scene passes from conscious phrasing to feeling so deep that

[207]

it can find expression only in action rather than words.

How completely, too, in this play, Shakespeare understands that subtlest of tasks for the dramatist, — the creation of atmosphere. I have already remarked how perfectly that opening scene of the quarrel in the streets creates the atmosphere of unrest, uncertainty, and imminent danger which the play needs as a background if the love of Romeo and Juliet is to have its full dramatic significance. Shakespeare depends much for his dramatic contrasts upon his sure creation of atmosphere. How carefully, too, he makes us feel the gayety of the preparations for the marriage of Juliet to the County Paris, knowing that we spectators are still torn with pity because we have just left Juliet lying in her chamber in a stupor. That is, whether he wishes atmosphere for a moment, for a scene, or as a background, he gains it, and with sure hand.

Yet, though Shakespeare in *Romeo and Juliet* so tells his story that he gives the play three permanent essentials of great drama, — atmosphere, perfect dramatic phrasing, and convincing characterization, — he was, of course, writing only for his immediate audience. Keenly sensitive to its likings and moods, he moulded his exposition to accord with these. This, the end of the play, for instance, proves. It shows that his audience was, above all, interested in a story play. It is perhaps true that *Romeo and Juliet* is still for us largely a story play, but to-day we do not care for that

long recapitulation at the end by the Friar of what has
already been shown us in action.[1] We close the play

[1] *Friar.* I will be brief, for my short date of breath
Is not so long as is a tedious tale.
Romeo, there dead, was husband to that Juliet;
And she, there dead, that Romeo's faithful wife:
I married them; and their stolen marriage-day
Was Tybalt's dooms-day, whose untimely death
Banish'd the new-made bridegroom from this city;
For whom, and not for Tybalt, Juliet pin'd.
You, to remove that siege of grief from her,
Betroth'd, and would have married her perforce
To County Paris: then, comes she to me,
And, with wild looks, bid me devise some means
To rid her from this second marriage,
Or in my cell there would she kill herself.
Then gave I her (so tutor'd by my art)
A sleeping potion; which so took effect
As I intended, for it wrought on her
The form of death: meantime, I writ to Romeo,
That he should hither come, as this dire night,
To help to take her from her borrow'd grave,
Being the time the potion's force should cease.
But he which bore my letter, Friar John,
Was stay'd by accident, and yesternight
Return'd my letter back.   Then, all alone,
At the prefixed hour of her waking,
Came I to take her from her kindred's vault,
Meaning to keep her closely at my cell,
Till I conveniently could send to Romeo:
But, when I came (some minute ere the time
Of her awakening), here untimely lay
The noble Paris, and true Romeo, dead.
She wakes; and I entreated her come forth,
And bear this work of heaven with patience:
But then a noise did scare me from the tomb,
And she, too desperate, would not go with me,
But (as it seems) did violence on herself.
All this I know, and to the marriage

P   [209]

either with the death of the lovers or with the coming of the Watch and the Prince. But any one knows that untrained listeners, such as children, deeply enjoy such a recapitulation. It looks as if in 1595 the Elizabethan audience liked to be reminded, as a play closed, of what had happened to all involved in the final tragic situation. To-day the intensity of our sympathy with Romeo and Juliet leaves us with no thought for any one else.

In this play, then, Shakespeare, though working for immediate results, has developed such insight into character, has so matured in power of phrase, and has so mastered the technique of the drama that the ephemeral causes for interest and popularity are as nothing in comparison with the permanent. What a contrast in this respect between *A Midsummer Night's Dream* and *Romeo and Juliet,* on the one hand, and, on the other, the preceding plays considered!

The Merchant of Venice, like *Romeo and Juliet,* is primarily a play of story rather than of characterization, undeniably fine as the characterization in both plays is. If any one has doubts as to this, let him consider carefully the relation of the last act to the other acts. The figure of Shylock, which has become for us central in the play because of the emphasis placed upon it by modern actors, is allowed to disappear at the end of Act IV.

> Her nurse is privy; and, if aught in this
> Miscarried by my fault, let my old life
> Be sacrific'd some hour before his time
> Unto the rigor of severest law.

teftum

porticus

sedilia

orchestra

ingressus

mimorum aedes

proscenium

planities fiue arena.

Ex obseruationibus Londinensibus
Johannis De witt

THE DE WITT DRAWING OF THE SWAN THEATRE IN 1596

The many queries sure to arise in the mind of any one who has been deeply interested in him are left wholly unanswered. That is not the method used by a dramatist when the characterization of a special figure is meant by him to be the prime interest of his audience. Indeed, when one notes that Shylock appears in but five scenes of the entire play, and that only two of these are long, it must be clear, even though his characterization be definitive, that the far greater emphasis on the love story of Bassanio and Portia shows what Shakespeare expected to win and hold the attention of the public. In that last act the figure of the merchant himself, Antonio, practically disappears; the emphasis is so placed by means of the complication of the rings that the love story compels attention to the very end of the play. It may be surmised that Shakespeare derived most personal satisfaction in creating Shylock, but that does not affect the fact that, with nice feeling for the everyday interests of his audience, he made his play primarily one of story rather than of characterization.

Moreover, in handling this story Shakespeare shows that he has now acquired in perfection the art of so interweaving in his narrative many different strands of interest that if the sources were not known, no one would suspect him of bringing together incidents and episodes not originally connected. In what was probably the original of the play, an Italian collection of tales, *Il Pecorone* of Ser Giovanni Fiorentino, there is no original for the Lorenzo-Jessica story. In the play the casket scene replaces source material distinctly salacious. Either some playwright whose play Shakespeare revised — for there is suspicion of a play on the same subject preceding Shakespeare's [1] — made both the addition to the story and this change in it or Shakespeare did. How much the addition of that Lorenzo-Jessica story accomplishes! As Professor Moulton has pointed out,[2] it bridges over the time which must elapse between the signing of the bond and its forfeiture; it fills time so that Antonio's losses do not seem improbably immediate; it brings out in contrast the tenderer side of Shylock; and it allows much poetry to come into the play. Considering the incompetence of the predecessors of Shakespeare, except Greene and Marlowe, in this matter of motivation and adjustment, it is probable that this competent use of the Jessica-Lorenzo story is wholly Shakespeare's. Nothing, too, is more characteristically Shakespearean than the way in which the poetic episode of the caskets replaces coarse material in the original. This same sublimation of the coarse to the richly poetic is what we shall find constantly recurring as we compare Shakespeare's sources and his finished products. As I have said before,

---

[1] Gosson, in his *School of Abuse* (1579), speaks of a current play, *The Jew*, "representing the greediness of worldly chusers and bloody minds of usurers"; and in the same year Spenser, in a letter to Gabriel Harvey, makes references which show that both knew a play containing the bond and probably the casket incidents.

[2] *Shakespeare as a Dramatic Artist*, R. G. Moulton, Ch. III.

it could not have been the public that forced this; it was Shakespeare's own instinctive sense of the dignity of his art and his enjoyment of poetry for its own sake. Finally, let me quote Professor Moulton's statement in his *Shakespeare as a Dramatic Artist* as to the plotting in this comedy, perhaps the most complex of any Shakespearean play, certainly the most so of any play we have thus far considered. Professor Moulton has pointed out that there are four divisions in the plot: the bond, the love of Bassanio and Portia, the love of Jessica and Lorenzo, and the episodes concerning the ring exacted by Portia from Bassanio at the close of the trial scene. "It is to be observed," says Professor Moulton, "that all four stories meet in the scene of the successful choice. This scene is the climax of the casket story. It is connected with the catastrophe in the story of the Jew: Bassanio, at the moment of his happiness, learns that the friend through whom he has been able to contend for the prize has forfeited his life to his foe, as the price of his liberality. This scene is connected with the Jessica story: for Jessica and her husband are the messengers who bring the sad tidings, and thus link together the bright and the gloomy elements of the play. Finally, the episode of the ring, which is to occupy the end of the drama, has its foundation in this scene, in the exchange of the rings, which are destined to be the cause of such ironical perplexity. Such is the symmetry with which the plot of *The Merchant of Venice* has been constructed: the incident which is technically its dramatic centre is at once its mechanical centre, its poetic centre, and philosophically considered, its true turning-point; while considering the play as a romantic drama, with its union of stories, we find in the same central incident all the four stories dovetailed together."

Such firm, deft plotting as this rests upon a perfect understanding by the dramatist of two things: his own artistic purpose and the relation of his public to his original material and the development he desires to give that material. For instance, Shakespeare added to his story because he knew his public liked a crowded plot and because the plot in its simplest form contained glaring improbabilities which demanded beguiling motivation. He gave his last act to a climactic presentation of the complication of the rings because he felt that his audience would find their keenest pleasure in the love story as such. But he dared to lift his audience far beyond its usual level by his constant, incisive touches of characterization, his substitution of the casket scene with its rich poetry for the coarse details of his source, his thoughtful comment on life, and by such splendid passages of poetry as "The quality of Mercy is not strained." Is there not here a perfect illustration of the right relation of the dramatist to his public? Considering his audience, regarding it, Shakespeare moulded his material so that while it delighted them as much or more than the work of his contemporaries, he yet accomplished in characterization what most interested him, and by poetry, philosophic comment, and ideality lifted his audience to an unwonted level of artistic appreciation.

This ability to hold at the same time two points of view — an absolute necessity for any great dramatist — is what this play constantly illustrates. It is shown in what I have already commented on; namely, Shakespeare's notable skill, for instance in the trial scene, in handling the same material so that it is tragic as seen and felt by Shylock, and richly comic as seen and felt by Gratiano and the other friends of Antonio. Moreover, in Shylock we have the first instance in the Elizabethan drama of a sympathetic presentation of an unpopular figure. It is true that in *The Jew of Malta* by Marlowe, the experiment seems to have been made in Act I and part of Act II; but thereafter Barabas becomes a figure which must have given delight to the Jew-baiters of the time. What made these Jew-baiters particularly numerous and fierce in 1594–1596 was the recent execution of Dr. Lopez, a Portuguese Jew, for alleged conspiracy against the life of Queen Elizabeth. 1595–1596 was an odd time for the presenting of a kindly portrait of an harassed and wily Jew, yet here it is. I am no believer in the theory that Shakespeare meant Shylock to be a comic figure. On that hypothesis, why the many appealing little touches such as the cry of Shylock when Tubal tells him Jessica has given his turquoise ring for a monkey, "I had it of Leah when I was a bachelor, I would not have given it for a wilderness of monkeys"? Perhaps Shakespeare's predecessors in their various Jew plays had made the usurer comic; his degraders certainly did in the seventeenth century; but no man with so just a sense of dramatic values as Shakespeare shows, in the trial scene, in his presentation of Shylock's disappointment, now tragically through Shylock's eyes, now through Gratiano's as amusing, could have written the lines of Shylock in this and other scenes merely to touch the risibilities of the Jew-haters in his audience. Neither in Shakespeare's day nor now does the fact that an audience can laugh at certain lines or scenes prove anything whatever as to the original purpose of the dramatist to make them laugh by these lines and scenes. If Shakespeare had wished to create laughter by Shylock, why did he keep him out of the fifth act, thus losing the many opportunities which his forlorn, defeated condition would have given to delight the Jew-baiters?

What clear insight into the effect of his material on his audience and, as a consequence, what a sure sense of climax the dramatist shows in the trial scene! In every way the audience is led at the outset to feel the hopelessness of Antonio's position, and very deftly the offer of double the original loan, which is refused, is made to serve both as a detail to emphasize Shylock's complete mastery of the situation and as a means of humiliation for Shylock at the end of the scene. When all seems ready for the catastrophe, the audience is kept in suspense by the arrival of Portia and Nerissa, but pleasurable suspense because of the handling of that incident. The strong, poetic appeal is made by Portia in the speech on mercy; once again, the audience thrills as it hears from Portia herself that the bond places Antonio absolutely in Shylock's power. Suddenly the solution is hinted in those simple words of Portia: —

> "Have by some surgeon, Shylock, on your charge,
> To stop his wounds, lest he do bleed to death."

But not yet does Shakespeare let his audience see the solution. He throws out the hint and passes swiftly to the farewell speeches of Antonio and Bassanio in which one is made to feel that Shylock will have his pound of flesh. Then, when three times the audience has been taken up to the critical moment, there comes with a shock of surprise probably as keen for the Elizabethan audience as for Shylock himself, the words of Portia: —

> "Tarry a little: there is something else.
> This bond doth give thee here no jot of blood;
> The words expressly are, a pound of flesh:
> Take then thy bond, take thou thy pound of flesh;
> But, in the cutting it, if thou dost shed
> One drop of Christian blood, thy lands and goods
> Are by the laws of Venice confiscate
> Unto the state of Venice."

But not even with this does Shakespeare allow the scene to end. Step by step, in perfect contrast with the way in which the net was drawn tighter and tighter about Antonio in the earlier part of the scene, it is now drawn about Shylock, to his increasing surprise, mortification, and hopelessness. He is not allowed to take the money Bassanio would willingly give him instead of the pound of flesh. He learns that whether he takes it or not, he has incurred the law for his design upon Antonio. He leaves the court room baffled, broken in spirit and in fortune. And then, with a swift turn, Shakespeare sets his audience laughing over the exchange of rings because they can see the awkward situation which Bassanio is preparing for himself. It is true that for a modern reader the full climax comes at the exit of Shylock, but that is not true necessarily for an audience which found its prime interest in the story and which delighted, as is shown us by Shakespeare's plays and those of other writers of his time, in sharp contrasts between the serious or tragic and the comic or grotesque.

Summed up in a word, all this accomplishment in *A Midsummer Night's Dream, Romeo and Juliet,* and *The Merchant of Venice* means mastery. In these plays Shakespeare has shown that whether working with a single strand or with many, he can develop a firm plot of compelling interest. *A Midsummer Night's Dream* proves that he has gained the power, which he had not acquired in *Love's Labour's Lost,* of developing a plot under hampering special conditions. All three plays demonstrate that by 1595–1596 he could develop his plots climactically, fulfilling all promises held out in earlier parts of the play, something he was unable to do in *The Two Gentlemen of Verona. Romeo and Juliet* and

The Merchant of Venice are evidence that what apparently was beyond his powers in *Titus Andronicus*, namely, giving complete convincingness to improbable or relatively impossible story, no longer troubles him. Moreover, not only is his characterization now so true that it is the largest element in metamorphosing the improbable into what is readily accepted, but he handles it with an emphasis as sure as that demonstrated in the treatment of the fairy group, the lovers, and the rustics in *A Midsummer Night's Dream*. In *Venus and Adonis* and *The Rape of Lucrece* he showed control of poetic narrative: this group of plays is proof that in the intervening years he has mastered the art of narrative in the drama. He has gained it thus far, for farce in *The Comedy of Errors*, for melodrama in *Titus Andronicus*, for fantasy in *A Midsummer Night's Dream*, for romantic story in *Romeo and Juliet*, and *The Merchant of Venice*. The secret of mastery in the drama, namely, emphasis, is his in 1595–1596. Perfect emphasis, dramatically speaking, is that presentation of one's material by which the dramatic purpose is accurately fulfilled, yet so as to hold from start to finish the sympathetic and rapt attention of the audience, while drawing from it the largest emotional return to be derived from the story under the conditions of presentation. Shakespeare's acquirement of perfect emphasis rested upon two things: in the first place, each new story which he had to tell he apparently undertook with no rigid preconception as to what a play must be. That is, he was totally without hampering preconceptions in regard to dramatic forms. On the other hand, he understood perfectly the conditions of the stage for which he was writing, and his relation to his audience was also one of sympathetic and kindly understanding. Resting on past experience with this audience, aided in part by certain principles of composition which he had found effective in his earlier efforts, but not holding rigidly to them if he saw any reason to depart therefrom, he faced each play as a special problem in technique. Is it not from this very fact that in every instance a Shakespearean play was practically an effort so to adapt a story to the stage that it should be as vivid as possible for a mixed audience, that a large part of Shakespeare's perennial hold on the public derives?

If, by 1596, Shakespeare is master of the technique of pure story-telling on the stage, what remains for him? Many reaches of character which he has not explored. As his experience with the chronicle plays suggested, exploration of those reaches could be so successfully phrased only in one of two forms which Shakespeare had not yet attained, — high comedy and tragedy. Subtler characterization leading to differentiation of dramatic forms is what lies ahead.

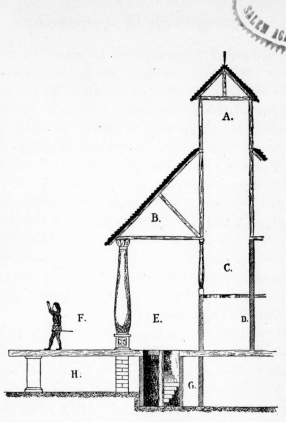

CROSS-SECTION OF THE ELIZABETHAN STAGE
(Adapted from a print by Brodmeier)

A. Loft, possibly used for painted cloths.
B. Loft for properties and machinery.
C. Balcony Stage.
D. Rear Stage.

E. Inner Stage.
F. Outer Stage.
G. Steps for Trap, etc.
H. Space under Front Stage.

CHAPTER VI

HIGH COMEDY

ALL of Shakespeare's work which in its extant form lies between 1597 and 1600 is marked by joyousness of spirit, indeed by an almost lilting gayety, combined with mastery of method. Nor, in saying this, am I thinking only of the plays which chiefly are the basis for my discussion of high comedy in Shakespeare, namely, *Much Ado about Nothing*, published in 1600 and probably written in the preceding year; *As You Like It*, entered for publication on Aug. 4, 1600, but "staied," and not printed until the folio of 1623; and *Twelfth Night*, which cannot be placed later than Feb. 2, 1602, when we hear of a performance of it at the Middle Temple, but very likely not its first. I am thinking also of the revision of *Henry V*, probably in 1599, of *The Taming of the Shrew*, and *The Merry Wives of Windsor*, both of which, as we have them, belong between 1597 and 1599.[1]

Whatever may be our feeling as to the proper classification of *The Taming of the Shrew* and *The Merry Wives*

---

[1] *All's Well that Ends Well*, even if its original form may go back to a date early in the nineties, in its existing form is usually placed *circa* 1602.

of Windsor, surely no one questions the right of *Much Ado about Nothing, As You Like It,* and *Twelfth Night* to rank as comedies and as probably the best comedies our language knows. If farce be, as it is defined, "the form that shows us possible people doing improbable things," it is easy to see that there is some reason for considering *The Taming of the Shrew* farce; but here, as elsewhere in Shakespeare, forms mingle, and the rich poetry and the elevated tone of that last scene, in which Katherine makes her submission, leave a critic feeling that probably he should compromise and call *The Taming of the Shrew* farce-comedy. Surely, too, even if one is certain one does not recognize in the Falstaff of *The Merry Wives* the shrewd, resourceful Falstaff of *Henry IV*, and balks a little, too, at believing even the Falstaff of *The Merry Wives* could so easily be led over and over into situations which any man of sense, especially in the light of this man's experiences, might expect to result disastrously, one is somehow unwilling to say that *The Merry Wives* is pure farce. The characterization is too real, the situations, except that centring about Herne the hunter, are too probable for pure farce. Rather compromise again becomes necessary: one declares *The Merry Wives* farce-comedy.

But what does this word "comedy" which one hears so constantly and so glibly bandied about mean? It is one of the hardest words to define satisfactorily that I know. Often it is used as if it meant no more than a play that does not end sadly,[1] yet surely one can recall plays, particularly in the modern drama, in which a story of present-day life unrolls seriously, even with tragic moments, but not to an ending tragic nor even sad. For instance, Mr. Pinero's *Lady Bountiful* does just that. Brieux' *Blanchette* is of the same kind. For that matter, so is *Measure for Measure*. What, then, is such a play? We usually dodge the issue by calling it *drame* in imitation of the French, society drama, tragi-comedy, or most vaguely of all, simply play. But this dodging shows that the distinctions between comedy and tragedy need determining. Most definitions of comedy, like most dramatic nomenclature, hark back to Aristotle, whose incisive distinctions, in his *Poetics*, as to tragedy in his own day have so much truth that they have fairly hypnotized later generations into talking as if the tragedy and the comedy of their own days could be ultimately analyzed and described in terms of Aristotle. The fundamental distinction which I laid down in the first chapter of this book pointed to the underlying absurdity of such use of Aristotle. Drama depends not merely on the dramatist, but also on his public, whose ideals may be vastly different from those of the Greek public. Even if the dramatist

---

[1] For instance, John Fletcher wrote in the address *To the Reader* prefixed to *The Faithful Shepherdess:* " A tragi-comedy is not so called in respect of mirth and killing, but in respect it wants deaths, which is enough to make it no tragedy, yet brings some near it, which is enough to make it no comedy, which must be a representation of familiar people, with such kind of trouble as no life be questioned."

derive his inspiration from the past, he must so express it that it shall not be wholly foreign to the instincts and ideals of his audiences.

Now, Aristotle says that "comedy aims at representing men as worse, tragedy as better, than in actual life." Elsewhere he says: "Comedy is an imitation of characters of a lower type, — not, however, in the full sense of the word 'bad,' the ludicrous being merely a subdivision of the ugly. It consists in some defect or ugliness which is not painful or destructive." That definition undoubtedly held true for the comedy of Aristotle's day, and accounts for Aristophanic farce as well as for Plautan comedy. Does it, however, without forcing, adequately account for Benedick, Touchstone, Viola, and Beatrice? Evidently, either Aristotle's definition was, after all, incomplete in its own day, or forms of comedy did not then exist which had developed in Shakespeare's work by 1600. Even when Dryden, modifying Aristotle a little, declared, in the latter part of the seventeenth century, that "Comedy presents us with the imperfections of human nature; [it] causes laughter in those who can judge of men and manners by the lively representation of their follies and corruption," is it not clear that Dryden is thinking rather of his own practice and that of his contemporaries than of the great comedies of Shakespeare? Nor do we make much headway when we pass to such a glittering generality as "Comedy shows us possible people doing probable things." Are we quite sure that if Shakespeare had not thrown his spell over us, we should be convinced of the probability of all those forest experiences of Rosalind or the love adventures of Viola? All these definitions smack too much of their period or author, and are not sufficiently inclusive. What room is there under them for the sentimental comedy of the eighteenth century, a comedy depending on a sensibility in its public which the Greek would not at all have understood and against which so genuine a sentimentalist as Goldsmith protests even within the century.

Is it not safest to say that the comic in general as distinguished from the tragic is a matter of the point of view from which the dramatist looks at his material and the emphasis he gives it? Some forty lines in the scene of *The Merchant of Venice* to which I have already often referred illustrate the truth of this statement.

Portia. And you must cut this flesh from off his breast:
The law allows it, and the court awards it.
  Shylock. Most learned judge! A sentence! Come, prepare!
  Por. Tarry a little; there is something else.
This bond doth give thee here no jot of blood;
The words expressly are "a pound of flesh."
Take then thy bond, take thou thy pound of flesh;
But, in the cutting it, if thou dost shed
One drop of Christian blood, thy lands and goods
Are, by the laws of Venice, confiscate
Unto the state of Venice.
  Gratiano. O upright judge! Mark, Jew: O learned judge!
  Shy. Is that the law?
  Por.   Thyself shalt see the act:

Q

For, as thou urgest justice, be assured
Thou shalt have justice, more than thou desirest.

> *Gra.* O learned judge! Mark, Jew: a learned judge!

> *Shy.* I take this offer, then; pay the bond thrice
And let the Christian go.

> *Bassanio.*   Here is the money.

> *Por.* Soft!

The Jew shall have all justice; soft! no haste:
He shall have nothing but the penalty.

> *Gra.* O Jew! an upright judge, a learned judge!

> *Por.* Therefore prepare thee to cut off the flesh.

Shed thou no blood, nor cut thou less nor more
But just a pound of flesh: if thou cut'st more
Or less than a just pound, be it but so much
As makes it light or heavy in the substance,
Or the division of the twentieth part
Of one poor scruple, nay, if the scale do turn
But in the estimation of a hair,
Thou diest and all thy goods are confiscate.

> *Gra.* A second Daniel, a Daniel, Jew!

Now, infidel, I have you on the hip.

> *Por.* Why doth the Jew pause? take thy forfeiture.

> *Shy.* Give me my principal, and let me go.

> *Bass.* I have it ready for thee; here it is.

> *Por.* He hath refused it in the open court:
He shall have merely justice and his bond.

> *Gra.* A Daniel, still say I, a second Daniel!
I thank thee, Jew, for teaching me that word.

Is it not clear that whether this scene is comic or
tragic depends on whether you look at it through the
eyes of Shylock or the eyes of Gratiano? Is it not
perfectly clear, too, that some of our later actors,
notably the late Sir Henry Irving, have emphasized
the lines of Shylock so deftly that the interruptions of

Gratiano, which doubtless delighted the audience of Shakespeare's day, become almost irritating to us? It is easy to believe, however, that before an audience, for some special reason stirred with race hatred against the Jew, that scene might be so emphasized as to bring shouts of delight after every speech of Gratiano, transmuting the tragic into the comic. We know, at any rate, that by the end of the seventeenth century Shylock had become a comic figure. But is all this more than saying that with any given incident which we wish to present on the stage, if we emphasize its serious significance, we write either insufficiently motivated serious drama, which is melodrama, or adequately motivated serious drama, which is tragedy, and if we treat the same incident for its potential amusingness, we may range from the exaggerated emphasis which means farce or extravaganza through all the region of comedy? I say "all the region of comedy," for we shall soon see that comedy subdivides and badly needs mapping. Primarily, then, the comic depends on the point of view of the writer, for this determines his selection of material, and on his emphasis, for this is the means by which he makes it serve the ends he has in view. The importance of emphasis in creating comic effect becomes obvious if one considers what would have happened if the scenes in which Maria, Sir Toby, and Feste torment Malvolio had not been so emphasized that the sympathies of the Elizabethan audience went with the tormentors. Misemphasis would have meant lack of sympathy and consequent indifference to the whole scene, or even, worst of all, sympathy for Malvolio. In the last case what was meant for a highly amusing practical joke would for the audience have seemed unpardonable tormenting. In brief, the comic is struck, like a spark, from the impact on an audience with well-understood ideals and sympathies by material carefully emphasized with regard to those ideals and sympathies. The comic is a coöperative process; like electricity, it requires a positive and a negative pole.

Now what had been the dramatic use of the comic when Shakespeare manifested in his three great plays, *Much Ado about Nothing, As You Like It,* and *Twelfth Night,* consummate power as a comic dramatist? We have already seen that the miracle plays, dealing with Biblical history, and the chronicle plays, dealing with legendary or veracious history that is not sacred, moved inevitably for one of their developments to the comedy of manners. That is, in representing the past in terms of the present, the miracle play gave the people, not shepherds of the East watching their flocks by night, but shepherds of the Conway and the Clyde; and the chronicle play gave, not the historical tatterdemalions who doubtless were in the army of *Henry IV,* but in Bardolph, Pistol, and even Falstaff himself, pictures from Eastcheap and the Bankside. At first these figures appear only in a scene, or in uncorrelated scenes, but gradually there develops the sub-plot of a comedy of manners, none too well connected with the main plot. Comic characterization which ranged from exaggeration to restrained and convincing art was well understood in some plays long before Shakespeare ever wrote a line. The scene in the Chester miracle play of *Noah and the Ark,* in which Noah's wife refuses to embark unless her gossips may accompany her, illustrates the fact that at a very early date selection and emphasis for comic effect were understood.

Noah. Wife, come in: why standes thou there?
Thou art ever froward, I dare well sweare;
Come in, on Godes name! halfe tyme it were,
For feare lest that we drowne.
   Noah's wife. Yea, sir, set up your sail,
And row forth with evil haile,
For withouten fail
I will not out of this towne;
But I have my gossips everyone,
One foot further I will not gone:
They shall not drown by St. John!
And I may save their life.
But thou letten them into thy chest,
Else row now wher thou list,
And getten thee a new wife.
   Noah. Shem, lo! thy mother is wrawe!
Such another I do not know.

So Shem and Ham both try to persuade her, but in vain, and the cheerful gossips sing a drinking song as the tide comes in. Then Japhet tries his fortune, only to have Mrs. Noah say: —

[229]

That will I not for all your call,
But I have my gossips all.
   Shem. In faith, mother, yet you shall,
Whether thou wilt or not.
   Noah. Welcome, wife, into this boat.
   Wife. Have thou that for thy note.
   Noah. Ha, ha, marry this is hot!

How much comic action those last few lines connote!

The effect here certainly depends on the point of view of the dramatist, for to Mrs. Noah the experience was certainly not amusing, and to Noah himself the last lines clearly show that it was painful indeed. The comic effect comes, too, from the emphasis, for only that is stressed which would be sure to raise a laugh from an audience of the time. Think how gruesome, even tragic, the scene might have been made for just the same audience by emphasizing the pettiness of this squabble in the presence of the impending cataclysm.

The pre-Shakespearean drama used freely, and sometimes with full intelligence, comic situation. It tended, however, as *Gammer Gurton's Needle* and the best plays of John Heywood prove, to turn to the exaggeration that means farce. In very many cases it could not, or it would not, so present its material that truth to life should keep it on the level of comedy. Rather, either wilfully, because of the sure response of the audience to farce, or inevitably because exaggeration is easier than the restraint of truth, situation in these plays ran to the farcical.

THE STAGE OF THE RED BULL THEATRE.

(This shows the curtains of the upper stage.)

Dramatic dialogue must first of all expound, making the story clear; if it fails to do that, no amount of characterization or cleverness in itself will compensate. Had the drama not grasped this requisite thoroughly, it could never have developed as it had by 1585. In addition, even as dialogue expounds plot, it should expound it in character for speakers. How well comic characterizing phrase was grasped even as far back as the miracle plays is shown by the extract from the Chester plays and by that line of the Third Shepherd in the Towneley Christmas play as he and his two companions see the sheep-stealer, Mak, approaching: "Is he commen, then let ilk one look to his own." Comic dialogue in this pre-Shakespearean drama ranges from mere punning to actual wit, but for the most part it shows the same tendency toward exaggeration, toward farce, as do situation and characterization.

By 1590 the forms which comedy will take by 1605–1610 may be discerned by him who looks back, though they were not clearly descried by the dramatists of that date. Farce, but rather as an element than as a form, is widespread. Even the comedy of humor was present, though, like the others, without individual form. A "humor" in comedy, as Congreve admirably defined it, is only " a singular and unavoidable manner of doing or saying anything peculiar and natural to one man only; by which his speech and actions are distinguished from those of other men. . . . Humor I take to be born with us, and so of a natural growth;

or else to be grafted into us, by some accidental change in the constitution or resolution of the internal habit of the body, by which it becomes, if I may so call it, naturalized."[1] Inasmuch as the comedy of manners must always rest on a just depicting of the humors of men and women, it, too, was present formlessly. This comedy of manners shoulders romance or history, as the play is *Common Conditions* with its rascally tinkers of the opening scene, or *The Famous Victories of Henry V* with its scenes of the Prince and his friends of the London slums. Romantic comedy shows, for instance, in the love story of this *Common Conditions* or in *Friar Bacon and Friar Bungay*. As I have already pointed out, in most of Lyly's comedies the love story was simply biding its time to break through its brilliant but stiff ornament that bore it down even like Tarpeia. Had Lyly thought rather of what his characters were than of what they said, he would have created high comedy. Under comedy as signifying only "humorous" characterization, we should in Lyly's plays be able to place only the sub-plots of his plays, which deal with his waggishly impudent pages and his adaptations of figures from the Latin comedy. His main plots show us, depending largely as they do for their effect on dialogue of a very mannered sort, that there may be another or other elements in comedy besides the mere humorous portraiture

[1] *Concerning Humour in Comedy. A Letter. Dramatic Works* (1773), Vol. II, pp. 224, 227.

which the comedy of manners rests on. The first additional element we recognize is, of course, dialogue. Lyly's work steadily illustrates the fact that both dramatist and audience had awakened to the fact that dialogue, in addition to its work in characterization and exposition, might give pleasure in and of itself for its ingenuity, its wit, and its beauty and style. There is recognition of this truth, as I pointed out in the first chapter of this book, in the work of Thomas Kyd also; so that even before Shakespeare wrote there had appeared in the dramatic treatment of material emphasized for its amusingness something besides comic situation and characterization, something besides dialogue that both expounded and characterized clearly, namely, a dawning appreciation of the value in comedy of dialogue at the time considered witty or in accord with ephemeral standards of style.

Before Shakespeare's day two evolutions were taking place in comedy, one very slowly during centuries, one rapidly between 1590 and 1605. Slowly, through a surer feeling for truth to life, greater ability in presenting it, and a growing appreciation of the value of literary restraint, farcical treatment of men and manners was changing to comedy of manners and to something vaguely like romantic comedy. Very rapidly, in the neighborhood of 1600, Jonson and Middleton developed from this comic material the comedy of manners: Jonson, because of his tendency to emphasize one characteristic at the expense of all others, kept closer to the exaggeration of farce than did Middleton, who painted broadly and impersonally. The slower development marks a differentiation of comic material; the quicker development is in providing forms for these differentiations. In the first evolution many men slowly intellectualize the low comedy of their fathers by bringing to it a sense of poetic beauty, a feeling for artistic restraint, and literary style. Through greater truth to life, an increasing sense of beauty and a developing perception of the value of the witty as contrasted with the merely humorous, low comedy by 1590 very nearly arrives at high comedy.

But we call both the romantic comedy of Shakespeare and the realistic comedy of Congreve, for instance in *The Way of the World*, high comedy. Unless there is to be confusion, high comedy evidently needs defining.

George Meredith, in that illuminating *Essay on Comedy*, which had the happy fortune to be born a classic, says that the test of true comedy is that it shall "awaken thoughtful laughter," and adds, "Believe that idle, empty laughter is the most desirable of recreations, and significant comedy will seem pale and shallow in comparison." Confine those definitions to high comedy, which is what Mr. Meredith is really considering, and they are indisputable. But what does he mean by "thoughtful laughter"? That the laughter results solely from the thought which went

into the design of the dramatist? Hardly, for, as
I have shown, there must be thoughtful design in all
dramatic composition, from farce to tragedy. Is it
that thinking over the scene after its performance we
realize its full comic import? Hardly, for no comedy
would be a lasting success, the full effect of which came
only when the public had left the theatre for some time.
No, the thoughtfulness of the laughter must mean that
the thought and the laugh are practically one, that
some instantaneous appreciation by us of a contrast,
a comparison, a relation, produces the laugh: "that
we simply do not laugh idly." That is the chief point,
that we do not laugh idly. Ask a child at the circus
why he is convulsed, ask his much older, uneducated
neighbor why he too is convulsed, when the clown
by a backhanded blow, "accidentally on purpose,"
fells the immaculately dressed ringmaster, and neither
of them can tell you anything except that it is "so
funny." Had one asked even the more intelligent members of an Elizabethan audience why they found the an-
tics of madmen or the demented unqualifiedly amusing,
they could no more have told you than any American
audience to-day can tell you why it finds mild drunkenness theatrically so irresistible, and why, in a farce or
comedy that has been hovering over the abyss of bore-
dom, the single expletive "damn" is often enough to
save the situation. Those are, of course, the simplest
forms of unthinking laughter. We rise from them
through better and better characterization, because

more and more incisive and subtle, to a point where the amusingness can exist only for him who can see comparisons, relations, or contrasts between what is represented on the stage and certain standards generally accepted, or clearly suggested by the dramatist.

That is, if one can appreciate only low comedy, one will enjoy in *Twelfth Night*, in the story of Malvolio, only the practical joke played upon him at the instigation of Maria; but if one have also the spirit of high comedy, one will get a keener and more delicate pleasure as one's thought recognizes steadily the delightful contrast between what Malvolio thinks himself, and what he is; what he thinks the effect he is producing, and the effect he really produces on Olivia. Or again, a large part of our delight in the wooing of Beatrice by Benedick and her treatment of him comes in our sense of the contrast between what they think the situation is and our knowledge of what the plotting of Don Pedro, Claudio, and Leonato have made it. For him who sees this contrast neither in *Twelfth Night* nor in *Much Ado about Nothing*, — and such contrast reveals itself in some instant of thought-producing laughter, — one of the springs of delight in these two plays is dried. High comedy in contrast to low comedy rests then fundamentally on thoughtful appreciation contrasted with unthinking, spontaneous laughter. Low comedy rightly produces only the latter, and always verges on the exaggeration of farce. The comedy of manners is a link: it may be low and run into farce; it may rise into high comedy; and we shall often find comedies which range from low to high if they have, as Shakespeare's have, two or more strands of plot. That is, the comedy of manners is not properly a category, as are high and low comedy. Rather the term identifies a kind of material which, according to its treatment, may range from farce through low comedy to high comedy. We have seen, then, that the comic is determined by the point of view of the dramatist as well as by the emphasis he gives his material, and we have learned that for high comedy the emphasis is given to rouse, not thoughtless, but thoughtful, laughter. Can we not determine additional characteristics of high comedy?

What part in producing this thoughtful laughter do character, phrase, and story necessarily play? From the very definition thus far built up for high comedy evidently characterization of a high order is an essential. In high comedy we deal not with the superficial aspects of character, not with mere typical acts such as Sir Toby Belch's drunkenness or Sir Andrew Aguecheek's cowardice, but with the complex moods of Rosalind, Viola, and Beatrice; with the contradictions of Benedick rather than the simple emotions of Claudio; with Orlando's lover's moods and Touchstone's fool's wisdom rather than with the feelings of Corin or William. Moreover, since we have already seen that dialogue may play an important part in comedy, and that dialogue when at its best must be not only a pleasure in itself, but in character, every figure of any consequence in a high comedy must be perfectly understood or the dialogue cannot combine these two qualities. Has one any doubt of Shakespeare's perfect understanding of all the intricacies of thought and feeling of Viola, Rosalind, and Beatrice? Moreover, the later history of the English drama has shown us that what is recognized as high comedy may be slight in story but, if it is to have any permanent hold on the public, must be strong in characterization. Had I time to analyze here Sheridan's *School for Scandal* or Congreve's *The Way of the World*, I could show easily that it is upon characterization those two plays rest fundamentally for their appeal to the public, though the fusillade of wit so distracts our attention from the underlying characterization that we recognize its importance only on analysis. Congreve offers only just enough plot to provide a framework for his characterization and phrase. Sheridan, it is true, offers much more, but still far less than Shakespeare.

But if the power of grasping and representing delicate and subtle shades of character is the first essential, phrase is the second. I say "phrase" intentionally rather than "dialogue," because there is in some of these high comedies, notably the Shakespearean, a charm that lies neither in the characterization nor the wit, but rather in the beauty of the phrase as phrase or the poetic content of the phrase as contrasted with its wit.

Do not these relations of story, phrase, and characterization in high comedy show why we call it high? Surely this comedy makes the highest demands on the literary and interpretative powers of the dramatist. He who is clever only in weaving plot filled with character types or with figures copied from simple originals cannot write it. He who lacks wit and skill in phrase is no master in it. On the other hand, this comedy demands an audience interested, even more than by plot, in fine shadings and contrasts of characterization, and possessing a sense of proportion and beauty. These facts point to a condition, apart from the dramatist, essential for high comedy. Mr. Meredith has stated that since the usual subject of high comedy is love, and women must consequently be important in it, for the success of high comedy a state of society is essential in which women are at least not looked down upon by men, but are their companions. It seems to me not quite true that high comedy results only when the love story is central in it; surely whatever makes us indulge in thoughtful laughter over our fellow human beings, whether the source of the comic lie in love or in other human relation or experience, is proper material. On the other hand, since love is the one common experience almost equally interesting to all audiences, it must naturally be the chief subject of high comedy. Now the love story means depicting necessarily the subtler moods of women under finer feelings stirred in them by men. It must be clear why not only an intelligent audience, but an audience with women in it, and cultivated women at that, is essential if high comedy is to flourish.

What better time could there be for the appearance of high comedy than the closing years of the reign of Elizabeth, when the great queen had given her country peace, when the drama had been fostered by her, when women like the Countess of Pembroke shared the literary enthusiasms of their brothers and friends? Moreover, the interest of the court in the drama as seen in the many performances at the royal palace and the houses of the nobility and in the attendance of men of fashion and university wits at the theatres, gave just the specially intelligent group in Shakespeare's audience which was needed if the more delicate appeal of high comedy was to be appreciated.

To what extent do the essentials of high comedy appear in *Much Ado about Nothing*, *As You Like It*, and *Twelfth Night*, and what is Shakespeare's special contribution, if any, to the form?

That Shakespeare's depicting of subtle and complex moods in his high comedies is masterly is universally admitted. That this success rests on his perfect understanding of his *dramatis personæ* is as widely acknowledged. As we have seen, it was nothing new in 1598 to treat a romantic story with puppets, or even with well-drawn types, for the speakers. There had been some plays, and there were many thereafter, in which characters thoroughly convincing within the scene or

The Stage used by the Elizabethan Stage Society

the act appeared in a romantic setting. Greene, on the one hand, and Dekker, Heywood, and Beaumont and Fletcher, on the other, bear witness to that. What was unheard of in 1598, and what remained exceedingly rare thereafter, was any play in which, against a romantic background, subtle and complex moods of men, and especially of women, were so portrayed that the characters grew even as the audience watched the development of the play. Complex character, true to life, not within the scene or the act, but developing as the play advanced and able to endure scrutiny and analysis for the consistency of its drawing from start to finish, — this was one of Shakespeare's contributions to high comedy. But his mastery of his art by 1598 enabled him to make this contribution to all of the dramatic forms in which he chose to work between that date and 1600.

The success of these high comedies rests quite as much on the fact that Shakespeare, consciously or unconsciously, probably the latter, appealed in the main in his characterization to permanent rather than temporary interests of an audience. It has been pointed out that "men manifest their stage of culture in nothing more than in what they laugh at." The clown in the Elizabethan drama is a survival of an appeal to a response once sure, but by 1600 waning. The American of the French stage in such a play as *L'Etrangère* of Dumas fils shows to-day by the languid interest he rouses in a French audience, how rapidly figures drawn, not from life but in accord with prejudices or momentary interest of the public, will lose their effect. Shakespeare himself offers instances of this. There is a notable example in the scene of *Twelfth Night* in which the chained Malvolio begs for paper that he may write to his mistress of his miseries. To an Elizabethan that scene of torment by Sir Toby, Feste, and Maria was extremely amusing, and consequently those three are in the foreground and Malvolio is more heard than seen. But times have changed, and the scene is either boresome or somewhat repellent to-day. I have often seen it fall flat. I believe, therefore, that Mr. Sothern is quite right in putting the tormentors at the back of the stage, and letting the audience see as well as hear Malvolio. The change, by creating sympathy for him, undoubtedly does violence to the original intent of Shakespeare, but by bringing the scene into accord with the sympathies of a modern audience makes it carry. Possibly all the Sir Toby-Sir Andrew scenes, unless played with a restraint perhaps not Elizabethan, and none too common on our own stage to-day, are in danger of overreaching at present; but the main story appeals as much as or more than it originally did. And this is true of the whole of *Much Ado about Nothing* and *As You Like It*.

The first reason for this permanency of interest is that Shakespeare does not deal in local types, nor even in English men and women. His people may be expatriated by translation, but they still remain so true to human nature that they delight strange audiences in foreign lands. No contrast could be greater than between his figures and Lyly's literary wraiths appealing not merely to their own decade but to the Court set, and even to one group within that set. Or contrast Shakespeare's work in these high comedies with Ben Jonson's comedies of manners, and the danger of the appeal to interest in local characterization is clear. Jonson, so far as his observation, strongly affected as it was by his reading of classic comedy, would permit, drew with photographic accuracy the people he saw in the taverns, the theatres, and the streets of the London of 1600–1610. With him story went for little. Dialogue interested him most when it was anatomizing character, even if at times he spoke himself rather than as fitted the character in question. What resulted? When, after a break of some years during which he was writing masques, he returned in 1620–1630 to writing plays, nobody would heed him. The people then wanted incident, story, more than characterization. He had no story of interest to tell, and he drew, as he had drawn ten or a dozen years before, humorous local figures. The people had lost their interest in such figures apart from plot, even as posterity has shown little interest in them except as pictures of the time.

Shakespeare had grasped a truth once admirably phrased by Madame Riccoboni in a letter to Garrick. "The taste of all nations," she wrote, "accords on certain points: the natural, truth, sentiment, interest equally the Englishman, the Russian, the Turk. But wit, badinage, the quip, pleasantry, change in name as the climate changes. That which is lively, light, graceful, in one language, becomes cold, heavy, insipid, or gross, in another. Everywhere humor depends on nothing, and often that nothing is local." Let us be honest with ourselves. Do all the speeches in these high comedies whose intent is evidently amusing really delight us to-day? Of course not, but we enjoy what the foreigner enjoys in such speeches, the character which comes out from behind them. They were like the masque of the Greek actor, put on to emphasize, to intensify, the effect a speaker was to produce. But the character behind was so truly, so finally drawn by Shakespeare that, even if special speeches have grown stale, our delight in Jaques, Beatrice, Rosalind, and Viola is abiding — be we Anglo-Saxon or Latin. Though the conditions in which a character may appear be unusual, Shakespeare finds the universal in the individual placed in those conditions. He does not stress the unusualness of the conditions; rather he relates them as closely as he can to our own experiences. This he does largely by painting for us not those details, those characteristics which mark off the figure from all other men, but rather his reaction as an individual on experiences, emotions, moods, common to all mankind. He does not deal in types, as *The Lover* of John

Heywood's interlude, nor in the slab-sided figures of the Jonsonian humor comedy, nor in unusual manifestations of rare or extraordinary qualities as do Chapman or Marlowe in their serious plays. Instead, he paints for us in individuals their manifestations of universal or typical moods, emotions, and states of mind.

Undoubtedly the prominence which Shakespeare gave the love story in his high comedies, as elsewhere in his plays, has much to do with their universal appeal. "All the world loves a lover" and always will. Now in the plays still extant which belong before 1600, the love story is but one element of interest, or had been treated for the incident it offered rather than the love motif, or had been subordinated to false standards of literary expression. By 1600 it had been given in the English drama much the dominating position it has since held in our drama. Putting aside the decided probability that Shakespeare was the person most responsible for this new emphasis, for the matter cannot be settled with our scanty supply of plays written between 1590 and 1600, it remains true that no other plays written by 1600 combine so much emphasis on the love story with such delicacy of feeling and such idealism of tone. Nearly all the later dramatists make the love story the centre of their plays, but it usually has its sordid side, and in Marston it is passionate enough to be called modern. Nowhere else than in Shakespeare does one find physical passion so purified and idealized. Even as Shakespeare gives the love story the greatest possible prominence, he frees it from its baser elements by skilful emphasis and elevated thought. On the side of characterization, then, Shakespeare's high comedies held many appeals to the public. The characterization in them is the equal of any the drama of any nation has to offer. With the love story as the central interest, something of which the public never tires, Shakespeare so emphasizes in the individual what is of universal and permanent appeal that his people surmount the barrier of a foreign language and withstand the passage of the decades.

What also distinguishes Shakespeare's high comedy is his use of plot. As I have already said, later high comedy usually shows a small amount of plot as compared with characterization and dialogue for its own sake. Is not this natural? Since high comedy depends fundamentally on delicate strokes of characterization, and there is but the space of five acts for all this exposition, if we increase the difficulty of our characterization and at the same time expand our dialogue, must not plot suffer except in the hands of a master in dramatic proportioning? It is just here that Shakespeare once more shows how firmly ingrained now was his acquired sense of the value for his audience of story. In not one of these three great plays has he been content with what a single source supplied him. For the love story of Rosalind, as provided him by Thomas Lodge in his novel *Rosalynde, Euphues' Golden*

Legacie, he has, at the least, so much developed
from bald hints Lodge's Jaques, Touchstone, the
rustics with their love story, and the Foresters, that
they seem his creations. Though Barnabe Rich seems
in his *Apolonius and Silla* to have supplied him with
the main story of *Twelfth Night,* he adds Malvolio and
all the group headed by Sir Toby. In *Much Ado* he
weaves three strands: the story of Hero and Claudio,
to be found in Bandello, though not taken directly
thence by Shakespeare; the love making of Beatrice
and Benedick, the exact source of which is not clear;
and the character studies of Dogberry and Verges,
evidently wholly Shakespeare's own. Note, too, that
even here in high comedy he thinks it worth while to
knit his work closely, for in *Much Ado about Nothing,* it
is Dogberry and Verges who overhear the plotting
of Conrade and Borachio, and so ultimately bring the
news that clears Hero from her disgrace; and it is the
blow falling on Hero which makes Beatrice and Benedick drop their pretences and, in order to prove her
innocence, come to an understanding. There again
we have a knitting of the parts of the plot similar
to that pointed out in *The Merchant of Venice.* In
Twelfth Night, too, remember it is the duel forced
upon Viola by Sir Toby that really brings about the
dénouement, since it is Sir Andrew's attack on Sebastian, whom he mistakes for Viola, which finally
brings brother and sister together. Lately it has been
more than once reported that *The School for Scandal*

no longer draws well. Congreve admitted that in his own day his plays were really successful only with the few. Of course, in both cases this limited popularity can be partly accounted for by what has already been said of the special audience which high comedy requires, but has not the absence of an absorbing story something to do with the lack of permanent and widespread success for these two plays? Some seventeenth-century verses tell us

> Let but Beatrice
> And Benedick be seene, loe in a trice,
> The Cockpit, Galleries, Boxes, all are full.

Evidently the public thoroughly appreciated that play. Watch an audience to-day at any one of these three comedies. How masterly is their planning for the public! Here is something for every one: he who cares most for story finds his satisfaction; he who delights in character may enjoy his fill; he who is pleased by witty and characterizing dialogue is not disappointed; and even he who loves poetry for its own sake is provided for. What wonder, when these plays also please the actor, because they are full of dramatic opportunity, that our public loves them to-day as well as did the public of the past?

In *Love's Labour's Lost* we saw Shakespeare led astray by ephemeral and false standards of style and wit, mistaking antithesis, alliteration, all the mannerisms of style of the moment, for real beauty of phrase, and even playing on words with the idea that this was wit. But in *The Two Gentlemen of Verona* he had already begun to understand that wit is not external in source but internal; that it is not general but individual, the intellectual reaction of an original mind on an idea or situation. Speech rightly to be witty must first of all, then, be in character. Shakespeare came soon to realize, also, that scenes of wit for their own sake, like those of Navarre and his lords and the Princess and her ladies, quickly weary; that it is safer to risk them only rarely, and to let a scene have the double value of interesting characterization through witty dialogue. Comparison of an extract from Lyly and some lines in Shakespeare treating an analogous idea will show the great superiority of the latter's matured method.

Phillida. Have you ever a sister?

Gallathea. If I had but one, my brother must needs have two; but I pray have you ever a one?

Phil. My father had but one daughter, and therefore I could have no sister.

Gall. [*Aside.*] Ay me, he is as I am, for his speeches be as mine are.

Phil. What shall I doe, either he is subtle or my sex simple.

Here Lyly is thinking only of the complication itself and of his mannered phrase. Shakespeare, taking this complication, so handles it that the plot moves on, the speeches characterize, poetic feeling fills the little scene, and the thought is phrased in exquisite poetry.

Duke.   Make no compare
Between that love a woman can bear me,
And that I owe Olivia.
   Viola.   Ay, but I know, —
   Duke. What dost thou know?
   Vio. Too well what love women to men **may owe:**
In faith, they are as true of heart as we.
My father had a daughter lov'd a man,
As it might be, perhaps, were I a woman,
I should your lordship.
      Duke.   And what's her history?
   Vio. A blank, my lord. She never told her love, —
But let concealment, like a worm i' the bud,
Feed on her damask cheek: she pin'd in thought:
And, with a green and yellow melancholy,
She sat like patience on a monument,
Smiling at grief. Was not this love, indeed?
We men may say more, swear more; but, indeed,
Our shows are more than will, for still we prove
Much in our vows, but little in our love.
   Duke. But died thy sister of her love, my boy?
   Vio. I am all the daughters of my father's house,
And all the brothers too; and yet I know not. —
Sir, shall I to this lady?

This is dramatic literature, for here the dramatic
moment is not clogged or destroyed, as often in Lyly
and many another Elizabethan dramatist, by the very
desire for literary beauty. Rather, the very beauty
of the expression helps to clearer, and therefore swifter,
presentation of the situation. This superiority in
phrasing results chiefly, too, from Shakespeare's assured
grasp on character. He does not look at a situation
for itself, nor merely as an opportunity for phrase. He
studies it primarily for what it may be made to reveal

The Stage used for Revivals of Elizabethan Plays at Harvard University

as to the characters involved. Entering into it completely with each of these, he expresses their individual reaction on it. Of course, his perfect feeling for the values of words in producing emotion and beauty aids, but it is, in the last analysis, Shakespeare's profound interest in character which lifts him from the dramatic phrase-maker to the master of dramatic phrase.

Nor does the effect of beauty produced by these three great comedies result wholly from the phrasing. It comes quite as much from the pervasive "sweetness and light." Reading these three plays, one recalls the statement of Maeterlinck: "Words are only a kind of mirror which reflects the beauty of all that surrounds it." Shakespeare has known how to put a certain uplift into his work. In the first place, his is the right attitude for the writer of comedy, whether high or low, and indispensable for the writer of high comedy, broad human sympathy, a readiness to believe in the good rather than the bad side of human nature. His, too, is so strong a sense of humor that he never loses his just sense of human values. Think how often the bad taste or misemphasis of an actor makes Sir Toby repellent. How delicate evidently must be the touches by which Shakespeare keeps free from the sordid, the base, the disgusting, in his material. Compare the story of *Apolonius and Silla* with the story of Olivia, Viola, and Sebastian, and at once the care is evident with which he excised the sordid, the suggestive, and the salacious, substituting, for instance in *Twelfth Night,* such poetic scenes as the interview of Sebastian and Olivia. Steadily he elevates his material, steadily his outlook on life is one of serene enjoyment of the follies and the love entanglements of his characters. It is, indeed, the cheery optimism of these plays which in part gives them their permanent hold. Who reads Jonson — still more, who reads the judicial Middleton — as compared with Shakespeare? Middleton's studies of the guller and the gulled about the Inns of Court in 1600-1608 are remarkable, but in giving pleasure they are not comparable with these comedies which are not of London life or English life, but of the land of romance toward which humanity, tired and discouraged by its fitful artistic excursions into what is called "the real world," gladly returns from time to time like the child at nightfall for its "one story more." Just here is another secret of the permanent hold of these plays: they are our most perfect specimens of dramatic story-telling for the children of a larger growth, which we all are in the last analysis. They raise no problems; they sweeten our feeling toward humanity; they lure us away to the restful land of romance.

We have seen that by 1594 Shakespeare was successful as an adapter of farce and melodrama; that by 1597 he was already masterly in his scenes of the comedy-of-manners type and as a dramatic story-teller able to adapt his work to any audience. Already he had taught his dramatic and his literary instincts to work in accord. By 1600 he calls into being a new form in English drama, high comedy, summoning it from the misty region of Lyly's imagination where it was lurking all unconscious of its mission. This form he stamped strongly with his own personality, not only in its genial attitude toward mankind and its witty and beautiful phrase, but also in its idealization of human passion. And all the three great comedies are marked by their clear and easily comprehended exposition of complex moods in a complicated story, the whole transfused with beauty of thought and phrase. Moreover, this union of plot, characterization, dialogue, and beauty has not been equalled by any English comedy since.

High comedy must always be difficult; it endeavors to popularize the intellectual, to bring the ordinary mind into touch with the subtle in life on its gayer side, and with the beautiful in dramatic art. What gave Shakespeare all this attainment in one of the two most difficult of dramatic forms, the other being tragedy? The toilsome acquirement we have been watching of the power to set more and more perfectly comprehended character, even in its subtlest moods of gayety, in a story of absorbing interest woven from many strands. It resulted from trained interest in character, trained poetic power, perfect technique gained from training, and from an almost uncanny knowledge of human nature, again the result of patient training of an originally keen sympathy guided by a maturing sense of humor. In ten years the growth from the ineptitude and the imitation of *Love's Labour's Lost* to the perfect accomplishment of *As You Like It, Much Ado about Nothing*, and *Twelfth Night* has been made. What remains for this master of dramatic technique, this creator of a new form in the drama of his day? He has yet to study the graver side of life as closely as the lighter, to perceive and draw forth the drama inherent in its subtlest moods. He has yet to lift melodrama and chronicle play to the level of tragedy.

CHAPTER VII

TRAGEDY

IN any attempt to formulate for ourselves Shakespeare's ideas of tragedy, two things are absolutely necessary: First, we must distinguish clearly between two words often used carelessly and as if properly interchangeable, namely the adjective *tragic* and the noun *tragedy*. In the second place, here, more than anywhere else perhaps, and certainly more than anywhere else except in the chronicle plays, one must endeavor primarily to judge Shakespeare's work not as a modern but as an Elizabethan.

The importance of distinguishing between *tragic* and *tragedy* becomes clear the moment that I make the statement on which in large part this chapter will rest; namely, that, though tragic situation was constantly evident in the plays before Shakespeare's time, there was no real tragedy except in Marlowe. Anything mournful, cruel, calamitous, bloody is *tragic* in the adjectival sense of the word. For instance, that repellent scene of *Titus Andronicus* in which Lavinia appears tongueless and with bleeding stumps for hands, or that in which she writes in the sand, guiding the stick held between her teeth with her bloody stumps, is tragic, but, as we have seen, *Titus Andronicus* is not a tragedy, but a melodrama. Accidents to people from the trolley cars are frequent enough and are often tragic, but in not all these cases is the maiming or the killing a *tragedy*. Of course, if the victim is some blind person, obliged because of limited means to make his way through the crowded streets of the city alone, and if his friends have marked, but he has been unwilling to admit, a growing deafness, then he accident partakes of the nature of tragedy, for preceding conditions have coöperated to bring about a result inevitable unless some special providence supervises or intervenes. That is, as I have already implied repeatedly, tragedy is a sequence of incidents or episodes so presented as to emphasize with seriousness their causal relationship.

Naturally, tragedy is slower in developing than farce or the low comedy that ultimately takes shape as the comedy of manners or of humors. It is always easier to photograph than to paint, for painting demands a trained judgment in selection and a knowledge of the laws of color required in photography, even nowadays, only from those who are endeavoring to break down the boundaries between photography and painting. Tragedy may very well be contemporaneous with high comedy. No matter how well these old writers in the miracle plays drew the farmers and shepherds of their day, the best of their accomplishment was far less difficult than to attempt to make clear the inevitableness of certain events in political history. They could duplicate from their own day some of the serious characters of Biblical history; they could present its tragic incident; but they made little or no attempt to motivate from scene to scene. The most wonderful of these old miracle plays, the so-called Brome *Abraham and Isaac*, was satisfied with showing in masterly fashion every shade of the interplay of emotions between father and son, as the former struggled between his affection for Isaac and his duty to God, and the latter hesitated between unquestioning obedience and a child's dread of physical pain and the unseen knife. The motivation goes wholly into making convincing the immediate mood presented. The moralities of course hovered always, when at their best, on the confines of tragedy. Indeed, on a first reading, such a play as *The Nice Wanton*, in which we learn how Ishmael and Delilah pay the penalty of their bad bringing up, may appear a real tragedy. Constantly, throughout this morality, we are made to understand that the evil results for the brother and sister spring from the slackness of the doting mother. In the recent performances of *Everyman* we beheld the tragic consequences for every man of a life such as the central figure led. These moralities, even if they deal with types, called, for instance, "Youth," "Idle Living," rather than with individuals, do try to drive home the significance of the actions seen. Whenever one of the authors says to his audience, "Pass your time as has my chief figure in idleness or riotous living and behold the

s [257]

disappointment and misery awaiting you," he is, at least, implying a great law of conduct. The fact is, the moralities may in a sense be called the Tragedy of Types. They have only to pass over to treating in historical or everyday situations the individual rather than the type, and real tragedy will be born. Yet for a form instinct with the spirit of tragedy, the morality was singularly resultless. The point is that the moralities were consciously tragic, consciously didactic, but only unconsciously tragedies. Moreover, plays replaced moralities because the people wearied of didacticism and wanted entertainment only. What tragedy there was in these moralities arose from their didacticism. Consequently, when their didacticism went, the glimmerings of tragedy went too. Instead, with the interest in Seneca and his bloody plays, with the coming of the romantic material provided by the floods of *novelle* coming to England from France and Italy, there ensued a frank revel in inadequately motivated emotion, in melodrama.

If a reader will recall *Titus Andronicus* for a moment, he will see just what I mean by melodrama, the form that stops at nothing to gain its effect. Melodrama is not simply the crowding of one striking situation upon another, — the funeral of the sons of Andronicus, the seizing of Lavinia, the marriage of Tamora, the killing of Bassianus, the mutilation of Lavinia, the madness of Titus himself, — but the happening of incidents for reasons only to a slight extent set working early in the play,— the hatred of Tamora for Titus and the anger of Saturninus at both his brother and Titus. In fact the latter plays a very small part in the after results: it is the hatred of Tamora, which gives the events what tragic motivation they have. It is curious, however, that some of the incidents most fateful for the later development of the story come from the mere love of Aaron for evil for its own sake, and the unbridled passions of the sons of Tamora. If all those later catastrophes came directly or indirectly from Tamora's scheming for revenge, then we should have a tragedy. This right feeling for tragedy appears first in Marlowe's *Tamburlaine*. In Part I all the important events spring from the hero's lust for geographical conquest. Part II shows a struggle between an individual and his environment in the sense of the working of the unseen forces of nature which govern life and death. That is, he is the first man to look behind the individual as a portrait, though not the first to look behind the type, and he is the first to look behind the individual not for moralizing but as a means to convincing characterization. That is, even when Shakespeare was working in *Richard III* and the earlier form of *Henry V*, the English drama had begun to grasp the idea of tragedy — a sequence of serious episodes leading to a catastrophe and all causally related. Yet it was evident only in Marlowe, and with him was only just beginning to deal with ordinary human passions rather than with extraordinary, such as Tamburlaine's greed of conquest, Faustus's mad love for all possible knowledge. The tragic in history had been understood for centuries, but except for *Tamburlaine* and *Edward II*, historical tragedy was in 1595 yet to be moulded from it.

As I have already pointed out, I believe there is great danger in generalizing as to Shakespeare's plays unless we first determine, so far as we can, both his purpose in writing a particular play and his relation in it to his audience. Remember, too, what I have already pointed out, that the plays I have in mind in this chapter, *Julius Cæsar*, *Hamlet*, *Macbeth*, *Lear*, *Othello*, and *Antony and Cleopatra*[1] can perfectly well, so far as the material from which they are made is concerned, be classed roughly with the chronicle plays we have already considered. They all came from chronicles of one sort or another. The chronicle might be of British history or of Roman, it might be legendary or veracious, but except for the better educated in the audience — the smaller portion surely — there would be no distinction between the veracious and the legendary. The only distinction made by the audience would be between the plays that treat of British history and those that treat the history of some other nation. How far can we be sure, then, that the public

---

[1] *Timon, Pericles, Troilus and Cressida, Measure for Measure,* and *All's Well That Ends Well* are excluded because probable collaboration in the first three, possible collaboration in the fourth, and the partial remaking in the fifth, make them more confusing than helpful in such a discussion as this.

THE HARVARD ELIZABETHAN STAGE, WITH THE CURTAINS DRAWN

in general when they first came to see these so-called tragedies expected anything different from what they had already seen in the tragic chronicle plays of Shakespeare? Remember that the play which preceded the Third Part of *Henry VI* was not, like *Henry VI*, called a chronicle play, but *The True Tragedy of Richard Duke of York*. Remember, too, that plays we now call tragedies, which were even so ranked in the folio of 1623, were not always so characterized when they first appeared. The title-page of *King Lear*, for instance, in the first quarto reads: "M. William Shakespeare, his true Chronicle History, with the life and death of King Lear and his Two Daughters." That is, till after 1608–1610, at least, there was no accurately differentiated use of the words *tragedy* and *chronicle play*, and there seems to have been no popular appreciation of the difference between tragedy and melodrama, for constantly we hear the Elizabethans speaking of plays as tragedies when they were merely forms of melodrama which verged on tragedy.[1] *Titus Andronicus* itself appears in the folio of 1623 among the tragedies. This, then, is the first point I want to emphasize: that it is doubtful whether the greater part of Shakespeare's audience, in seeing the tragedies I have

[1] See John Fletcher's wholly uncritical definition of comedy as a play ending pleasantly, and a tragedy as a play closing with deaths. Note, p. 223. Thomas Dekker, on the title-page of *Old Fortunatus*, which begins with the death of the titular figure, and ends with the death of Ampedo, describes it as a " pleasant comedie," because for the greater part its interest is light rather than serious.

in mind in this chapter, felt it was seeing anything whatever except specially interesting specimens of the chronicle plays which dealt not with English kings and nobles of relatively recent times, but of foreign lands or of a period so remote as almost to be mythical. That is, there was in the public mind of 1603–1608 no such sharp break as we feel between Shakespeare's chronicle plays and what posterity distinguishes as his tragedies. To my mind the great tragedies were for the public of their own day primarily not tragedies at all, but merely more masterly specimens of dramatic story-telling than the plays which had preceded them. I say "more masterly" in the sense used by the Elizabethan audience: they were better because they recounted in absorbing and final fashion stories involving both the most intense and the most subtle emotions.

Is not that just what we have a right to expect from Shakespeare after his development from *Love's Labour's Lost* to *Much Ado about Nothing?* Why should he feel, simply because he turned from comedy to serious work, that his public would be satisfied with less story than he provided in the crowded plots of *Much Ado* and *Twelfth Night?* Must it not have become one of the premises of whatever theory of dramatic art he may have evolved by 1600 that under ordinary stage conditions, spare whatever else he might, he could not for an Elizabethan audience spare story? Recall the pains he took to crowd it even into that performance for a special occasion, *A Midsummer Night's Dream.* Could

[262]

one think of denying that these tragedies, one and all from *Julius Cæsar* to *Antony and Cleopatra*, are jammed with incident and, as we should now expect, with incident so related as to be worthy the name of plot? If story was not the chief interest of his audience in listening to plays, why was it that he lingered at the end of *Romeo and Juliet* to let the Friar tell the audience again just what it had already seen? That is much like the child who waters his lemonade when it gets low in the glass that he may prolong his pleasure. Note that also in *Lear*, not very far from the end, there is, technically speaking, a somewhat similar situation. Why should we have a scene in which Edgar tells Albany much that is already well known to us [1] unless Shakespeare felt that the public so loved story for its own sake that it would take great pleasure in seeing how all the unhappy strokes of fate seemed working to a happier ending.

For myself, I feel for two reasons sure that for the general public these tragedies were primarily dramatic stories rather than tragedies. In the first place, I believe this because, if the next time that a reader attends a Shakespearean performance he will sit, not in the orchestra or in the first balcony, but in the cheap seats where many people are getting their first or their early impressions of Shakespeare with no critical training and no historical background, he will find that what they are watching and what they are en-

[1] Act. V, Sc. 3, ll. 180–221.

joying is not the characterization of Hamlet, of Lear, of Macbeth, or Othello, but the stories in which these men are the central figures. To them these plays are transcripts from an older life, but transcripts, as Miss Elizabeth McCracken has shown in a delightful essay on *The Play and the Gallery*,[1] of large meaning for them. And this is true, not because they feel themselves to be possible Lears, Macbeths, or Hamlets, but because the situations and the incidents of the stories so grip their imaginations that they place themselves in them, deducing rules of conduct. Just here one cannot afford to forget what our return to the crude romantic fiction of these last ten years demonstrates; that the world in general finds its delight from fiction, not in character, but in story, not in coming to understand the character of him or her who did this or that, but in reading what was done. Can anything show this more clearly and finally than the romantic novel of to-day with characters who might easily be given type names, but which abounds in exciting incidents neatly woven into a compact plot. It is, broadly speaking, only the trained and critical part of an audience which thinks more of characterization than story. Relatively, too, how small that part is!

My second reason for believing that to the Elizabethan public these tragedies were merely specially absorbing story-telling is the way in which this idea helps to solve the problem many modern critics find

[1] *The Atlantic Monthly*, 89 : 497–507.

in Shakespeare's fourth act. These writers say that in *Julius Cæsar, Macbeth,* and *Antony and Cleopatra,* the fourth act seems to drag, clogging the movement of the play. As a result, there has been some inclination to formulate for Shakespeare a rule of technique which aimed to reach the strongest scene of the play at the end of Act III and to allow a subsidence of emotion in Act IV. First of all, one must remember that all this talk of acts and scenes in Shakespeare's plays rests on a very insecure basis. Though *Othello, Lear,* and *Macbeth* are in the Folio divided into scenes as well as acts, *Hamlet* is not divided at all beyond the second scene of the second act, and *Antony and Cleopatra* has no division except the first scene of the first act.

Any one who has worked much on quarto Elizabethan plays needs no proof that in many cases the scenes were first marked off when the manuscript was prepared for the printer. The very absence, so evident in Elizabethan plays, of the modern effort to get a strong climax at the end of the act as marked, strengthens one's doubt whether the dramatists of Shakespeare's time had at all the same idea of an act that we have to-day. For them it was probably more a period of time than a literary unit. When it is easy to divide one of their plays into acts according to modern ideas, that is much more probably the result of their recognition of permanent laws governing dramatic exposition within the space of two and a half hours than because they had our notion of an act. Before we try to formulate Shakespeare's weakness, according to present-day standards, in the fourth act of *Macbeth* and *Julius Cæsar* into a conscious method, we must remember this fact and another.

Critics seem sometimes to forget for the moment that in the tragedies, from *Julius Cæsar* to *Antony and Cleopatra*, Shakespeare was creating modern English tragedy, and that since he grew in all the other forms he attempted, he was probably not perfect in this at the start. We expect to-day to get up to our strongest situation in the fourth act, working out the dénouement in the fifth, or even, if we are very skilful, to hold our strongest complication for the fifth act, thereafter unravelling our plot with the utmost rapidity till the final curtain. We, however, are not path-breakers; we tread a well-beaten road, — indeed, a region so well mapped that we may choose the way by which we will travel it. Shakespeare transformed a path which was nothing more than Marlowe's connecting of chance openings in the woods into a clearly marked way; he made melodrama and chronicle play into tragedy. But surely any man who creates does it through effort, experimentation, and even failure. Shakespeare comes up to a strong situation at the end or near the end of what we usually call his third act, and there faces an absolute necessity of dramatic composition. He must set working at once the causes and conditions which are to bring about the dénouement in the fifth act. In *Hamlet, Lear,* and *Macbeth* his fourth act serves just this purpose. The ideal work, technically, is that which we find in *Othello.* Here, even as we reach a high point of interest in the third act, we pass on immediately in the fourth act to more striking scenes, which in turn lead to the fifth act. But if a dramatist has not gained complete control of the technique of a difficult form, tragedy, particularly in treating subjects far more difficult than those attempted by any of his contemporaries, of course his fourth act may seem to drag for him who cares more for characterization than for story, and who applies the standards of modern drama. In *Othello* it is true that we pass instantly from the handkerchief complication at the end of the third act to the development of that complication in the fourth act. That is just why the play seems so swift, so climactic, in a word so modern in its treatment. It should be noted, however, that *Othello,* like most modern tragedies, has a single plot and but one group of figures. That resemblance is significant.

If a dramatist's plot, as was the case in most of Shakespeare's tragedies, is woven of many strands, and he has just brought the story of Lear or Hamlet to a fine climax in Act III, he must necessarily give immediate attention in Act IV to Ophelia or to Edmund and Edgar. It is much easier to get climax, a swift and unbroken movement, in manipulating a plot of a single interest than with a complicated plot. Moreover, urged on by the demand of our public for such movement, we have studied the art of swift, climactic exposition. Had Shakespeare's audience cared, above all else, for the characterization of Macbeth, they would have found the fourth act poor; but caring primarily for the complicated story, they found it far from dull.

My own feeling is that common sense as applied to this matter of third act and fourth act in Shakespeare will show that he had no rule for reaching his strongest scene in Act III and no scheme for allowing a subsidence of emotion in Act IV, but that he produced in *Julius Cæsar* a fourth act probably not entirely successful even in its own day; in *Macbeth* a fourth act certainly unsatisfactory to-day, but in 1600–1610 as effective as, I am sure, were the fourth acts of *Lear*, *Hamlet*, and *Antony and Cleopatra;* and in *Othello* wrote a fourth act perfect for all time.

First of all, let us make sure whether our approach to these tragedies is that of the Elizabethans. Have we not grown used to seeing some distinguished actor or actress emphasize a particular character in one of them with such interpretative art that the play henceforth stands in our minds as first of all a great study in human passion or desire? That surely is what has made Professor Bradley, the most interesting of our recent writers on Shakespeare's dramatic art, say: "One reason why the end of *The Merchant of Venice* fails to satisfy us is that Shylock is a tragic character and that we cannot believe in his accepting his defeat and the conditions imposed on him. This was a case where Shakespeare's imagination ran away with him, so that he drew a figure with which the destined pleasant ending would not harmonize." Could anything mark more clearly a judgment affected by such presentation of Shylock as Sir Henry Irving's? Shakespeare run away with in a play plotted with the utmost ingenuity and skill, a play in which the salacious, permeating in the original, is painstakingly excluded! Surely not.

Suppose one's interest in *The Merchant of Venice* chances to be quite as much in the love-story of Bassanio and Portia as in Shylock, would one then worry about Shylock after his defeat? I have shown that it is just this love-story which Shakespeare makes the unifying thread for the play. I purposely classed *The Merchant of Venice* with the plays of story, for I believe it to have been written not as the play of Antonio, of Shylock, of Portia, or of any individual in its list of characters, but as a very dramatic love-story made possible by the unstinted friendship of a merchant of Venice. Surely so skilled a playwright did not name his plays idly.

Apply this idea that the tragedies were to the Elizabethans primarily stories on the stage, not above all else characterization, to the often-heard criticism that Shakespeare reaches his real climax in the third act, letting interest fall off in the fourth, or only keeping it steady till the fifth act. Even those who make this criticism admit that the interest does increase in *Othello*, and it is hard to see how they can effectively attack the fourth act of *Lear* with its madness of Lear and the reunion with Cordelia. They point out, however, that in the fourth act of *Hamlet* the Prince is absent during the greater part, only appearing in one or two brief early scenes, in which he baffles those who would talk to him of the murder of Polonius and makes clear that he is leaving for England. The greater part of the act is given to the madness of Ophelia. These critics say, also, that the fourth act of *Julius Cæsar* is made up of three scenes which, though interesting in themselves, give a broken effect to the act and are in decided contrast to the excitement at the close of Act III, when the people are crying, under the stimulus of Antony's speech, for revenge on the murderers of Cæsar. No one, certainly, in reading the fourth act of *Antony and Cleopatra*, can fail to see the scrappiness of the fifteen scenes which make it; and in *Macbeth* it is quite true that in the fourth act Macbeth appears only in the scene of the second interview with the witches, and rather as a part of the scene than dominating it. The rest of the act is given up to the murder of Lady Macduff and her child and the interview in England between Malcolm and Macduff. After the powerful scene of Macbeth and the ghost of Banquo, near the end of Act III, this act does seem tame. But let us approach these plays in a different

Two Title-pages of Academic Plays showing their Stages

(The Centre print, of the hall at Hampton Court, shows that the end of the hall could easily be made to duplicate the stage of *Messalina*.)

mood. First of all, we are Elizabethans seeing them on a stage which allows the scenes to follow one another almost instantly. They have not, therefore, the effect of detached and separate pictures, but rather, instantly following one another, make us, as in *Antony and Cleopatra*, swiftly understand, as we watch Antony under many different conditions, his gnawing shame for his cowardice at Actium, or give us speedily and vividly bits of information which we must comprehend if the events of the fifth act are to be clear to us. Remember, too, that for the audience these plays are still chronicle plays, and to it the chronicle play, even in *Henry IV*, apart from the comic figures, meant incidents of historic truth or approximate truth related, if at all, by some one figure passing through most of them and affecting, or affected by, the others.

What makes that fourth act of *Julius Cæsar* ineffective to-day, is what may have made it ineffective in its own day, that just when we have been wrought up to the keenest interest in what the mob will do to the murderers of Cæsar, we are asked to let that pass for good and all. Instead, we are given two short scenes which merely prepare for the fighting in the fifth act, and a long scene of the quarrel between Cassius and Brutus, delightful in itself, but purely episodic. It does bring out the sensitiveness and the underlying sweetness of Brutus, it does count in characterization; but it does not move the story toward its close, make a dramatic climax after Act III, or in any way fulfil the exciting promises of that third act. The fact is, of course, that from the moment the fourth act begins, the play lacks the unifying influence of Cæsar, and we are forced to make one of those awkward changes of interest midway in a play which are usually fatal to any unity of effect. For whether we like Cæsar or not, the first three acts tell his story rather than that of Brutus, and the last three acts belong to Brutus more than to any other character.

In *Macbeth* to-day we greatly miss the central figure in two of the three scenes of the fourth act, for it has become for us primarily a play of character. Moreover, in the second meeting with the witches, hearing again what we think we heard more effectively earlier, we feel as if the play, midway, were starting over again. But call *Macbeth*, not a study in character or in two characters, not a tragedy showing the deteriorating effect of crime and the retribution that inevitably follows, but the "Story of Macbeth," as *Richard II* and *King John* were the stories of those kings, and it is clear that, of course, the fourth act must treat the second interview with the witches, the murder of the child of Macduff, and the scene between Macduff and Malcolm. Those incidents were in the old chronicle; they were essential parts of the story of Macbeth. Why leave them out any more than certain of the main incidents in the story of *Richard II, Henry VI,* or *Henry VIII?* Consider, however, the bearing on this question of the suspicion that back of some of these plays lay other plays on the same subjects. In that case there were two good reasons why Shakespeare should embody in his work some scenes that we to-day in a character-study, but not in a play primarily of story, might omit or subordinate: namely, that the audience had liked those scenes in the past; and above all, because, as Professor Campbell has well said, "Whatever is believed to have happened, however strange, is accepted as possible." To the less-trained Elizabethan mind, to have seen something acted in a play called a chronicle play was equivalent to attestation of its truth. They had duly inherited the attitude of the priest in Warwickshire generations before, who, preaching on the articles of the creed, said to his congregation, feeling sure that the performances by guilds at Coventry of a play on the creed were well known to his audience, "These articles ye be bound to believe, for they be true and of authority, and if you believe not me, then for the more surety and sufficient authority go your ways to Coventry, and there ye shall see them all played in Corpus Christi Plays." Considering some of the improbabilities in *Hamlet*, *Macbeth*, and *Lear*, one understands that inevitably parts of these earlier dramatic presentations must be seen in any revision or fresh dramatization of the story. It is again the situation Shakespeare faced in making over the two Titus stories. No matter how scrappy the fourth acts of *Macbeth* and *Julius Cæsar*, can we deny their theatrical effectiveness for an uncritical audience or their value as illustrative material — the murder of Lady Macduff, the second meeting of Macbeth with the witches, the quarrel between Brutus and Cassius? Certainly not. And what for an Elizabethan audience was true of the fourth act of *Macbeth*, must have been true of the fourth act in *Lear* and *Hamlet;* that is, an Elizabethan audience, as long as in the space of two hours and a half an interesting story revealed itself in interesting scenes, did not prefer characterization to incident, did not bother itself at all about act divisions, and worried neither itself nor the dramatist over climactic movement, but was content to let the story double back on itself or even offer an excursus if the dramatist so willed. But be the scene essential or an excursus, it must be interesting.

My own belief is, that certainly not till Shakespeare had written most of his tragedies, did he have any theory of tragedy whatever, but rather that his tragedies are a perfectly natural and normal development from the serious side of the chronicle plays, just as we have seen that his high comedies were a normal development from the work of Lyly on the one hand, and on the other the chronicle plays on their lighter side. In the first place, to-day, how much thinking about theories of tragedy do dramatists busy themselves with before they write? They see or hear something which suggests a plot to them, and they fall to working, reworking, and moulding it for presentation on a stage they know to a public they understand. For them their work resolves itself into problems of characterization, of structure, and, perhaps, of interesting presentation to their well-known audience of essentially undramatic states of mind. Now and again, as they face this or that problem, they may get a suggestion from the practice of Shakespeare or somebody else in the past, but they are not guided in their work by definitely formulated theories of tragedy. Entering their situations through their characters, or discerning clearly the characters essential to the situations originally in mind, the best dramatists are unsatisfied till they understand these characters, not only within the scene, but as developing or disintegrating from the beginning to the end of the play. Moreover, they are unsatisfied till they know, at least, the chief characters in their relations to the other people of the play. Given all that grasp of character, and it is hard, at least, not to stumble on some underlying law of conduct. Stumbled upon, it forthwith unifies the hitherto seemingly scattered tragic incident into tragedy. This statement is, I believe, borne out by the fact that the play, before 1600, in which Shakespeare goes deepest into life on its serious side, is, except in one detail, perfect tragedy. I mean, of course, *Romeo and Juliet*. At the moment when it is necessary that Romeo shall have news that Juliet is waiting for him in the tomb of her fathers, the swift, relentless logic of the play breaks down. Thus far everything that has happened has been an inevitable consequence of a secret marriage between the son and the daughter of two houses at deadly feud. Grant Tybalt's state of mind when Romeo and Juliet first meet, and that first meeting must sooner or later lead to bloodshed and tragic consequences. We have seen, too, how carefully Shakespeare has motivated Romeo's relation to the killing of Tybalt so that his banishment, granted the earlier scenes, comes as something well-nigh inevitable. But what is it which prevents Romeo from getting the news that his wife is merely stupefied, not dead? Merely a device of the dramatist; there is no inevitableness in this whatever. Friar John, sent to Mantua with the letter from Friar Laurence, seeks a fellow-monk as companion, only to find himself in a plague-stricken house, whence the authorities will not allow him to come out till Romeo, warned by his servant, Balthasar, of the death of Juliet, has returned to Verona to die. That turn in the play is at the will of the dramatist, is melodrama, and it breaks the chain of circumstance necessary for perfect tragedy. Grant that, as Professor Bradley skilfully argues, such blind strokes of chance do occur, is it not likely that had Shakespeare been developing his material in accord with any theory of tragedy, he would have seen to it that the march of events was as thoroughly motivated here as elsewhere in his work of the same date? Conceive that, entirely unthinking of tragedy as anything but a serious play ending in death, he was absorbed in depicting with perfect understanding the figures he found in his original, and in setting them in a dramatic version of compelling interest, and it is clear that the flaw in the logic of events occasioned by the detail as to Friar John would not give him a moment's pause.

Surely by 1600, when Shakespeare had gone farther than any of his contemporaries in farce comedy and high comedy, and fully as far in chronicle history and melodrama, he must have felt free simply to give himself to his desire to understand complicated human nature in intense situations and to working out the problems of dramatic presentation it offered. That is exactly what I believe he did, given either by the mere process of maturing with the years a deeper insight into human nature or sobered and matured by circumstances in his own life or about him. After all, there was no real break between his chronicle plays, strictly speaking, and his tragedies. The two parts of *Henry IV* belong in 1597 and 1598, the making over of *Henry V* falls in 1599, and *Julius Cæsar* belongs in 1600 or 1601. We have had evidence that even as the chronicle plays developed, Shakespeare's interest in prince or noble as human being had come to supersede his interest in him as king or ruler. Harry Hotspur is after all, next to Falstaff, the sympathetic figure in the First Part of *Henry IV*, and the scenes in which he is best depicted show him least as the historical figure, most as the man. After all, have we not here the real underlying difference between the tragedies

[277]

and the chronicle plays? It would have been possible, of course, to write a play on the reign of Lear; Shakespeare chose to make his whole play turn on what happened after the abdication of power. It is as if in *Richard II* he began the play just as Richard resigns his crown to Bolingbroke, and then act by act showed the many humiliations for Richard resulting therefrom. In the tragedies the dramatist has broken away from history as history, and uses it even as he would the common experience of everyday life in the comedy of manners, simply as so much illustrative material by which to make clear the character he is expounding. That is, in the tragedies, history past and present, facts and fiction, have all been fused for Shakespeare into possible material for studies of character, and what he is interested in is expounding circumstance in terms of character. I am almost willing to say that had any Elizabethan asked him what his tragedies meant, he would have phrased his answer in something equivalent to this, "To expound circumstance in terms of character." Nor is he any longer connecting his scenes merely by the fact that some one figure moves through them, produces them, or is affected by them; but character has become the prime subject of study. So far as the insistent demand of his public for story will permit, his scenes are but carefully chosen mirrors, indices, of character. Perceiving certain truths of conduct behind individuals in fictitious or historical circumstance, he sets himself

to recreate for us the person whom he sees so that the
meaning he has for Shakespeare shall be equally clear
for us. That is, the audience was interested in story;
Shakespeare had become primarily interested in character; and just in that contrast lay the chief technical
problem he must solve in the composition of his tragedies. Character is most easily expounded by analysis,
description, and monologue, but not even the Elizabethans would stand page after page of monologue.
Description must be sparingly used, and the audience
must see not the analysis, but rather in action the results of it. That is, the characterization must be set
in an illustrative story of strong dramatic action. Indeed, this group of tragedies shows Shakespeare's
gradual attainment of the power successfully to serve
two masters at once. By crowding his plays with story,
he strove to keep his audience attentive even as his
scenes developed states of mind in some central figure
or figures. And those states of mind he pictured by
action.

Once more, also, as in the high comedies, he makes
in the same play more than one appeal to his public.
In these tragedies if we want story, here it is; if we
want characterization, we find it; nor do we find un-
relieved tragedy, but tragedy is lightened by comic
contrast; and if we seek poetic beauty, the plays are
rich in it. He who wishes to know how a dramatist
may write what he wants and at the same time provide
what is sure to hold the public attentive should study

these tragedies. In them an analysis of character so minute that it tends to become undramatic is set in story so full of illustrative incident that the public of Shakespeare's day, as I have already said, probably considered these plays perfect pieces of story-telling. That we do not find some of them, such as *Julius Cæsar* and *Macbeth*, wholly flawless does not prove that they are failures, but merely, in *Julius Cæsar*, that no difficult task is usually accomplished at the first attempt, and, in *Macbeth*, that to-day the more critical are so much more interested in character than story as to resent the presence of certain scenes which, while they round out the story, distract attention from the central figure. The difference means that had Shakespeare written for the more critical of our public to-day he would have had a much easier task than the Elizabethans allowed him in working out the characterization which primarily interested him.

Nor does it seem to me likely that Shakespeare ever evolved any detailed theory of tragedy. After all, the most richly creative minds leave the formulation of their practice to the men who glean after them. It is certainly curious that repeated efforts to phrase such a theory for Shakespeare seem to have been futile. They point, for instance, to the fact that all these tragedies deal with people of high estate, that they all involve a clash of wills of some kind, or that it is questionable whether any idea of morality entered into Shakespeare's tragic purpose. But all that does not

An "Elizabethan Stage," which shows an effect gained from a "painted cloth" in the upper stage.

really differentiate Shakespeare. The first clause is axiomatic for all except the most modern tragedy; the second is but one of the broadest of the definitions of tragedy; the third simply raises the eternal question whether art may or must be moral. When any attempt is made to distinguish between Shakespearean tragedy and the tragedy of the Greeks, one finds critics indulging in large generalizations or shading off into vagueness. The fact is, in a sense *Macbeth* is Greek, if what we mean by Greek is saying that tragedy is the fulfilling, struggle though the individual may, of a blind fate. For does not the whole tragedy of *Macbeth* depend upon the fact that the messages of the witches fulfil themselves relentlessly in spite of all the scheming and the crime with which Macbeth tries either to thwart them or to force on them his own interpretation? Surely Macbeth is not exactly our present-day idea of tragedy. On the other hand, it is the struggle between a man's temperament and his environment which one sees in *Hamlet*. Possibly that classifies *Lear*. But can we perfectly place *Julius Cæsar* as a tragedy of fate or of the struggle between the individual and his environment? Brutus perhaps shows the latter, not Cæsar. The chief interest of the play seems to me, apart from its admirable characterization, that it shows the chronicle play resolving itself into tragedy by means of emphasis on the essentially human side of the characters involved. Is it easy to find in the early part of the play the tragic causes which render necessary all the later catastrophes? Is it not a play unlike either *Richard III* or *Henry V* on the one hand, since Julius Cæsar dies in the third act and Brutus by no means dominates all the acts, and on the other, unlike *Hamlet* or even *Antony and Cleopatra*, which after all, so far as the dramatist is concerned, primarily exist to show and explain the moods of a main figure? Is it not true that in the loose coördinating of its scenes, all of which are, however, illustrative of the conspiracy against Cæsar, its rise, its height, and its failure, we look back to the earliest forms of the chronicle play, even as in such episodic scenes as the quarrel between Brutus and Cassius we foreshadow the subtle characterization of the later tragedies? It is a natural and an easy transition for the public to tragedy from the chronicle play. But just how are *Lear, Othello,* and *Antony and Cleopatra* to be classed? In these is no blind edict of fate working itself out, as was the case in *Macbeth;* nor is one quite content to say that each is a struggle between a man's temperament and his environment. For tragedy in the sense in which we have been using it, the disastrous results in Othello should come because we see in action the truth of the warning of the father of Desdemona to Othello, "She has deceived her father and may thee." But Desdemona is innocent enough, and the marriage would not have resulted badly had there been no Iago. The tragedy here arises not from a temperament struggling against its environment or against a blind decree of fate, but in a struggle of temperaments. Were there no Iago to plot and plan and lie, whence would come the tragedy in *Othello?* Were there no Goneril and Regan, where would be the tragedy of *Lear?* And the whole tragedy of *Antony and Cleopatra* lies in the completeness of Cleopatra's benumbing control over Antony. But is all this more than saying that Shakespeare discovered all the sources of tragic story rather than assumed or insisted that all tragedy flows from one fountain head? Tragedy involves a struggle, a clash of wills. We may have the human being in clash and conflict with the consequences of some event in which he had no part and for which he was in no way responsible. The Greeks called that fate; we call that the tragedy of heredity. The individual may be in conflict with the will of the community; that is what we have in Ibsen's *Enemy of the People.* The individual may be torn by the conflict of his own emotions, the warring within himself of idealism and brutishness; or, he may be partly torn by this and partly by the clash between his own desires and the will of the community. We see both in *Hamlet.* Or the conflict may come between two temperaments which cannot be brought together without baleful influences for one or both. That we have in *Antony and Cleopatra* and *Othello.* Beyond these I know no source for tragedy. In other words, Shakespeare's use of tragic material is inclusive, as might be the case with a man who does not start with a definite theory of tragedy and thus develop one source only. Deeply and sympathetically interested in human nature and increasingly attracted by the alluring problems in characterization which tragic material offered, Shakespeare devoted himself for a series of years to presenting whatever tragic story offered him a particularly subtle and consequently attractive problem in characterization. Naturally he used now this source of tragedy, now that, till he exhausted all.

Is it likely, when the problems raised are so different, the sources of tragedy used so contrasted, that it will be possible to formulate a satisfactory theory of Shakespearean tragedy? I think not. I doubt if it troubled Shakespeare at all whether his public heard of these plays as tragedies, chronicle plays, or merely as plays. What interested him was that the plays should keep his audience so attentive from start to finish by a story full of interesting incident that the character-study he wished to make could clearly and convincingly reveal itself. Each new play was to him a fresh problem to be separately conquered, though of course every preceding conquest made his judgment surer and his hand firmer. Into the characterization he put all that experience and sympathy had given him in knowledge of the human heart and all the philosophy his observation of life had brought him. He clothed his plays, too, in poetry of constantly increasing compactness, connotativeness, and beauty. That by which, above all, he made his plays carry for the great general public was what in *Love's Labour's Lost* and *The Two Gentlemen of Verona* he did not at all understand; what he failed to attain in the pure chronicle play as long as he was hampered by his sense of fact; but what he depended on in his high comedies, namely, plot. Through this deft plotting he was able to present to the public of 1601–1608 plays that, so far as genuine tragedy is concerned, used all its sources. All, too, he used successfully. Since his day, tragedy has but used the same sources, fitting its material to its special audience and stage conditions. Shakespeare is the first modern master of tragedy.

CHAPTER VIII

LATE EXPERIMENTATION

THE high comedies and the tragedies of Shakespeare give us in perfect union, story, characterization, and poetry of phrase and informing spirit.
This perfection of accomplishment, we have seen,
rests on minute care for the technique of the drama,
and in turn this care for technique was called into
being by Shakespeare's desire to fulfil at one and
the same time his own wishes as to characterization
and the wish of the audience for story. These facts
must not be forgotten in any consideration of *Coriolanus*, usually assigned to 1609; *Cymbeline*, generally
assigned to 1609–1611; *The Winter's Tale*, 1610–1611;
and *The Tempest*, 1611. In considering these plays
in relation to their immediate predecessors, one is
constantly puzzled, and sometimes fairly baffled, by
the differences.

What was the mood, for instance, in which *Coriolanus* was written? I might have emphasized earlier,
had space permitted, the increasing compactness
between 1598 and 1608 of Shakespeare's expression,
but why should a man as thoughtful as he heretofore
of his audience, so far forget it in this play as often

to write without lucidity and in phrases extremely difficult to deliver? Dialogue for the stage, as Mrs. Craigie has pointed out in the preface to *The Ambassador*, must always "show consideration for the speaking voice." It matters not if the speech have imagination, interest, charm; it is not dramatically perfect unless it be emotional rather than intellectual. Now who could have known this better than the Shakespeare of the high comedies and the great tragedies? Yet, listen to this from Menenius telling to the rabble the fable of the belly and the other members.

> I will tell you,
> If you'll bestow a small (of what you have little)
> Patience awhile, you'll hear the bellies answer.

Or why does Coriolanus, who at times is so simple as to be final in phrase, utter such Browningesque lines as the fourth and the fifth of the following?

> Let them pull all about mine ears: present me
> Death on the wheel, or at wild horses' heels;
> Or pile ten hills on the Tarpeian rock,
> That the precipitation might down stretch
> Below the beam of sight, yet will I still
> Be thus to them.

It is in this same play, too, that Shakespeare clouds a dramatic effect by a phrase perfect in characterization. Coriolanus (I, 9) has just returned to the main army after his successful entrance into Corioli. Wearied with the heat of battle, impatient of the praises of all about him, he has only one request to make, — that a poor man of the town who used him kindly may not be kept prisoner. One expects the scene to end, as for mere dramatic effectiveness it should, with the naming of his benefactor by Coriolanus and the exit of some messenger to release the captive. Coriolanus says:

> I that now
> Refused most princely gifts, am bound to beg
> Of my lord general.
>   *Cominius.*   Take it: 'tis yours. — What is it?
>   *Coriolanus.* I sometime lay, here in Corioli,
> At a poor man's house; he us'd me kindly:
> He cried to me: I saw him prisoner;
> But then Aufidius was within my view,
> And wrath o'erwhelm'd my pity. I request you
> To give my poor host freedom.
>   *Com.*   O, well begg'd.
> Were he the butcher of my son, he should
> Be free as is the wind. Deliver him, Titus.
>   *Lartius.* Marcius, his name?
>   *Cor.*   By Jupiter, forgot: —
> I am weary; yea, my memory is tir'd.—
> Have we no wine here?
>   *Com.*   Go we to our tent.
> The blood upon your visage dries; 'tis time
> It should be look'd to. Come.

How perfectly that "By Jupiter, forgot" conveys the complete physical weariness of the man, how admirable it is as a close in a scene of characterization, but how completely it lets down the action of the scene. Here, for the moment, Shakespeare's steadily increasing interest in characterization becomes so absorbing as to make him forget that for the bulk of his audience the action of his scene was still of prime importance. The appeal of Volumnia to Coriolanus which turns him from his proposed attack on Rome is supposed in the play to have a persuasive power which many a reader or auditor has not recognized. Yet this failure of a speech or scene to produce just the effect with which it is accredited by the dramatist is most unusual in the later work of Shakespeare. The tendency, too, of the main characters to indulge in long speeches is also noteworthy, for that tendency has been decreasing as Shakespeare's work matured. It is striking, also, that in this play the dramatist's imagination seems more restrained than is usual with him; many of the best speeches, for instance, that of Coriolanus offering his services to Aufidius (IV, 5) and the yielding of Coriolanus to the appeal of Volumnia (V, 3) in the scene just referred to, repeat Plutarch, Shakespeare's source, almost word for word. In sharp contrast to all this, however, the original material has in places been rearranged for greater dramatic effect, and the play lacks neither scenes of power nor passages of deep insight into character. Nor is it possible to say that this contradictoriness of effect results from some hasty revision, careful in places and neglectful in others, for faults and merits alike are part of the very texture of the play.

Indeed, is not the effect of *Coriolanus* in itself dubious? Here is a story as single in its interest as that of *Romeo and Juliet* or *Othello;* all interest concentres on Coriolanus. What is he? A man who reveals at our first sight of him an intense pride of rank and an almost uncontrollable temper. And what else for some three acts does the play tell us with marked emphasis, except that he is a courageous and splendid fighter? When, too, because unable to control his temper, he has unwittingly lent himself to the machinations of Sicinius and Brutus and has been banished, does he bide his time till the large party of friends he has in Rome can bring him back? Not at all. Strive to palliate his conduct as we may, he is at heart the basest of human creatures, a man ready to sell his country from the mere desire for personal revenge. What controls him, too, at the crises in his life — first, when he must return to beg pardon from the people for his insults, and, secondly, when he is asked to withdraw his troops from before Rome? Merely personal affection for his wife and mother. He is no architect of his own fortunes, no ruler of his own fate, and one does not feel any large measure of sorrow when he is struck down by the angry Volscians whose confidence he certainly has betrayed. He never rises above the immediate emotion. What curious material for the hero of a play, — for he is the hero in the sense that he is the central figure. He has none of the elements of popular appeal of *Henry V*, or even of *Richard III*. He is that poorest of human products, a creature so uncontrolled and with so little knowledge of his real self that he has not the strength to be mainly good or mainly bad. Contrast his popular appeal with that of the other two plays of single story. *Romeo and Juliet* has two exceedingly attractive central figures, and their story and their emotions are the most permanently interesting for the public of any which exist. Who is there who cannot somewhat enter into sympathetic understanding of Othello? Surely jealousy, which this strongly attractive central figure feels, was no exclusive possession of the Elizabethans. But *Coriolanus* is a tragedy of pride of birth. Under any conditions it must appeal to only a small portion of the audience. It would seem that Shakespeare must have realized this was just the story which needed contrasting strands of interest if it were to be carried to popular success. Yet he did not supply them. Or was he experimenting, trying to see what could be done for his public with a figure which he knew for them was essentially uninteresting?

Perhaps we shall have more light on this play if we look at the other three plays of the final group. Is it not a little curious that, after writing mainly tragedies from 1601 to 1608, Shakespeare, between 1608 and his retirement from the stage in 1611, should write chiefly plays of a highly romantic order? The possible exception, *Henry VIII*, is a chronicle play of the old-fashioned type. Why this reversion to an earlier mood? The cause is, I believe, very commonplace, but effective. About 1608 the English public evidently experienced one of those revulsions from dramatic scrutiny of the graver or grimmer sides of life such as the public knows periodically.[1] Ten years ago, for instance, we were flooded with plays that held up for our scrutiny the sadder and the seamier sides of life. As a public we forced these plays off the stage by our delight in the mere romantic story-telling that came in among the novels and by our satisfaction with the adaptations promptly made from these novels. I can remember when the New York managers declared it not worth while to read a manuscript of a play adapted from a novel. Who brought the change ten years ago? You, reader, and I, and the many others who make the hydra-headed composite called the public; because when somebody risked publishing some very romantic stories of adventure, we bought them by tens of thousands and so led somebody else to risk presenta-tion of one of these stories as a play. Then we flocked so greedily to see this play that the deluge of bad adaptation of poor fiction which has followed was let loose. It is certainly a very striking fact that not only did Beaumont and Fletcher, about 1608 or 1609,

---

[1] For the probable work of Beaumont and Fletcher in fostering this change see *The Influence of Beaumont and Fletcher on Shake-speare*, A. H. Thorndike (1901).

come into prominence writing plays of an intensely romantic order, but that just as Shakespeare shifted from his tragedies to romantic comedy, Thomas Middleton shifted from realistic studies, in the comedy of manners, of the seamy side of London life, to very romantic stories. It is perhaps, worth noting, too, that that other arch-realist, Ben Jonson, left playwriting in 1614 for a long term of years, during which he was working upon masks only. It looks very much as if we faced another illustration of the fact that no dramatist, however great, can produce wholly out of relation to his audience. What makes it seem, perhaps, even more likely that Shakespeare's change was not wholly free, is that these later comedies have an underlying gravity of tone far different from the three great comedies considered in Chapter VI. He does not really change: like the perfect host, he merely tries to subdue his mood to that of his guests.

Yet detail after detail in these late plays show that he was not as flexible nor as sympathetic with the moods of his audience as heretofore. For instance, compare his treatment of the story of Imogen in *Cymbeline* [1] with the handling of the story of Clau-

---

[1] It is, perhaps, worth noting, as bearing on what was said in Chapter VII about the way in which fact and fiction, history and legend, had all become for Shakespeare by 1602 simply so much raw material from which a careful study of character might be made, that this very interesting play is about equally compounded of parts from *Holinshed*, the chronicler, and a tale which appears, in one form, as the ninth novel of the second day in Boccaccio's *Decameron*.

dio and Hero in *Much Ado about Nothing*. In *Cymbeline* the story which might easily have become a tragedy holds the central place, and the best characterization goes into the figures who make it. Study the emphasis in *Much Ado about Nothing* and it is clear that the Hero and Claudio story is steadily subordinated to the scenes which make for entertainment and amusement and that its figures are the most lightly characterized of all. Moreover, note that in *Much Ado about Nothing* the audience is carefully kept so informed that even while the people on the stage suffer for the wronged Hero, the audience knows that Hero will be righted. In the story of Posthumus and Imogen the audience is, till the last scene, by no means so sure of the ending. Notice, also, the break in the middle of *Cymbeline*. We hear early of the disappearance of the two sons of the king, but we never see them until the third scene of the third act. The fact is, of course, that we have in a sense reached the climax of the Posthumus-Imogen story at the end of Act II, when the former discovers, as he thinks, Imogen's unfaithfulness. We shift in this third act our interest somewhat, or at least we divide it between Imogen and the group of dwellers in the cave, even as, more markedly, midway in *The Winter's Tale*, we drop the story of Hermione and Leontes and take up the story of Florizel and Perdita. Yet so interestingly is the transition made in *Cymbeline* that, as one reads, it is usually passed unnoticed. Seeing the play, one is conscious of a diffusion of interest in the last three acts as contrasted with the singleness of purpose in Acts I and II.

Cymbeline is, however, noteworthy among these late plays as showing both that even at the end of his career Shakespeare held, in spite of *Coriolanus*, to the principle that story is of prime importance in dramatic composition, and also that if he wished, he could work even at this late day with the greatest possible deftness. No student of dramatic composition who is struggling to bring a play of many strands to a perfect close should fail to study very carefully the relation of the last scene of all in *Cymbeline* to the whole play. As Professor Wendell has pointed out,[1] there are some twenty-four distinct situations in the dénouement clearly and effectively developed to an interesting close in which everybody has been accounted for. This is as it should be in any straightforward story-telling for the stage.

There has been, of course, endless discussion as to the real purpose of Shakespeare in writing *The Tempest*. Did he, or did he not, have some subtle meaning in Caliban and his other figures? Is the play an allegory of life? Such attempts to give the play a deeper meaning than have the other plays are natural enough. How could a man of nearly fifty who for more than twenty years had been searching the hearts of men and presenting to the public the results of his scrutiny, fail to think deeply on

[1] *William Shakespeare*, Barrett Wendell, pp. 358–361.

[295]

human life? How could he help letting something of his thought find expression in the figures of his late plays even if the prevailing purpose was that of the mere story-teller? Such momentary glimpses of the wider vision of the dramatist are nearly inevitable in the late work of almost any matured dramatist of power, but they do not necessarily mean either a cryptogram or a theory of philosophy. The very simple immediate conditions from which *The Tempest* grew Mr. Sidney Lee has well stated: —

"In the summer of 1609 a fleet bound for Virginia, under the command of Sir George Somers, was overtaken by a storm off the West Indies and the admiral's ship, the 'Sea-Venture,' was driven on the coast of the hitherto unknown Bermuda Isles. There they remained ten months, pleasurably impressed by the mild beauty of the climate, but sorely tried by the hogs which overran the island and *by mysterious noises which led them to imagine that spirits and devils had made the island their home.* Somers and his men were given up for lost, but they escaped from Bermuda in two boats of cedar to Virginia in May, 1610. The sailors' arrival created vast public excitement in London. At least five accounts were soon published of the shipwreck and of the mysterious island, previously uninhabited by man, which had proved the salvation of the expedition. 'A Discovery of the Bermudas,' otherwise called the 'Ile of Divels,' written by Sylvester Jourdain or Jourdan, one of the survivors, appeared as early as October. A second pamphlet describing the disaster was issued by the Council of the Virginia Company in December, and a third by one of the leaders of the expedition, Sir Thomas Gates. Shakespeare, who mentions the 'still vexed Bermoothes' (I, 1, 229), incorporated in 'The Tempest' many hints from Jourdain, Gates, and the other pamphleteers. The references to the gentle climate of the island on which Prospero is cast away, and to the spirits and devils that infested it, seem to render its identification with the newly discovered Bermudas unquestionable. But Shakespeare incorporated the result of study of other books of travel. The name of the god Setebos whom Caliban worships is drawn from Eden's translation of Magellan's 'Voyage to the South Pole' (in the 'Historie of Travell,' 1577), where the giants of Patagonia are described as worshipping a 'great devil they call Setebos.' No source for the complete plot has been discovered, but the German writer, Jacob Ayrer, who died in 1605, dramatized a somewhat similar story in 'Die Schöne Sidea,' where the adventures of Prospero, Ferdinand, Ariel, and Miranda are roughly anticipated. English actors were performing in Nuremberg, where Ayrer lived, in 1604 and 1606, and may have brought reports of the piece of Shakespeare. Or perhaps both English and German plays had a common origin in some novel that has not yet been traced."[1]

[1] *Life of William Shakespeare*, S. Lee, pp. 252–253.

That is, *The Tempest* was primarily a play written to take advantage of a necessarily ephemeral interest in the shipwreck of certain Britishers on the Bermuda isles. Naturally, Shakespeare particularly made use of the rumor that the islands were haunted by spirits and devils. Considering carefully the dramatic possibilities of the different groups which make the story, one sees, I think, that no group is developed to its full extent, but rather that the different groups exist in order to give needed variety and to provide contrasting opportunities for Ariel and his crew to play tricks upon now this group and now that. Early we start, with Ferdinand and Miranda, a love story that might easily lead to many complications, but it drops into the background. The plan of Caliban, Stephano, and Trinculo to kill Prospero and Miranda might easily result in a number of scenes; it produces one in which they are nearly routed by the fairies. The group of shipwrecked royalty might easily provide much more story and incident than it does. Now, inasmuch as we know from preceding analyses, how deftly Shakespeare could develop and interweave two or more strands of story, giving to each its full development, either he is indifferent here or his purpose was not primarily to tell the story of any one of these groups, nor even a composite story involving them all.

On the other hand, play *The Tempest* as a fairy tale, and watch the result. Present that opening scene of the shipwreck so that it means the breaking up of the real world, a passing into the unseen; and then, not emphasizing the humanity of the figures of the play, give Caliban prominence as a mere monster; play with particular emphasis the scenes in which Prospero talks of his magic power and the scenes demonstrating that gift; fill the stage, not with visible fairies in gauze dresses, dancing ballets, but with voices coming from above, below, to right, to left, with possibly a rush of light figures now and then across the stage, and I believe we have the right presentation of the play. It is, as always with Shakespeare, a story play, but this time a fairy story. Yet present *The Tempest* as we may, once more we seem to have left the close interweaving of the earlier plays, the minute care for structure.

What is one to think technically of *The Winter's Tale*, so perfect in its atmospheres, — of gloom in the first part, of careless gayety in the second? Why should a play in most respects so perfect, apparently wantonly disregard a fundamental fact of dramatic composition known, as we have seen, to Christopher Marlowe twenty years before? I mean, of course, the law that to shift interest in the middle of a play is always undesirable. We saw Marlowe transcending it in *Edward II* by disregarding historical sequence, and by careful preparation. There is never a performance of *The Winter's Tale* in which this curious shift of interest from Hermione and Leontes to Florizel and Perdita is not noted, and as a real blot on something which would otherwise be a pure artistic pleasure. No dramatic justification for it has yet been discovered.

Wherever we turn, then, among these four plays, we are conscious of change or puzzling conditions. We confront in *Coriolanus* and in *The Winter's Tale* dramatic methods strangely in contrast to those to which Shakespeare has accustomed us; we find that even such delightful reading as *Cymbeline* and *The Tempest*, when acted, produces a certain dissatisfaction. I believe the difficulties with *Cymbeline* and *The Tempest* can be done away with by the idea I have reiterated, namely, that the Elizabethans, taking them purely as stories, were satisfied or delighted, while we, looking for some central interest or some central character, find them less satisfactory in action than when read. But are the other two plays to be accounted experimentation or growing indifference to the desires of an audience? In connection with this query it is interesting to consider the careers of two such contrasting figures as Henrik Ibsen and A. W. Pinero. In each case a period of early experimentation was followed by a time of admirable technique which accompanied a naturally firmer and deeper presentation of character, and there followed on these two stages a third sharply contrasted with the second. It is as if in the plays of Ibsen from *The Lady of the Sea* onward, he broke loose from dramatic convention and said, "Let me tell my story in the easiest way for me which yet makes possible perfect characterization." And in *Iris* and *Letty* of Mr. Pinero one misses, in that curious epilogue to *Letty* and in the dependence in *Iris* on the lapse of time between Acts III and IV, much of his old care in dramatic construction. It is as if both these men said: "To construct carefully is necessary for the most exacting critics in my audience; it is necessary in order to satisfy me artistically; but I see that my audience, absorbed in story as it is, and mesmerized to complete acceptance of my figure, if the character is well done within the scene, is much more easily satisfied. I, too, will be satisfied with as little structure as the greater part of my audience. It will give me more time for characterization within the scene." Or is this change in all these cases, instead of a growing cynicism, a spirit of bold experimentation resulting from a realization that inasmuch as the dramatic laws could not find expression without the individual worker, a more daring attitude toward dramatic composition may reveal that simpler ways, if rightly handled, are just as good as more complicated? There is, of course, no final statement to be made on this for Shakespeare, but it is certainly significant that Fletcher, who in 1600 was just coming into popularity, is noted for his dependence, not upon his characterization as a whole, but rather upon his very effective development of the single scene. On the whole, it seems wisest to call all these years, 1608–1612, mature experimentation.

By 1611 Shakespeare had sold his shares in the Globe and the Blackfriars theatres and was retiring to New Place, Stratford, for five years of life as a country gentleman. Different dramatic conditions, signified by the change in public taste in plays, were arising. Shakespeare may have foreseen, so sensitive had he been to his public, that it was becoming more and more responsive, not to the play as a whole, but to the immediate effect, a condition that characterizes the public in the years from 1615 to 1640. He may even have felt the rivalry, for the public is fickle, of some of the younger men. Does not the large amount of suspected collaboration or revision of other men's work in the years 1600–1608, as compared with the period 1594–1600, point in the same direction? Grant that, in order to meet the exacting demands on his time of such complicated dramatic problems as *Hamlet, Lear, Macbeth,* and *Antony and Cleopatra,* Shakespeare made up the amount of production expected from him annually by his company, by collaborating or revising in *Troilus and Cressida, Timon, Pericles,* and even *Measure for Measure,* or grant that in them he yielded to the natural desire of certain dramatists and his own company in particular that he should lend the spell of his name to these plays. In either case the relative successes, at least, of these revised or genuinely collaborative plays, as well as many of the successes of his contemporaries, must have made Shakespeare see that, so far as popular acclaim was concerned, he could satisfy his standards of characterization with far less deft structure and pervasive artistry. What is more natural for a man who has sounded the depths of human feeling in the tragedies, and has faced successfully the most complicated problems of technique, than that he should, as the public interest forces him to return to an earlier romantic mood, both experiment in technical problems, and in his mere story-telling, though it steadily shows all of his old mastery of character and at times all of his old knowledge of his audience, grow a little more personal in phrase, and somewhat careless as to the minute details of technique which had helped to give him his supreme position?

It is certainly interesting that all these four plays, though two at least, *The Winter's Tale* and *The Tempest*, were decidedly successful in their own day, are but rarely revived. Does not that look as if their success depended more upon special conditions in the audience of their time than upon permanent elements of successful appeal when presented on the stage? It is doubtful how far even the master of technique may break free from the principles he has toilsomely acquired; it is indubitable that, whatever his success when he does break through, his experimentation forms no excuse for ignorance of these

[303]

same principles by a beginner. He who builds for the moment may construct as did the contemporaries of Shakespeare, may have as little artistic conscience as Dekker or Chapman, but he who builds for posterity must keep his standards unswervingly as high as did Shakespeare between 1595 and 1608 in the uncollaborative work. After all, even genius does not so much create the laws of a literary form as reveal them. Fundamentally, the laws are determined, not so much by the practice of the genius as by the relations of the public to the particular form.

After this careful technical consideration of the greater part of Shakespeare's plays how can we maintain that this man had no idea of art for art's sake? Grant that in the last three or four years of his writing he grew weary, even became perhaps a little irritated with the unappreciativeness of the great part of his audience, which could not discern the subtleties by which he gained his best artistic effects and surpassed the men whom they, probably, too often held his peers, nevertheless we have seen him steadily, from 1598 to 1608, for ten long years, fighting the fight to combine in his plays the largest degree of public favor with the highest degree of artistic accomplishment. If he had no feeling for his art as an art and for its dignity, why did he wait till after 1608 before he relaxed his structure and took the easier way in play-writing? One has only to turn to the pages of these other dramatists who surrounded him, who had their successes in their own time and who have their deserved following of readers even to-day, to see that what most distinguishes Shakespeare from them is not simply a profounder knowledge of human life, — theirs is sometimes as profound as his for the moment, though not like him sustainedly, — but the sense he leaves in the best of his plays of some underlying artistic ideal which brings those plays to a roundness and a completeness artistically almost never seen in the work of these other men. Remember, too, that it was he who wrote of

> Desiring this man's art and that man's scope,
> With what I most enjoy, contented least,

and remember that he is absolutely the only person in the entire list of so-called Elizabethan dramatists who raises pure farce to the level of literature. This he did in *The Comedy of Errors*, *The Taming of the Shrew*, and *The Merry Wives of Windsor*. Could any man do that who did not know the mood the lines I have just quoted convey? Who better knows that mood than the man who loves and respects his art for his art's sake?

The significance, the very great significance, for Shakespeare's rapid growth as a dramatist, of the freedom with which he could use whatever came to his hand that was not the property of some rival company, must at last be evident. At a time when, as we have seen, plot was everything for the public in a play, conceive the difference it would have made in the productiveness of even Shakespeare himself had he been obliged first to spin his story, then to characterize it carefully, next to fit it to the conditions of his audience and of his stage, and finally to inform it with the spirit of poetry which came to be the final stamp he placed upon his work. Of course, with no dramatist is there just that sequence in composition: the processes run together; but even he who has tried to write one play can attest that conceiving his story was the most time-consuming process of all. One of the foremost English dramatists told the writer recently that when once he had schemed his story and could begin to see his characters in the definite situations of his play, the mere writing of the dialogue took but a short time. The first stage of all to-day, finding the story, was for Shakespeare, as we have seen in almost every play of his, no real task at all. For him the first stage was judging what the story needed to make it dramatically effective for his audience.

The importance for any dramatist of the conditions of his stage, the practice of Shakespeare illustrates. We have seen that the curious arrangement, as it seems to us, of outer, inner, upper, and back stage made perfectly possible a rapid succession of scenes, impossible for us at the present day, thus allowing that fourth act of *Antony and Cleopatra* to produce a totally different impression from the misleading one it gives upon our modern stage with its necessarily long waits for the shifting of scenes, its excisions, or its rearrangements. I could wish very much that what I have been pointing out might make a reader feel that to tamper with the order of Shakespeare's scenes in the plays written after he had attained mastery of his art is, dramatically, utterly unpardonable. Condense we must at times, because of the cumbersomeness of this scenery-ridden modern stage, but we may condense with discretion and success. One point which I have been steadily trying to make is that in the great majority of his plays Shakespeare consciously aimed at a total effect from the thoughtful and skilled handling of a multitude of details. Change his order, cut out whole scenes, and the very effects for which even Shakespeare labored become impossible.

I need not dwell upon the effect of the absence of elaborate scenery in producing the descriptive quality of Shakespeare's plays, nor need I emphasize probably, that the relatively small size of most of the theatres and the use of a stage thrust out far into the pit made possible a certain intimacy and delicacy of effect which did much to offset the fact that the theatres were open to the sky and not so easy to hear in as our own theatres. One sometimes wonders that the Elizabethan audience was sensitive enough to enjoy the scenes of quiet poetical

monologue or of delicate touches of characterization, but one wonders no longer after seeing a careful
revival of one of these plays, — not simply the curious
archæological botches which are too often palmed
off on an unsuspecting public as Elizabethan stages.
Some years ago, when Ben Jonson's *Silent Woman* was
revived at Harvard University, the professional actors,
when they first saw the wide expanse of undecorated
stage and the eager pittites sitting close up to the
very edge of it, almost refused to carry on their work.
They said: "These people are too close; we have
nothing to set our imaginations afire. All this will
chill us inevitably into tameness." But at the end
of the first act, to which they had been forced, they
came off tingling with enthusiasm and delight because, as one of them said: "Why, I have never
known anything like this. There are no footlights
to get over, there is no proscenium arch to frame
us in. As quick as I do anything the audience comes
back at me with a response. Those old fellows certainly knew the right conditions for the actor." A
slight tendency in the last few years to produce plays
less elaborately, to let the play depend more on its
text and the actors who interpret it, is but a return
to that stage which gave us the best drama that
we have ever had and which affected advantageously
the work of Shakespeare himself. I am not urging
a return to Elizabethan stage conditions, but that
the plays of any period can be judged accurately

only under the stage conditions for which they were
written, and that we should not to-day, both in revivals
and in plays of the present, swamp what is essential
and distort the intended effect by an over-elaborate
presentation.

And the public! Shakespeare seems to have had
the genius for meeting their interests which to-day
marks the great editors. To just what extent he led
and to what extent he followed in the vogue of the
chronicle history, farce, and the later romantic plays,
it is now impossible to say, but we know that his
first real success came in skilful compliance with
the fondness of the public of 1590–1600 for erotic
verse; that there are striking resemblances between,
for instance, the *Philaster* of Beaumont and Fletcher,
and his own *Cymbeline;* and that at the time when
As You Like It was making such a success there
were two plays called *The Downfall* and *The Death
of Robert Earl of Huntington*, which showed a crude
use of woodland scenes suggestive of those of the
Duke and his followers in Shakespeare's play. Thus
one might trace analogue after analogue between
his work and that of the other men who surround
him or precede him. To what extent he was creditor
and debtor we shall now never know. The important point is that in every case he "imitates inimitably" something which thus becomes in the highest
degree worthy of imitation.

Shakespeare's public permitted at first a slowness

of exposition which to-day we find irksome; it was responsible for his curious occasional recapitulation, as in *Lear* and *Romeo and Juliet;* it gave him a license for monologue and poetic description which we to-day do not sanction. But the same sympathetic regard for the likings and habits of mind of his audiences which made Shakespeare comply to this extent, carried him from the immediately to the permanently significant in the relation of the public to a play. Seeing that comic relief made his plays more acceptable to his public Shakespeare provided it and thereby added something permanently effective for the Anglo-Saxon mind. Unless reiteration be of no avail, I have made evident that not merely to Shakespeare, but to all the Elizabethan playwrights, the drama was the art of the story-teller, not of the characterizer or of the poet except in a secondary degree. That largely accounts for the failure of the novel to develop in the days of Elizabeth and James, and if we may go on and say that for the great bulk of humanity the drama will always remain the art of the story-teller, we shall understand perhaps better than we have before why with the rise of the novel in the early part of the eighteenth century the English drama fell decade by decade into an increasingly degraded condition until it became a mere mummer and jester of His Majesty the People. We shall perhaps understand better, too, the real meaning of Shakespeare's development and shall be able more sensibly to appreciate his plays, judging them from the standpoint of their own day and not from our own. Perhaps, also, we shall begin to see why some suspect that as the novel, after its superb accomplishments in England for two centuries, peters out into that flabby inanity of the modern magazine, the storiette, the much older art which no time or change has been able to kill, the drama, is in sight of a new period of rich and significant development.

Shakespeare's experience with his audiences of course revealed to him the permanent principles of dramatic composition. It showed that mere fable, story, is not enough in play-writing. For the best results there must be clear exposition, which depends on underlying unity, — which in turn depends on carefully considered structure. That structure, in its turn, rests on proportion and emphasis. The fable or story before it can become, dramatically speaking, plot must be so proportioned as to tell itself clearly and effectively within the space of two or two and a half hours; and this exposition must be emphasized with regard to the tastes and prejudices of the audience, as well as the artistic purpose of the dramatist, if it is on the one hand to win success with the public, and on the other to be differentiated as high comedy, tragedy, melodrama, or farce, and not remain a hodge-podge. Shakespeare's practice proves, too, in regard to the underlying principles of dramatic composition that a play succeeds best when a central figure or group of figures, or a unifying idea, focusses the attention of the spectator. Shakespeare's experience shows, moreover, that a play must have movement, gained by initial swift, clear exposition and a skilful use of suspense and climax. And finally, this body of farces, chronicle plays, comedies, and tragedies demonstrates that in drama characterization is the ladder by which we mount from lower to higher in the so-called forms, and that a predetermined point of view is the means by which the dramatist so emphasizes his material as to differentiate it in form.

How normal, too, the whole development! Dominated, at first, by the literary and the dramatic standards of the day, influenced in comedy and tragedy by the leaders of his time, Lyly and Marlowe, Shakespeare felt his way haltingly through the beginnings of high comedy and through melodramatic presentation of history to straight story-telling in *A Midsummer Night's Dream* and *The Merchant of Venice*, and by his thorough grasp on character in *Romeo and Juliet* perhaps unconsciously discovered tragedy. Is it not logical, too, that when other men were busily writing the comedy of manners, as was the case with Jonson and Middleton and even Thomas Dekker, or melodrama as with George Chapman or John Marston, Shakespeare accomplished most in the two forms which chiefly depend, not on mere story, but on characterization, and characterization often so subtle that it can be presented only by a master of technique? I refer, of course, to high comedy and to tragedy. In tragedy he simply has no rival in the English language. Within the field of romantic high comedy he has but one real competitor, John Fletcher, and no peer. As Professor Schelling has said, Shakespeare "building on what he found, essaying no miracles, unerring master of every possibility of his art, yet contravening no natural law, reached what had seemed the unattainable not by the cataclysm of irresistible genius and inspired haphazard, but by the orderly processes of growth."[1]

It is time we ceased to talk as if he who writes successfully for the public must be competent only for a low level of literary work. It is equally true that, incited thereto as we are by clever advertising, we should stop rating as literature whatever the public acclaims. The dramatic artist sees in his environment what is significant or may be made significant for his particular public. The great dramatist so presents what in his own day, or the day he chooses to depict, is permanently significant that its significance becomes permanently recognized. Neither task may a dramatist accomplish if he does not enter into the minds of his audience and even as he writes regard their tastes, their prejudices, and their ideals. But there can be no content for his soul if in this writing he sacrifices the literary

[1] *The English Chronicle Play*, F. E. Schelling p. vii.

and the dramatic ideals which have come to him as an inheritance from his predecessors, and more particularly as the results of his own years of toilsome devotion to his chosen task. In nothing does Shakespeare proclaim his genius more than in his repeated winning of popular acclaim for fulfilment of his artistic desires. His original equipment, as seen in the Shakespeare of 1590–1593, in its sensitiveness to impressions, its power of literary expression, and its human sympathy, was promising but not extraordinary. The fruit of the years of patient regard for the tastes and the ideas of his public, of toilsome endeavor, of constant striving in many forms toward clearer and clearer dramatic ideals, was the development of inborn capacity into genius and the primacy of the English drama.

APPENDIX

THIS INDENTURE made the eighte day of Januarye, 1599, and in the two and fortyth yeare of the reigne of our sovereigne ladie Elizabeth, by the grace of God Queene of England, Fraunce and Ireland, defender of the fayth, &c. Between Phillipp Henslowe and Edward Allen of the parishe of St. Saviours in Southwark, in the countie of Surry, gentleman, on thone parte, and Peter Streete, citizen and carpenter of London, on thother parte, Witnesseth; that whereas the said Phillipp Henslowe and Edward Allen the day of the date hereof have bargained, compounded, and agreed with the said Peter Streete for the erectinge, buildinge, and setting up of a new House and Stage for a playhowse, in and uppon a certeine plott or peece of grounde appoynted out for that purpose, scituate and beinge near Goldinge lane in the parish of Saint Giles without Cripplegate of London; to be by him the said Peter Streete or some other sufficient workmen of his providing and appoyntment, and att his propper costes and chardges, (for the consideration hereafter in these presents expressed) made, builded, and sett upp, in manner and form following: that is to saie, the frame of the said howse to be sett square, and to conteine fowerscore foote of lawful assize everye waie square, without, and fiftie five foote of like

[315]

assize square, everye waie within, with a good, suer, and stronge foundacion of pyles, brick, lyme, and sand, both withoute and within, to be wrought one foote of assize at the leiste above the ground; and the saide frame to conteine three stories in heigth, the first or lower storie to conteine twelve foote of lawful assize in heighth, the second storie eleaven foote of lawful assize in heigth, and the third or upper storie to conteine nine foote of lawful assize in height. All which stories shall conteine twelve foot and a half of lawful assize in breadth throughoute, besides a juttey forwards in eyther of the saide two upper stories of tene ynches of lawful assize; with fower convenient divisions for gentlemens roomes, and other sufficient and convenient divisions for twoopennie roomes; with necessarie seates to be placed and sett as well in those roomes as throughoute all the rest of the galleries of the said howse; and with suche like steares, conveyances, and divisions without and within, as are made and contryved in and to the late-erected play-howse on the Bancke in the said parish of Saint Saviours, called the Globe; with a stadge and tyreinge-howse, to be made, erected and sett upp within the saide frame: with a shadow or cover over the saide stadge; which stadge shall be placed and sett, as alsoe the stearcases of the saide frame, in such sorte as is prefigured in a plot thereof drawen; and which stadge shall conteine in length fortie and three foote of lawfull assize, and in breadth to extende to the middle of the yarde of the said howse: the same stadge to be paled in belowe with goode stronge and sufficyent new oken boardes, and likewise the lower storie of the said frame withinsied, and the same lower storie to be alsoe laide over and fenced with stronge yron pyles: And the said stadge to be in all other proportions contryved and fashioned like unto the stadge of the saide Playhouse called the Globe; with convenient windowes and lights glazed to the saide tireynge-howse. And the saide frame, stadge, and stearcases, to be covered with tyle, and to have a sufficient gutter of leade, to carrie and convey the water from the coveringe of the said stadge, to fall backwards. And alsoe all the saide frame and the stearcases thereof to be sufficyently enclosed without with lathe, lyme, and haire. And the gentlemens roomes and two-pennie roomes to be seeled with lathe, lyme, and haire; and all the flowers of the saide galleries, stories, and stadge to be boarded with good and sufficient newe deale boardes of the whole thicknes, where neede shall be. And the said howse, and other thinges before mentioned to be made and doen, to be in all other contritivions, conveyances, fashions, thinge and thinges, effected, finished and doen, according to the manner and fashion of the saide howse called the Globe; saveinge only that all the princypall and maine postes of the saide frame, and stadge forward, shall be square and wrought palaster-wise, with carved proportions called Satiers, to be placed and sett on the topp of every of the same postes: and saveing alsoe that the saide Peter Streete shall not be charged with anie manner of paynteinge in or aboute the saide frame, howse, or stadge, or anie parte thereof, nor rendering the walles within, nor feelinge anie more or other roomes then the gentlemens roomes, twoo-pennie roomes, and stadge, before mentioned. Nowe thereuppon the said Peter Streete doth covenante, promise, and graunte for himself, his executors, and administrators, to and with the said Phillip

[317]

Henslowe, and Edward Allen, and either of them, and thexecutors, and administrators of them, by these presents, in manner and forme followinge, that is to say; That he the saide Peter Streete, his executors, or assigns, shall and will at his or their owne propper costes and chardges, well, workman-like, and substantially make, erect, sett upp, and fullie finishe in and by all thinges accordinge to the true meaninge of theis presents, with good stronge and substancyall new tymber and other necessarie stuff, all the said frame and other works whatsoever in and uppon the saide plott or parcell of grounde, (beinge not by anie authoritie restrayned, and having ingres, egres, and regres to doe the same,) before the five and twentyth daye of Julie, next comeing after the date hereof. And shall alsoe att his or their like costes and chardges provide and find all manner of workmen, tymber, joysts, rafters, boords, dores, bolts, hinges, brick, tyle, lathe, lyme, haire, sande, nailes, lead, iron, glass, workmanshipp and other thinges whatsoever which shall be needful, convenyent and necessarie for the saide frame and works and everie parte thereof: and shall alsoe make all the saide frame in every poynte for scantlings lardger and bigger in assize than the scantlings of the timber of the saide new-erected howse called The Globe. And alsoe that he the saide Peter Streete shall furthwith, as well by him selfe as by suche other and soe manie workmen as shall be convenient and necessarie, enter into and uppon the saide buildinges and workes, and shall in reasonable manner procede therein withoute anie wilfull detraction, untill the same shall be fully effected and finished. In consideration of all which buildings and of all stuff and workmanshipp thereto belonginge, the said Philip

Henslowe, and Edward Allen, and either of them, for
themselves, theire and either of theire executors and administrators, doe joyntlie and severallie covenante and
graunte to and with the saide Peter Streete, his executors
and administrators, by theis presents, that the saide Philip
Henslowe, and Edward Allen, or one of them, or the executors, administrators, or assigns of them or one of them,
shall and will well and trulie paie or cause to be paide unto
the saide Peter Streete, his executors or assignes, att the
place aforesaid appoynted for the erectinge of the said
frame, the full some of fower hundred and fortie poundes,
of lawfull money of Englande, in manner and forme follow-
ings; that is to saie, at suche tyme and whenas the tymber
woork of the saide frame shall be raysed and sett upp by
the saide Peter Streete, his executors or assignes, or within
seaven daies then next followinge, twoo hundred and
twentie poundes; and att suche time and when as the said
frame-work shall be fullie effected and finished as is aforesaid, or within seaven daies then next following, thother
twooe hundred and twentie poundes, withoute fraude or
coven. Provided allwaies, and it is agreed betwene the
said parties, that whatsoever some or somes of money
the said Phillip Henslowe, or Edward Allen, or either of
them, or the executors or assigns of them or either of
them, shall lend or deliver unto the saide Peter Streete, his
executors or assignes, or any other by his appoyntment
or consent, for or concerninge the saide woork or anie parte
thereof, or anie stuff thereto belonginge, before the raise-
ing and setting upp of the saide frame, shall be reputed,
accepted, taken and accoumpted in parte of the first payment aforesaid of the saide some of fower hundred and fortie

poundes: and all such some and somes of money as they or anie of them shall as aforesaid lend or deliver between the razeing of the said frame and finishing thereof, and of all the rest of the said works, shall be reputed, accepted, taken and accoumpted in parte of the laste payment aforesaid of the same some of fower hundred and fortie poundes; anie thinge above said to the contrary notwithstandinge. In witness whereof the parties abovesaid to theis present indentures interchangeably have sett their handes and seales. Yeoven the daie and yeare above-written.[1]

CONTRACT FOR BUILDING THE HOPE THEATRE

Articles covenanted, granted, and agreements concluded and agreed upon this nyne and twentythe daie of August, Anno dmni, 1613, between Phillip Henslowe of the parish of St. Saviours in Southwarke within the countye of Surrie Esquier and Jacob Maide of the parish of Saint Olaves in Southwarke aforesaide, waterman, on thone partie, and Gilbert Katherens of the said parish of St. Saviours in Southwarke, carpenter, on thother partie, as followeth, that is to saie.

Imprimis, the saide Gilbert Katherens for him, his executors, administrators, and assignes, doth covenant, promise and graunt, to and with the saide Phillip Henslowe and Jacob Maide, and either of them, the executors, administrators and assignes of them and either of them, by theise presents, in manner and forme following, That he the saide Gilbert Katherens, his executors, administrators,

---

[1] *Malone's Shakespeare* (1821), Vol. III, Prolegomena, pp. 338–343.

or assignes, shall and will at his or their own proper costes
and charges uppon or before the last daie of November next
ensuinge the daie of the date of these presents above-
written, not onlie take downe or pull downe all that game
place or house wherein beares and bulls have been heretofore usually bayted, and also one other house or stable
wherein bulls and horses did usuallie stande, sett, lyinge
and beynge uppon or near the Banke syde in the saide
parish of St. Saviours in Southwarke commonlie called or
knowen by the name of the Beare garden, but shall also at
his or their owne proper costes and charges uppon or before
the saide last daie of November newly erect, builde, and
sett up one other game place or plaie house fitt and convenient in all thinges both for players to plaie in and for
the game of beares and bulls, to be bayted in the same; and
also a fitt and convenient tyre house and a frame to be
carryed or taken away and to stande uppon tressels good
substantiall and sufficient for the carrying and bearing of
suche a stage; and shall new builde erect and sett up again
the saide plaie house or game place neere or uppon the
saide place where the same game place did heretofore
stande. And to builde the same of suche large compasse,
forme, wideness, and height, as the plaie house called the
Swan in the libertie of Paris Garden in the saide parishe of
St. Saviours now is. And shall also builde two steare casses
without and adjoyning to the saide playe house in suche
convenient places as shal be most fitt and convenient for
them to stande uppon, and of such largnes and height as the
stear casses of the saide play house called the Swan now are
or be. And shall also builde the *heavens* over the saide
stage, to be borne or carried without any postes or sup-

porters to be fixed or sett uppon the saide stage: and all
gutters of leade needfull for the carryage of all such raine
water as shall fall uppon the same, And shall also make
two boxes in the lower most storie, fitt and decent for
gentlemen to sitt in; And shall make the partitions be-
tweene the roomes as they are at the saide play house called
the Swan. And to make turned cullumes [columns] uppon
and over the stage, And shall make the principalls and
fore front of the saide plaie house of good and sufficient
oken tymber, and no firr tymber to be putt or used in the
lowermost or under stories, excepte the upright postes on
the backe parte of the saide stories: all the bindinge joystes
to be of oken tymber, the inner principall postes in the
first storie to be twelve footes in height and tenn ynches
square; the inner principall postes in the midall storie
to be eight ynches square : the innermost postes in the
upper storie to be seaven ynches square; the —— postes
in the first storie to be eight ynches square in the seconde
storie seaven ynches square, and in the upper storie six
ynches square. Also the brest summers in the lowermost
storie to be nyne ynches deepe and seaven ynches in
thicknes and in the midall storie to be eight ynches depe and
six ynches in thicknes: the byndinge joistes of the first storie
to be nyne and eight ynches in depth and thicknes, and in
the midell storie to be viii and vii ynches in depth and thicknes. Item, to make a good sure and sufficient foundacion
of brickes for the saide playe house or game place and to
make it xii ynches at the leaste above the grounde. Item
to new builde erect and sett up the said bull house and
stable with good and sufficient scantling tymber plankes
and bordes and partitions, of that largenes and fittnes

as shall be sufficient to kepe and hold six bulls and three
horses or geldinges, with rackes and mangers in the same.
And also a lofer [louvre] or storie over the saide house as
nowe it is. And shall also at his or their owne proper coste
and charges new tyle with Englishe tyles all the upper roofe
of the said playe house, game place, and bull house or
stable. And shall finde and paie for at his like proper costes
and charges all the lyme lears, sand, brickes, tyles, laths,
nayles, workmanshippe and all other thinges needfull and
necessarie for the full finishinge of the said playe house, bull
house and stable And the saide playe house or game place
to be made in all thinges and in suche forme and fashion
as the said playhouse called the Swan, the scantling of the
tymbers, tyles and foundations as is aforesaide, without
fraud or covin. And the saide Phillip Henslowe and
Jacob Maide and either of them for them thexecutors administrators and assignes of them and either of them, doe
covenant and graunt to and with the saide Gilbert Katherens his executors administrators and assignes in manner
and forme followinge, that is to saie, that the saide Gilbert
or his assignes shall or may have and take to his or their use
and behalfe not onlie all the tymber, benches, seates, slates,
tyles, brickes, and all other thinges belonginge to the
saide game place, bull house or stable, and also all suche
old tymber whiche the saide Phillip Henslowe hath latlie
bought being of an old house in Thames Street, London,
whereof most parte is now lying in the yarde or backside
of the said Beare garden. And also be satisfied and paid
unto the saide Gilbert Katherens his executors administrators or assignes for the doinge and finishinge of the
workes and buildings aforesaid the sum of three hundred

and three score poundes of good and lawful monie of Englande in manner and forme followinge, that is to saie, in
hande at then sealing and delivery hereof three score
poundes whiche the said Gilbert acknowledgeth himselfe
by theyse presentes to have received. And moreover to
paie every weeke weeklie duringe the six weekes unto the
saide Gilbert or his assignes when he shall sett workmen to worke uppon or about the buildinge the premisses
the somme of tenn poundes of lawfull monie of Englande
to paie them their wages yf theyre wages doth amount
unto so muche monie. And when the saide plaiehouse
bull house and stable are reared, then to make up the saide
wages one hundred poundes of lawfull monie of Englande,
and to be paide unto the saide Gilbert Katherens or his
assignes. And when the saide plaie house bull house and
stable are reared, tyled, walled, then to paie unto the said
Gilbert Katherens or his assignes one other hundred poundes
of lawfull monie of Englande And when the saide plaie
house bull house and stable are fullie finished builded and
done, in manner and forme aforesaide, then to paie unto
the saide Gilbert Katherens or his assignes one other hundred poundes of lawfull monie of Englande, in full satis-
facōn and payment of the saide somme of ccc lxli. And
to all and singuler the covenantes, grauntes, articles, and
agreements, above in theise presentes contayned, whiche
on the parte and behalfe of the saide Gilbert Katherens his
executors administrators or assignes, are and ought to be
observed, performed, fulfilled, and done, the saide Gilbert Katherens bindeth him selfe, his executors, administrators, and assignes, unto the saide Philipp Henslowe and
Jacob Maide, and to either of them thexecutors admin-

istrators and assignes of them or either of them, bytheise presentes. In witness whereof the saide Gilbert Katherens hath hereunto sett his hande and seal the daie and yere first above written.

The marke [G K.] of Gilbert Katherens.[1]

[1] *Malone's Shakespeare* (1821), Vol. III, Prolegomena, pp. 343–347.

INDEX

INDEX